Urban Smellscapes

We see the city, we hear the city but, above all, we smell the city. Scent has unique qualities; it is ubiquitous, persistent and it has an unparalleled connection to memory, but it is usually overlooked in discussions of sensory design. What scents shape the city? How does scent contribute to placemaking? How do we design smell environments in the city?

Urban Smellscapes makes a notable contribution to the growing body of literature on the senses and design by providing some answers to these questions and informing the wider research agenda regarding how people sensually experience urban environments. This book is the first of its kind in examining the role of smell specifically in contemporary experiences and perceptions of English towns and cities, highlighting the perception of urban smellscapes as they relate to place perception, and describing the contribution of odour towards overall sense of place. With case studies from factories, breweries, urban parks and experimental smell environments, *Urban Smellscapes* identifies processes by which urban smell environments are managed and controlled, and gives designers and city managers a number of tools to actively use smell in their work.

Victoria Henshaw is a Lecturer in Urban Design and Planning at the University of Sheffield. She writes the blog Smell and the City. Her work centres on sensory perception and the design and management of cities, and has featured widely across the media including the *Independent* and BBC Radio 4 (UK), American Public Radio, Radio New Zealand and ABC Radio Australia (Perth). Prior to entering academia Victoria worked in town centre management and urban development.

Urban Smellscapes

Understanding and designing city smell environments

Victoria Henshaw

Routledge
Taylor & Francis Group

NEW YORK AND LONDON

First published 2014
by Routledge
711 Third Avenue, New York, NY 10017

Simultaneously published in the UK
by Routledge
2 Park Square, Milton Park, Abingdon, Oxon OX14 4RN

Routledge is an imprint of the Taylor & Francis Group, an informa business

Library of Congress Cataloging in Publication Data
Henshaw, Victoria.
Urban smellscapes : understanding and designing city smell environments / Victoria Henshaw. -- First edition.
pages cm
Includes bibliographical references and index.
1. Odor control. 2. City planning. 3. City and town life.
4. Smell--Psychological aspects. I. Title.
TD886.H46 2014
711--dc23
2013005106

ISBN: 978-0-415-66203-1 (hbk)
ISBN: 978-0-415-66206-2 (pbk)
ISBN: 978-0-203-07277-6 (ebk)

Typeset in Goudy Oldstyle Std
by Saxon Graphics Ltd, Derby

Printed and bound by CPI Group (UK) Ltd, Croydon, CR0 4YY

Dedicated to my family

Contents

List of illustrations   xi
Acknowledgements   xiii

1 **Introduction**   1

PART I
Smell, society and cities

2 **Perspectives on smell and the city I**   9

  2.1 Historical cities 11
  2.2 Legislation and policy relating to odour 13
  2.3 Odour classification, language and measurement 15
  2.4 Odour and urban design practice and theory 19
  2.5 Conclusion 22

3 **Perspectives on smell and the city II**   24

  3.1 Qualities of the sense of smell 24
  3.2 Olfactory performance 26
  3.3 Smell and memory 31
  3.4 Smell perception 32
  3.5 Place perception and odour 36
  3.6 Odour sensitivity 37
  3.7 Conclusion 40

4 **Smellwalking and representing urban smellscapes**   42

  4.1 Smellwalk case study: Doncaster, England 47
  4.2 The mapping and representation of urban smellscapes 54
  4.3 Conclusion 56

PART II
Smell sources in the city

5   **Air quality, pollution and smell**   59

　5.1 *Doncaster's historical pollution 60*
　5.2 *Traffic odours – a trade-off for city life 68*
　5.3 *Air pollution and the sense of smell 76*
　5.4 *Pedestrianisation, air pollution and judgements of place 78*
　5.5 *Air pollution and the design and control of urban smellscapes 81*
　5.6 *Conclusion 83*

6   **Food and smell**   85

　6.1 *Markets 86*
　6.2 *International food and cultural districts 93*
　6.3 *Odour extraction and ventilation 102*
　6.4 *Convenience food, fast food restaurants and odour values 106*
　6.5 *Food and smell – discussion 110*
　6.6 *Conclusion 111*

7   **Urban policy and smell**   113

　7.1 *The twenty-four-hour city and odour 113*
　7.2 *Smoking and odour 119*
　7.3 *Waste production in twenty-four-hour cities 125*
　7.4 *Case study comparison – Doncaster's Priory Walk and Silver Street 130*
　7.5 *Discussion 138*
　7.6 *Conclusion 140*

PART III
Smellscape control, design and placemaking

8   **Processes of odour control in the city**   143

　8.1 *Separation 144*
　8.2 *Deodorisation 149*
　8.3 *Masking 153*
　8.4 *Scenting 154*
　8.5 *Scenting the skies? 163*
　8.6 *Conclusion 167*

**9   Designing with smell: Restorative environments and
     design tools**   **169**

     9.1 Air and wind flow 170
     9.2 Restorative odours 173
     9.3 Smell design tools 186
     9.4 A new approach to odour in urban design 192
     9.5 Conclusion 193

10 Odour, placemaking and urban smellscape design   **195**

     10.1 The contribution of odour to placemaking 197
     10.2 Urban smellscape design: A practice of value or question? 201
     10.3 The strategic context for designing urban smellscapes 205
     10.4 Urban smellscape design process and tools 210
     10.5 Conclusion 220

11 Conclusion   **221**

     Glossary   225
     References   227
     Index   244

Illustrations

Figures

1.1   Ganesh Festival, La Chappelle, Paris 2009. ©melodybuhr   2

1.2   A little girl walks through the waste, the Zabaleen, Cairo. ©jamiefurniss   3

2.1   Urban odour descriptor wheel (Curren *et al.* 2013)   17

2.2   Mobile olfactometry: the Nasal Ranger. ©St.CroixSensoryInc.   19

3.1   Smell perception – summary of influencing factors   26

4.1   Section from commentated smellwalk in Montreal. Montreal 2011. ©natalieb   46

4.2   Doncaster smellwalking route and stopping points   50

4.3   Odours detected during urban smellwalks (UK/US/Canada/Europe)   53

4.4   Smellmap, Paris 2011. Kate McLean, Sensory Maps   56

5.1   Doncaster town centre circular road (an AQMA)   62

5.2   Colonnades, Doncaster   80

6.1   Doncaster Markets   88

6.2   Doncaster Fish Market   89

6.3   Smithfield Market, London   91

6.4   Copley Road, Doncaster   94

6.5   Manchester's Chinatown   99

6.6   Back of house ventilation: Manchester's Chinatown   103

7.1   Traditional pub and modern bar frontages, Doncaster   114

7.2   Smoking in outdoor café areas, Doncaster   124

7.3   Urilift, a public urinal which lowers into the ground. ©Urilift BV   130

7.4   Street cafés, Priory Walk, Doncaster   131

7.5   Silver Street, Doncaster (public highway)   132

7.6   Alleyway, Silver Street, Doncaster   137

8.1   Management and control processes: urban smellscapes   144

8.2   Smoking booths, Arlanda Airport, Stockholm, Sweden. ©Finnavia&Finnair   147

8.3   Waste disposal bins, Manchester   150

8.4   Commercial scenting in bus stops, London, February 2012   160

9.1 The smellscape as a composition of different notes
     (image drawn by Nabil Awad)   172
9.2 Small-scale planting in Doncaster's primary retail core   179
9.3 Frenchgate, Doncaster   181
9.4 Water-feature in public space, Manchester city centre   183
9.5 Immersive restorative experience, Manchester's urban canals   184
9.6 Air flow and odour concentration (image drawn by
     Nabil Awad)   187
10.1 Perfume fountain, Grasse, south of France   196
10.2 Chanel No.5 traffic island feature, Grasse, south of France   196
10.3 Mariatorget, Stockholm, Sweden. Image by Holgar Ellgaard   207
10.4 Sound speakers in a sonic garden, Venice, Italy.
     ©architetturasonora   207
10.5 Processes of urban smellscape design   211
10.6 Sensory notation tool: radar diagram (Lucas *et al.* 2009)   213
10.7 Sensory experience ratings across site, Doncaster   214

Charts

3.1 Participant smell performance self-assessments
     (Doncaster, 2009)   28
3.2 MOST favourite odours of one hundred participants   34
3.3 LEAST favourite odours of one hundred participants   35
3.4 Contrasting ratings of MOST and LEAST liked odours of
     one hundred participants   35
4.1 Place and smellscape liking rating – averages per area
     (1: very much disliked, 5: very much liked)   52
7.1 Place and smellscape liking – Priory Walk/Silver Street
     (1: very negative, 5: very positive)   133
7.2 Environmental quality: Priory Walk   133
7.3 Environmental quality: Silver Street   133
7.4 Odours detected and perception: Priory Walk   136
7.5 Odours detected and perception: Silver Street   136

Acknowledgements

In writing this book, I have been indebted to many – closest to home, my family for their unconditional support, and in particular Tony, our three sons Brodie, Alistair and Oliver, and my parents Victor and Pauline.

This book is based upon original research first undertaken as part of a doctorate at the University of Salford and supported by a grant from the Engineering and Physical Sciences Research Council (EPSRC). I am particularly grateful to my doctoral research supervisors Professor Trevor Cox and Dr Andrew Clark for their support, and to Dr Mags Adams who co-supervised the early stages of the study.

I would like to thank the University of Manchester for its support in financing the Smell and the City Project, and my colleagues there, in particular Professor Simon Guy, Dr Albena Yaneva, Professor Dominic Medway, Chris Perkins and Professor Gary Warnaby for their support. I would also like to acknowledge the support and advice provided by Professor Craig Watkins and Professor Jean Grugel at the University of Sheffield.

I am extremely grateful to Doncaster Metropolitan Borough Council for supporting the fieldwork and particularly for providing access to meeting and interview space while I was undertaking my research in Doncaster. I would particularly like to thank Jeff Prior for all his help, advice and friendship, and all those who gave up their valuable time to participate in the study.

I also wish to acknowledge the researchers and academics involved in the Vivacity2020 study directed by Professor Rachel Cooper at Lancaster University. I would specifically like to thank those who were involved in the research, design and implementation regarding environmental quality, most notably Dr Mags Adams and Gemma Moore who undertook the Vivacity2020 interviews in Manchester, Sheffield and Clerkenwell, London.

Finally I would like to thank my friend, the designer and cartographer Kate McLean, for her support and kind agreement to use a detail from one of her beautiful smell-maps on the cover of this book.

1

Introduction

One sunny afternoon in July 2012, my family and I made our way through Paris on a very busy Metro train after cheering on the spectacular final stage of the famous Tour De France cycling race. Still in celebratory mood, we were temporarily distracted from our revelry when we realised that our station connecting us to the Gare du Nord was closed. Instead we spilled out of the train, along with dozens of other travellers, one stop earlier than planned. No sooner had the doors opened than the strangest incident occurred. I'm not sure what I became aware of first: a dry, dusty, powdery smell hung in the air; all around, people started coughing and sneezing; my nose tickled and I experienced a tingling, almost burning sensation in the back of my throat, similar to the feeling you might get when breathing in pepper. As I fought the urge to gag and splutter along with my fellow commuters in a desperate attempt to expel whatever substance we were breathing in, I sought out other sensory information to inform me of the source of our collective displeasure, but I could not identify anything abnormal. However, as we descended from the platform among the building rooftops and down towards the street, the source of our discomfort became more apparent.

Despite many previous trips to Paris over the years, this multi-cultural neighbourhood was not one that I had visited before. The area teemed with people; groups of men stood together outside food stores, women and children congregated outside sari shops, and stores with peeling paint sold halal meat and unfamiliar foodstuffs. Heavily congested roads ran alongside and through the area dividing the thronging crowd, and primarily static vehicular traffic emitted fumes onto the pedestrian pavements where people walked laden with assorted coloured plastic bags. My family and I were outsiders in this area and our response to the alien odours hanging in the air reinforced this unfamiliarity. What I had first thought might be the product of some kind of mischievous act was revealed as the combined odours of strong food spices, dust and car fumes. Such encounters are not unusual in the Barbes Rochechouart and La Chappelle area of Paris where we had found ourselves, and are further pronounced during the annual Ganesh Festival when thousands of people descend on the area to celebrate the birthday of this popular Hindu god and camphor is burned as the procession moves through the streets (see Figure 1.1). These odours are not

Figure 1.1 Ganesh Festival, La Chappelle, Paris 2009 ©melodybuhr

those traditionally associated with Paris, represented in popular culture by its street cafés, Gauloises cigarettes and pissoirs; instead they are significant of a changing city and the differences between people and their perceptions of smells.

This incident reminded me of a presentation I attended some years ago in London, delivered by Jamie Furniss, then of Oxford University, on his ethnographic work with Zabaleen communities in Cairo, Egypt (see Figure 1.2). Zabaleen translates as 'garbage collector', and the community lives and works among Cairo's waste, sorting it into different types as part of a recycling initiative driven by economic necessity rather than environmental urgency. Furniss highlighted the objectionable smell of these districts, and explained how he had to learn from and deal with his physical response to the strong odours in undertaking his research (Furniss 2008). This presentation led me to think about the role of smell in cities and urban life, and to wonder how people would respond should the odours from the Zabaleen communities leak into the city's wealthier neighbourhoods. I set out on a quest to better understand experiences of smell in the city, and came to appreciate that these occur as a result of the coming together of people, odours and the environment, occurring at specific points in space and time. I also set about investigating the current and potential consideration of smell within my own broad disciplinary sphere of interest, that of the design and management of urban environments. This book is the product of my research.

Figure 1.2 A little girl walks through the waste, the Zabaleen, Cairo ©jamiefurniss

The smell environments of towns and cities are incredibly important and combine with other sensory information to impact directly on people's everyday experiences of urban life and their perceptions of different places, streets and neighbourhoods. However, when I mention to people that I research smell in cities, they invariably raise an eyebrow and question why it might be important to consider the role of odour in urban environments. Some suggest that we would be better off if we couldn't smell the pollution, the waste or the cigarette smoke frequently associated with urban life. Although these comments originally surprised me, I now appreciate that they are entrenched in society's preoccupation with the way things (people, environments and objects) look, and, to a lesser extent, the way they sound. I also now understand that such comments are influenced by some of the special characteristics of the sense of smell. As Richard Sennett (1994) identified in *Flesh and Stone*, where he examines the (dis)placement of the body in the city over time, city leaders and built environment professionals do not fully consider the physicality of the body within the environment, and as a result, opportunities to create different, stimulating and appropriate places for humans to inhabit within the city are missed.

First, however, it is necessary to clarify what I mean when I refer to 'built environment professionals', and to explain what I believe such professionals and students of related disciplines might gain from this book. I consider the term 'built environment professionals' to encompass everyone who is involved in the planning, design, development, control, maintenance and marketing of urban environments, whether on an immediate day-to-day basis or in terms of medium to long term planning, and according to a variety of scales from specific sites up to the level of the whole city. This term therefore primarily includes city planners, architects, urban designers and city managers, but it also extends to city engineers, geographers, marketers and those with a general interest in urban studies. I believe all of these professions have suffered from disciplinary perspectives which ignore opportunities presented by the sense of smell, and I hope this book will provide valuable information to support them in re-thinking their approaches and avoiding potential pitfalls along the way.

Clearly, the importance of delivering urban environments which meet our needs has never been greater. In 2008, for the first time in human history, the world's population became predominantly urban (United Nations 2008). With the emergence of global 'megacities' such as Mumbai in India, Shanghai in China and Lagos in Nigeria, urban densities around the world look set to continue to grow, thereby creating new ways of living and presenting fresh challenges in city design and management. Much previous research into the sensory aspects of urban life has focused primarily on negative characteristics, frequently labelling these as 'environmental stressors'. Such environmental stressors include undesirable environmental stimulation such as unwanted noise and vibration, and, from an olfactory perspective, poor air quality and 'nuisance' odours. However, just as Schafer (1994) and his colleagues on the World Soundscape Project in Vancouver, Canada made notable steps in highlighting the positive role that 'sound' as opposed to 'noise' can play in environmental experience, smell too has a positive role to play in city life.

'Smellscape' is a term originally coined by Porteous (1990), which can be likened to the visual landscape of an area as recorded in a photograph or painting. Porteous used this term to describe the totality of the olfactory landscape, accommodating both episodic (fore-grounded or time limited) and involuntary (background) odours. However, as Rodaway (1994) highlights, the urban smell environment is not as continuous, integrated and clear as visual, auditory and tactile space, and it is therefore impossible for a human being to detect the entire smellscape of an area as a whole at any one point in time. Following Porteous, when I mention urban smellscapes in this book, I am referring to the overall smell environment, but with the acknowledgement that as human beings, we are only capable of detecting this partially at any one point of time, although we may carry a mental image or memory of the smellscape in its totality. However, more of that later.

Although previous studies have assisted in developing a deeper understanding of the senses in environmental experience and design, few have focused specifically on the sense of smell. Sensory studies scholar Constance Classen (*et al.* 1994, 2005a) and historians Emily Cockayne (2007) and Jonathan Reinarz (2013) have written of everyday historical smell experiences of the city, with others writing of the experiences of specific (usually minority) groups (Classen 1999; Cohen 2006; Manalansan 2006). Low (2009) has examined smell experiences in contemporary Singapore, Grésillon (2010) in Paris, and Mădălina Diaconu *et al.* (2011) in the parks, coffee shops and public transport of Vienna, Austria. However, further and more detailed investigation of the smell characteristics of towns and cities is required, with the specific aim of informing urban design and management practices carried out on a day-by-day basis. In this book, I seek to contribute in broad terms to theory and practice by exploring the role of odour in towns and cities. I will do so by documenting and investigating different interpretations of odours in the urban environment, investigating relationships between urban smellscapes and city experiences and perceptions, and identifying ways of better incorporating smell into city design decision making processes and practice through the introduction of different tools for designing urban smellscapes.

I will draw on observations of urban smellscapes from across the world, some of which I gained alone or with others while undertaking urban 'smellwalks'. However, primarily I focus on two separate but related empirical studies carried out in English cities, which I outline in detail in Chapter 4 alongside a description of smellwalking as a method for researching the urban smellscape.

I have organised this book into three parts, each including three individual chapters. It is designed to allow the reader to either peruse the book from start to finish should they wish, or to dip in and out according to their own specific requirements or interests. Part I (Chapters 2, 3 and 4) provides key context for understanding urban smellscapes, bringing together existing but previously disparate knowledge on the sense of smell and its relationship to city experience and perception. Chapter 2 focuses on the city, Chapter 3 emphasises the human sense of smell and how it works, and Chapter 4 outlines the method of 'smellwalking', used as a valuable mechanism for documenting place specific detections and meanings of odours. Part II (Chapters 5, 6 and 7) explores contemporary experiences of smell in the city according to source type, including air quality and pollution, food, and those odours produced as a consequence of urban policies such as anti-smoking legislation or the encouragement of twenty-four-hour cities and related evening economy activities. Part III (Chapters 8, 9 and 10) draws from the discussion in previous chapters in identifying existing odour control processes in the city, highlighting material factors of influence and some tools by which built environment professionals might seek to positively affect urban smellscapes, and also offering insights into the role of odour in placemaking.

In short, this book investigates the factors at play in everyday experiences and perceptions of odour in the city. Although it does so by drawing in detail from smell experiences in English cities, the issues raised and the design solutions identified are of international relevance and application, as illustrated in the form of supplementary examples from across the world. Ultimately, in writing this book, I seek to engage with others with a passion for cities including academics, researchers, built environment students and professionals, helping to develop practices that better respond to the olfactory challenges and opportunities presented in designing more humanistic and enjoyable places in the city.

Part I

SMELL, SOCIETY
AND CITIES

2

Perspectives on smell and the city I

> When I first began to explore sensory deprivation in space, the problem seemed a professional failure – modern architects and urbanists having somehow lost an active connection to the human body in their designs. In time I came to see that the problem of sensory deprivation in space has larger causes and deeper historical origins. (Sennett 1994: 16)

Advice issued by a UK insurance company in 2008 for claims relating to sensory loss estimated the monetary value of the total loss of the sense of smell at £14,500 to £19,100. This compared to £52,950 to £63,625 for the total loss of hearing, and up to £155,250 for the total loss of sight. Only taste was valued lower than smell at £11,200 to £14,500 (Fox Claims 2008), which is an interesting valuation in its own right given the close associations between smell and taste (smell is responsible for between 70 and 90 percent of taste). It is a sad fact that across the Western world smell is not only one of the most marginalised of the widely recognised five senses, but also the one that people are most willing to lose (Vroon 1997).

I know a philosopher, Marta Tafalla from Barcelona, who has congenital anosmia, meaning that she was born without a sense of smell. She has concluded in her investigations into aesthetic experience that the world is both a less beautiful and a less ugly place without a sense of smell (Tafalla 2011). In my own research I have found that the very way that the sense of smell operates means that it frequently isn't until people lose their ability to smell the world around them that they come to appreciate the important role and influence it has in our everyday lives. The low value that we place on this sense raises important questions as to whether smell truly is of less meaning and use in society today, or whether this lack of appreciation is instead the product, a side-effect, of the prolonged development of built environments that fail to delight our nostrils, tickle our trigeminal nerves and stimulate our olfactory imaginations.

To begin to get under the skin of this issue, we have to look back in history to gain an understanding of why smell is held in such low regard. The reduction of many positively perceived roles for odour in modern Western society has been well documented by others such as Classen *et al.* (1994: 88–91), Zardini

(2005: 277) and Drobnick (2006). Rather than attempting to cover the entire content of their substantial works, I will instead draw out and summarise those key points that are of relevance to the design and management of the built environment.

In the seventeenth and eighteenth centuries, the enlightenment period marked a societal move towards a civilized and humane society which prioritised the 'noble' senses of sight and hearing over the 'lesser' senses of smell, touch and taste. However, this reduction was not isolated to the epistemological approach and production of a certain kind of knowledge during this period; it also became contained within physical built environmental form. In effect, society sought to differentiate humankind from the wider animal kingdom through the rejection of internal bodily chemical senses, viewed as animalistic by figures such as Hegel and Freud (Mavor 2006), in favour of vision and hearing that allow some distance between what is perceived and the person perceiving it. Unlike sight, where a viewer is able to choose what they view and look away if a sight or landscape offends them, our sense of smell cannot be switched off and instead draws in odours indiscriminately whether we perceive them to be good or bad (Engen 1991: 8). In short, we can see that the visual landscape is separate from our bodies and we have some control over our engagement with it. In contrast, we are constantly immersed in the smellscape as we breathe in and out; it is immediate, and it becomes part of our bodies as an integral aspect of the act of detection.

The enlightenment period also brought a view of the natural role of women as being determined through physical and biological factors. The senses of smell, touch and taste became seen as feminine and 'witchlike' (Le Guerer 1993: 3–7, Classen 2005b) with sight and sound considered to be more rational masculine senses. As the dominant group in society (white upper-class men) attempted to exercise control and authority over women through relegating them to the confines of the private domestic sphere, they also sought to control other groups and minorities such as the working masses, ethnic minorities, the elderly and those living and working in the rural hinterlands. These groups also became associated with smell (Cockayne 2007), both as sources of odour themselves and as being more reliant upon smell in their experiences of the world. Reinarz (2013) documents how smell was used well into the twentieth century in reinforcing racial stereotypes in both the US and UK, with immigrants being asked to make themselves available for 'sanitary salvation' as part of what was considered at the time to be part of a process of civilization.

The prioritisation of vision in particular over the other senses was fully embraced by modernism (Barbara and Perliss 2006, Urry 1999: 394–395), leading to the further rejection of positive roles for odour in progressive, high quality urban environments. The resulting ocular-centricity, or as Rodaway (1994: 160) terms it, '...a kind of hyper-realisation of vision', is argued by

Sennett (1994: 16) to have subsequently dominated town and city design. Indeed, Hall argued in 1969 (in Howes 1991) that not only do built environmental practices prioritise the visual above other senses, they also seek to suppress smells in public places, resulting in '...a land of olfactory blandness and sameness that would be difficult to duplicate anywhere else in the world. This blandness makes for undifferentiated spaces and deprives us of richness and variety in our life.' Pallasmaa (2005: 12) explains: 'An architectural work is not experienced as a series of isolated retinal pictures, but in its fully integrated material, embodied and spiritual essence.'

The combination of such ocular-centric architectural practice with a reductionist approach to odour has important consequences for the differentiation between places, and subsequently also for place identity and meaning. However, it is not a universal phenomenon and it certainly has not always been the case in urban planning and city life.

2.1 Historical cities

As Classen *et al.* (1994), Cockayne (2007) and Reinarz (2013) write at length, cities in the past were highly odoriferous sites fuelled by gatherings of large numbers of people in concentrated areas and supported by a cycle of food and goods supply, waste production and removal. From the 'intolerable odours' of nineteenth century Paris and 'the monstrous city' of London (Reinarz 2013), pre-industrial towns and cities across Europe were extremely smelly by today's standards. Strewn with excrement, mud, decomposing animals, meat, vegetables and blood, the pigs that rooted around in the street for organic matter offered only small comfort in reducing the filth among which urban dwellers went about their daily lives. Traditional industries such as tanneries, breweries and tallow-chandlers were located cheek by jowl with residences. Diseases, believed to be carried in the air through foul smells, were rife, and fears of odorous miasmas rising from the ground were heightened during epidemics (Cockayne 2007).

Industrialisation in particular, dubbed the 'excremental age of architecture' by Barbara and Perliss (2006: 30), brought pollution of the air as a by-product of burning coal in the home and in industry, impacting on both air quality and light. It was the smell rather than the smoke that people disliked most since diseases were feared more than respiratory illnesses (Cockayne 2007). Growing urban densities exacerbated the situation, and during one particularly warm summer in the 1850s the Houses of Parliament in London considered moving location due to the stench emerging from the River Thames, which was polluted with sewage and other waste (Steel 2008). However, the period was experienced differently by different people, with location, class, age and education all playing a role in influencing experience. The views of the enlightenment period were adopted by the aristocracy and the growing middle classes, and with this came an attempt to separate sources of smell through zoning activities, particularly those that were the most 'noisome' (Cockayne 2007). Underpinned by a growing recognition of the importance of personal and social hygiene in public health (Howes 1991: 145), sanitation efforts saw the introduction of city-wide sewerage systems into major European cities first, and subsequently into other cities across the Western world. However, the stinks didn't disappear overnight; they did return in subsequent decades, but they were now less connected with disease (Reinarz 2013).

Close proximity to smelly industries started to impact on property values, and as a result the poor became the most likely residents of the most densely populated and worst-smelling neighbourhoods, with the wealthy located in the west of most towns and cities to benefit from the prevailing westerly winds. Urban management processes and legislation were developed including an emphasis on odour release control through practices such as industrial zoning and street cleansing regimes (Rodaway 1994: 151–153). Across the Atlantic, cities such as New York and Chicago were designed with smell and air quality in mind, and the positioning of New York's grid layout was arranged 'in particular to promote the health of the city' by allowing for the 'free and abundant circulation of air' (New York Commissioners, quoted in Burrows *et al.* 1999: 420).

As new building techniques and materials allowed buildings to grow upwards towards the sky, balconies provided the opportunity for the wealthy to gaze at the wider populace without having to breathe in their 'polluting odours' at ground level (Urry 2003). Parks and gardens were also introduced into towns and cities as the wealthy considered these to provide 'lungs' for the city (Sennett 1994, Classen 2001), a means of accessing fresh-smelling air with perceived health benefits. Following compulsory purchase, such green areas in the UK were often created in areas previously inhabited by the poor.

It is therefore important that we dispel any notion of utopian urban smellscapes of the past where all odours were good. Rather, cities can be identified by their very nature as having always been sites of olfactory conflict, where negatively perceived odours combined with those that were more culturally acceptable. However, what is notable and unique about contemporary urban smellscapes is that the interrelated effects of modernism, city design and urban management practices have reduced the perceived role of odour to one that is limited and seen as having a generally negative influence within the urban environment.

2.2 Legislation and policy relating to odour

Most existing legislation and policy from around the world relating to environmental odour is dominated by considerations of air quality and the control of pollutants released into the air. Many of these legislative instruments refer to the presence or level of specific chemicals known to be harmful to humans, the environment and the atmosphere, including chemicals released from vehicular traffic or heavy industrial processes. Since the industrial revolution, air-borne pollutants, and more recently those from traffic emissions, have harmed health by impacting upon a variety of respiratory diseases and thereby increasing mortality rates. The World Health Organisation (2008) estimates that poor air quality is annually responsible for approximately two million premature deaths worldwide.

Issues of environmental degradation and climate change have moved increasingly into the international political arena, stimulating a series of high-profile international agreements (ASEAN 2008, UNFCCC 2008, European Parliament 2009). These agreements influence regional policies in most developed areas, the content of which is relatively consistent. For example, the European Union has issued a number of directives placing requirements on its member states to assess, provide information and work with other member states in reducing levels of key identified air pollutants such as sulphur and nitrogen dioxides, particulate matter and volatile organic compounds such as benzene (see http://www.airqualitynow.eu). Although individual member states are able to respond to these directives via different local mechanisms, this top-down approach has produced broadly similar activities on the ground such as the measurement of key air pollutants in cities and the identification of pollution hotspots.

Across much of the developed world air quality has improved through the burning of cleaner fuels, the decline of heavy industry and the location of power stations away from urban areas. However, increasing levels of vehicular traffic continue to pose a major threat to clean air, despite emission reductions from improvements in vehicle design. In contrast, throughout the developing world many countries have limited air quality legislation or enforcement in place. Emerging megacities such as Mexico City in Mexico, Lagos in Nigeria and Mumbai in India are regularly reported as suffering from air so polluted that it can be difficult to see through the smog (a combination of smoke and fog; a similar situation occurred in London in the 1950s). The Chinese city of Beijing made significant efforts to improve its air quality during the lead-up to the 2008 Olympic Games. Following the introduction of initiatives such as the halting of construction on some sites, closing some power plants and factories and limiting the amount of road traffic during the period immediately before the Games, air quality in the Chinese capital improved significantly

(Cornell University 2009). The Chinese authorities also introduced a policy for increasing sanitation and cleanliness in the city in preparation for the Olympics, including setting new standards of hygiene in public toilets with an aim to reduce the levels of offensive odours emitted (Bristow 2012).

Despite the profile of these emerging megacities as highly polluted places, information compiled by the World Health Organisation (2011) identifies the world's most polluted cities in terms of poor air quality as being smaller, less high-profile cities located in countries such as Iran, India and Pakistan. Generally across the world major towns and cities do suffer from poor air quality, with the input from traffic emissions to overall air pollution being proportionately highest in such areas (Harrison 2000).

One of the most significant factors featuring in air quality complaints is odour (Bokowa 2010, McGinley et al. 2000), but despite this fact its inclusion in law is extremely variable. In a review of legislation from Asia, Australia, Canada, Europe, New Zealand and the United States, Anna Bokowa (2010) identifies that the accommodation of odour in environmental legislation ranges from receiving no specific mention at all in some countries, through to the incorporation of extensive details specifying requirements for testing, modelling, control and monitoring mechanisms in others. Of the legislation with specific mention of odours, definitions of odour pollution centre on the release of substances or odours with the potential to harm human and environmental health or to cause discomfort to humans, often termed as 'nuisance' or 'annoyance'. This is an important point because odour is considered to have both the ability to cause direct harm to people, such as would be the case if a person was to breathe in and smell a toxic substance such as ammonia or smoke, and also to cause indirect harm by stimulating annoyance. The World Health Organisation defines the annoyance threshold for odour nuisance as being at a level where five percent of a specified population experience annoyance for two percent of the time (Nordin and Lidén 2006: 141). Some legislation, such as that in the UK, deems that nuisance can be experienced by individuals rather than being defined by its effect on a percentage of the population, although it is stipulated that this must be at a reasonable level rather than that of an 'over-sensitive' person, and it must be detectable by others such as trained public officials.

Odour control is also sometimes incorporated into planning or development law. In 1995 the Dutch government set specific targets for reducing levels of odour annoyance from industry, agriculture and roads, to a maximum of twelve percent of its population in 2000 and for none of its population to suffer from serious odour annoyance by 2010 (Lagas 2010). It enforced this restriction using a number of different legal mechanisms, including spatial planning. Although there were some notable reductions in odour pollution complaints as a result of the legislation, these did not reduce to the targeted amounts because of development pressures and the increase in proximity between residential and office premises and odour-producing sources as a product of growing urbanisation (*ibid.*). More generally, the trend to locate most odour-producing sources away from urban centres in developed nations has resulted in the majority of the remaining urban odour-producing sources being businesses preparing and selling hot food, retailers, pubs and clubs, and residential properties.

Unlike visual aspects of the environment, such as the protection of views of notable buildings or particular skylines in a city, the vast majority of legislation or policy relating to urban smellscapes places an emphasis on the control of odour emissions rather than highlighting any potentially positive roles that smell might play. One notable exception is a policy produced by the Japanese Ministry for the Environment, which identifies the role of 'good fragrance' as well as the management of offensive odours in a high quality environment. The Japanese government coordinated an initiative encouraging local citizens 'to participate voluntarily in local activities to understand the importance of preserving a good odour environment and to secure a better living environment through the reduction of offensive odours' (Japanese Ministry for the Environment, date unknown). As a result the government identified 'One Hundred Sites of Good Fragrance' across Japan, with sites listed in each of Japan's forty-seven prefectures. Sites include those with smells from a wide variety of sources, such as: *vegetation*, e.g. 'Japanese beeches and dogtooth violets of Mount Kenashigasen' and 'a hundred thousand peach blossoms at a glance'; *food*, e.g. 'grilled sweetfish from the Gogasegawa River' and the 'Nabu rice cracker of Morioka'; and *natural environment characteristics*, e.g. the 'steam of Beppu's eight springs' and 'the scent of rocky coast at Iwami Tatamigaura'. The list also includes urban odours such as the 'early morning market and traditional cityscape of Hida Takayama', 'Kanda's streets of used bookstores' (Tokyo), and the 'scents of liquor and soy sauce from Kurayoshi white-mud wall storehouses'. In identifying these sites the government and local citizens make visible the presence of these odours, and in doing so they increase the likelihood that these will be considered in any future development or design in those areas.

2.3 Odour classification, language and measurement

An inherent issue that city authorities face when attempting to control and enforce odour law and policy is the notorious difficulty of recording, measuring, describing and classifying odour. This issue is complicated even further when attempting to gain an understanding of the complexities of human perceptions of the urban smellscape. The delivery of a unified odour categorisation system has long eluded scientists, with systems being more revealing of those producing the odours than of the nature of the odours themselves. For example, Aristotle classified odour into seven categories: aromatic, fragrant, alliaceous (garlic), ambrosial (musky), hircinous (goaty), repulsive and nauseous (Landry 2006: 62). In contrast, the Kapsiki in Cameroon classify odours into fourteen categories, including mèdèke (the smell of various animals), rhwazhake (the smell of urine), 'urduk'duk (the smell of milk) and ndaleke (the smell of rotting meat or a corpse) (Classen *et al.* 1994: 111). Odour is clearly embedded within culture and belief systems, and unlike air quality levels, which can be monitored using devices set to detect levels of specific chemicals in the air, smells do not lend themselves easily to quantitative measurement.

Exacerbating this issue even further, most modern European languages have an insufficiently developed vocabulary for smells. In addition to the 'tip of the nose problem', which occurs when we detect a smell but are unable to identify and name exactly what it is (partially a result of the processing of smell through the brain's emotion centre in the limbic system), the description of odours can be very difficult. This is further compounded when differentiating between descriptions of the sense of smell, the act of smelling and the smell itself, and confused by everyday use of the verb 'to smell'. Fox (2006: 26) highlights that the statement that something 'smells' is generally interpreted negatively unless it is clarified; '...to give praise, we must specify that they "smell good" or "smell nice" ... Smells are guilty until proven innocent.'

Dann and Jacobsen (2003) observe that people frequently highlight potential sources of smell rather than odour qualities in their descriptions. Terms such as sulphurous, eggy, floral, earthy or nutty are used, and people also fall back on descriptive terms from other senses such as sweet, bitter, dry, light or fresh (Classen *et al.* 1994: 109–110). In an attempt to overcome this problem, academics at UCLA have developed a number of odour descriptor wheels including the words people use to describe specific odours along with their chemical names, and linking these back to potential sources or area types (Suffet and Rosenfeld 2007). Alongside odour descriptor wheels for drinking water, waste water and compost, they have developed another for urban odours (Curren *et al.* 2013; see Figure 2.1).

Further attempts to measure the smell environment were made by researchers at the Technical University of Denmark in the late 1980s and 1990s, focusing primarily on indoor air pollution but also relating to outdoor air pollution. Fanger (1988) introduced the idea of the 'olf', a unit he defined as the emission rate of air pollutants (bioeffluents) from one standard person, identified rather specifically as a sedentary white-collar worker with a skin surface area of 1.8 metres who takes 0.7 baths per day (Fanger *et al.* 1988). Fanger and his colleagues also introduced the 'decipol', defined as '...the pollution caused by one standard person (one olf) ventilated by 10 litres of unpolluted air' (*ibid.*: 1). The air pollutants or bioeffluents to which they referred were described as being

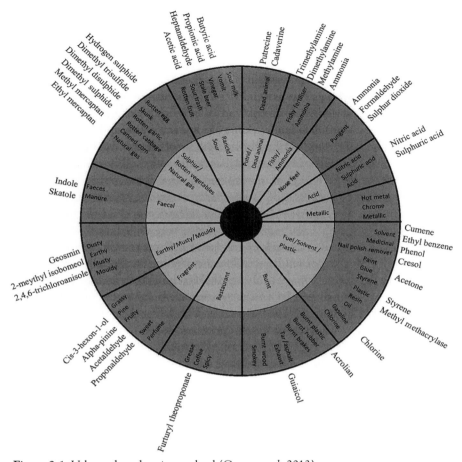

Figure 2.1 Urban odour descriptor wheel (Curren *et al.* 2013)

detected through the nose, and although they were not identified as such, the notions referred primarily to the measurement of odours. Fanger further extended his work to the quantification of non-human odour sources including tobacco smoke, building materials, furnishings and industrial pollution sources (*ibid.*: 5). Although Fanger and his colleagues made a useful contribution to the research of air quality in indoor environments specifically, their work focused upon the quantification of odour intensity rather than individual differences in the perception of odour qualities (as being positive/negative/neutral and so on).

The typical method by which city officials such as environmental officers assess ambient environmental odour is through their own sense of smell, via a 'sniff test'. The Chinese city of Guangzhou was reported by the BBC in 2007 to have trained 'noses', each professionally certificated for three years to sniff out sources of industrial odour pollution including that emitted by rubber factories, oil refineries and rubbish dumps (BBC 2007a). Unlike soundscapes, which can be recorded through the use of sound recording equipment, the human sense of smell is currently the most sensitive tool available for assessing smellscapes, distinguishing between odours and accommodating contextual information. However, the assessment of odours by people rather than machines is occasionally criticised, described as inconsistent, subjective and leading to uncertainty in decision-making processes (Yang and Hobson 2000). With advances in technology, quantitative tools for measuring, predicting, assessing and making odour-related decisions are becoming increasingly common with some city authorities stating a preference for the use of predictive models where feasible (Fraser 2002). Such tools are argued by Yang and Hobson (2000), Fraser (2002) and Nordin and Lidén (2006) to have the potential to provide an objective, consistent approach to assessing environmental odours, increasing the value for money of resulting odour control or reduction measures. However, Yang and Hobson (2000) acknowledge that these approaches, including olfactometry (an instrument used to detect the presence of odour compounds, strength and dilution), hydrogen sulphide measurements (measuring the presence in the air of this specific chemical compound, associated with sewage treatment plants, landfill sites and other such industrial plants), estimates of emission rates and dispersion modelling all have '...considerable margins of error which should not be ignored' (*ibid.*: 105).

Such models are based on an assumption that odour emissions should not exceed a maximum concentration level at specified sites, usually those where people such as residents or workers are located (DEFRA 2010: 33). Complex statistical models provide the opportunity to analyse the possible impacts of odour-producing businesses prior to their existence, as well as to examine the potential effectiveness of related abatement measures. They take into account such factors as wind flow, odour dispersal and the location of people, and are usually interpreted using a site-specific analysis of dose-response relationships (Miedema *et al.* 2000). Until recently, existing businesses were assessed using a 'sniff test' on site, or samples of air containing potentially offensive odours were collected at sites in special containers, taken back to the laboratory and analysed either by human panels of trained sniffers or by machines. The samples would be assessed for factors such as concentration (strength/intensity) and hedonism (enjoyment). However, new mobile olfactometers such as the 'Nasal Ranger' (see Figure 2.2) are starting to emerge, facilitating the mechanical assessment of odour dilution (as opposed to odour identification) on site and in real time. Such tools are increasingly used across the US both by odour producing businesses and by city officials (Weber 2011, The History Channel 2012).

Figure 2.2 Mobile olfactometry: the Nasal Ranger ©St.CroixSensoryInc

2.4 Odour and urban design practice and theory

Just as in legislation, positive roles for smell in urban design, planning and policy documents are rarely considered, and I know from personal experience that during the years I worked in developing and regenerating sites within cities, smell was something that we scarcely, if ever, thought about. As a result, important place identity odours might easily be destroyed or overlaid, without the professionals involved ever being aware of their existence. This possibility is acknowledged by the conservation body English Heritage (2010: 11) in its guide to carrying out assessments of historic areas: '...static visual attributes are supplemented or modified by a range of other factors derived largely from movement, sounds and smells, including such things as ... perfumes arising from gardens and the smell of certain industrial processes or effluents.'

More commonly, however, when odour is mentioned in the built environment literature it is generally in negative terms. In a text on public places, Carmona *et al.* (2003: 238) include a figure by the Government Office for London (1996) entitled 'The core contributors to the quality of London's urban environment', highlighting smell alongside noise and air pollution as a 'maintaining influence' in need of reduction. Henri Lefebvre (2009: 198) observes this negative status and perceived role for smell, commenting that '...the sense of smell had its glory days when animality still predominated over "culture", rationality and education – before these factors, combined with a thoroughly cleansed space, brought about the complete atrophy of smell.' Rodaway (1994: 151) argues that Lefebvre's argument is too simplistic and suggests that smell has instead been redefined within the spectrum of sensory experience, organised according to different strategies of smell control. In Chapter 8 we will examine some practical examples and the impact of these odour control processes in modern cities.

Whether they are the result of conscious or unconscious decisions made within the framework of a reductionist or strategic approach to odour, built environmental practices are today argued to be creating increasingly homogenised, sterile and controlled environments, suffering from what Drobnick (2002: 34) identifies as '...an alienating sense of placelessness'. The situation is compounded by forces of globalisation, argued by the New Economics Foundation (2005: 6) to have turned forty-one percent of the UK's surveyed towns into 'clone towns', defined as '...a place that has had the individuality of its high street shops replaced by a monochrome strip of global and national chains.' Such changes are also suggested to be contributing towards the homogenisation of olfactory environments (Illich 1986, Gill 2005, Reynolds 2008) as retailers of fast food and scented products release odours into the city. This phenomenon is discussed further in Chapter 8.

Processes of globalisation are further argued to result in the development of public spaces that exhibit an idealised cosmopolitan image of their respective neighbourhoods and cities. This is what Degen (2008) terms 'the Global Catwalk' for investment and tourism, which often ignores or intentionally overwrites local community use and place attachment. As a result, towns and cities combine both global and local elements that co-exist within the urban fabric (Smith 2007: 101), and as Relph (1976: 140) comments: '...there is a geography of places characterised by variety and meaning, and there is a placeless geography, a labyrinth of endless similarities.'

Placemaking has emerged as a central theme in urban design, aimed at rediscovering, enhancing, protecting or creating locally significant place-related meanings. Fleming (2007: 14) describes place as being '...not merely what was there, but also the interaction of what is there and what happened there'; this is therefore heavily situated within individual and social experience and memory. As I will go on to outline later, the sense of smell has a special and highly celebrated link with memory and place perception, but as Phyllis Lambert of the Canadian Centre for Architecture writes in Zardini (2005: 14–15), 'the whole gamut of "sensorial" phenomena that figure prominently in daily experience ... are strikingly absent from urban studies.'

Some urban and architectural theorists offer useful observations when thinking about the role of smell in experiencing and designing urban environments. Rasmussen (1959) describes architecture and city design as functional arts that should appeal as much to the ear as they do to the eye. He talks in detail about the feel of material textures underfoot, although he falls short of considering the sense of smell in his work. In her seminal text 'The Death and Life of Great American Cities', Jacobs (1961) stresses the importance of the human dimension and difference while also making observations on the opportunities and limitations of visual order in the city. Lynch (1960) and Cullen (1961) both focus primarily on visual dimensions of urban design, but they do so in very different ways: Lynch through engaging with local communities and representing his ideas on the image of the city in the abstract form of a plan, and Cullen by sketching his experience of the street as he navigates his way through the space. Pallasmaa (2005) tracks the ocular-centric approach in architectural theory and practice and places the body as central in designing architectural space. He briefly highlights smell in the second part of his celebrated short book 'The Eyes of the Skin', referencing associations between memory and smell and highlighting the sterility of modern architecture when compared to the provocative emotional imagery conveyed by a consideration of smell in other art forms such as poetry (*ibid.*: 54–56).

More recently, urban design and architecture theorists and practitioners have turned their attention more directly towards the senses. A number of studies have investigated the role of sound in urban environments (e.g. Schafer 1994; Kang and Yang 2003, Davies *et al.* 2007) and the bio-climate and thermal properties of urban space (e.g. Nikolopoulou 2003, 2004; Nikolopoulou *et al.* 2001; Nikolopoulou & Lykoudis 2007; Tahbaz 2010; Tseliou *et al.* 2010). In his edited text Zardini (2005) argues for a more sensory approach to urban design with an aim to '...analyse urban phenomena in terms of luminosity and darkness, seasons and climate, the smell of the air, the material surfaces of the city, and sounds.'

The documentation of the range and meaning of odours in contemporary urban environments remains limited, although some urban theorists have provided useful observations regarding the relationship between cities, place and smell. Landry (2006: 61–68) highlights his experiences of urban odours in his book on the art of city making, describing the 'globalized' smells of petro-chemicals, fruits, vegetables and spices from markets, and odours from stores, restaurants and breweries. Barbara and Perliss (2006) draw together previously disparate knowledge on place and odour associations across time and space, including fascinating interviews in 'smelly' sites with perfumers, architects and those working in such areas as New York's meat packing district and the Hermes leather production centre in Paris. Malnar and Vodvarka (2004) go further in developing a theory on the role of the senses in architecture, with specific reference to the different perceptual qualities of sensory modes and including reference to the sense of smell. They consider odour as having immediate, ambient or episodic qualities referencing the strength of smells in three dimensional space. They also propose tools for recording sensory evaluations of space, as do Lucas and Romice (2008) in their sensory environmental notation system.

However, this developing body of work on the senses and urban design is frequently patchy with regard to the issue of individual, social and cultural perspectives on odours and how these might be accommodated when thinking about the meaning of different smells in cities and potential effects on everyday urban design practices. One very interesting project in this field is the Tastduftwien (taste-smell-Vienna) project, carried out in Vienna, Austria and led by philosopher Mădălina Diaconu. The project explored and mapped odour and touch in the city, investigating memories and the varied meanings of odour with local residents (Diaconu *et al.* 2011). It examined odour experiences in parks and gardens, public transport, cafés, popular public spaces, vintage shops and playgrounds. The project also highlighted a link between odour scenting and potential allergic reactions, an issue we will discuss in further detail later in this book, and touched upon the implicit use of olfactory design in the built environment in the form of air conditioning and ventilation units.

French architect Suzel Balez (2002) also explored experiences of smell from the specific perspective of architectural design in her unpublished doctoral research implemented within the enclosed environment of an indoor shopping centre in Grenoble, France. Balez undertook walks with people through the shopping centre and identified thirty-two different olfactory effects, which will be explored in further detail in Chapter 10 in relation to the design of outdoor urban environments.

2.5 Conclusion

In an age when cities are playing an increasingly important role in everyday human experiences and much investment has taken place in city infrastructure, I join a growing number of architects and urbanists in calling for the development of a new sensory approach to urbanism which provides a means by which people might '...enhance their polysensoriality of the city and imagine how to design or redesign it in sensuously fitting and stimulating new ways' (Howes 2005: 330). In exploring historical perspectives on smell and identifying current architectural, urban design and management practices embedded within social and cultural thought, values and norms, one can begin to appreciate that city design, and specifically the urban dweller's experiences of smell in the city, could be other than they are. The focus on smell as a factor of primarily negative influence places limits on opportunities for other, potentially positive roles for olfactory encounters in everyday urban life, but this does not mean that smells no longer exist in the city. Instead, I suggest that smells come about as an unintended consequence of architectural and urban design, with a variety of odour management strategies currently under way within the city.

Before moving on to explore people's experiences of different odours and identify the strategies under taken in managing urban smellscapes, I will first outline some qualities of the sense of smell and highlight factors of influence in smell perception, examining how these may relate to theories of place perception and thus the urban imagery.

3

Perspectives on smell and the city II

In this chapter I draw from different disciplines, including the natural and social sciences, psychology and built environment disciplines, to describe how the sense of smell functions, its different qualities and factors of influence in olfactory performance. I do so by exploring characteristics of the odour, the various environments we inhabit, and individual factors such as age, gender and sensitivity to smell.

3.1 Qualities of the sense of smell

The mechanism by which the sense of smell operates has for a long time eluded science; in the 1940s Boring observed that research into olfaction had progressed only to the same scientific level as had been achieved for sight and sound by the mid-eighteenth century (in Porteous 1990: 23). Indeed, it is only in recent years that a dominant theory has been widely accepted by the scientific community about how this sense works. The sense of smell functions by drawing information from two key smell sensing organs: *olfactory receptors* provide the primary source for detection, with additional information provided through the *trigeminal nerve*.

Buck and Axel won a Nobel Prize in 2004 for their pioneering work investigating the olfactory system, specifically their research outlined in a paper published in 1991. They discovered a large group of around one thousand genes relating to an equivalent number of olfactory receptor types, each located within receptor cells. Each receptor is highly specialised and detects only a limited number of odours. When a smell is inhaled, it travels through the nose and is dissolved in nasal mucus. Information is passed through neurons to the receptors and on to the olfactory bulb which is located in the limbic system, known as the emotional centre of the brain. This relays information to other parts of the brain to form a pattern, and it is this pattern that the brain recognises, drawing from previous memories of encounters with that odour (Buck and Axel 1991). Hirsch (2006: 187) claims that the olfactory receptors enable the average person to differentiate between approximately ten thousand different smells, although the concentration of an odour is important.

Normally, a human is able to detect odours in concentrations as low as a few parts per billion when diluted in air (DEFRA 2010: 8), and other animals can detect much lower concentration levels (BBC Radio 4 2009). This is a product of humans having significantly fewer receptors than many animals (Herz 2006: 191, Chudler 2010), although the sophistication of the human brain allows olfactory information to be interpreted and used in a more complex manner.

The second lesser known element of the sense of smell is the trigeminal nerve, which is the nerve responsible for sensation in the face. Olfactory nerve endings on the trigeminal nerve are able to detect even low concentrations of some odours, producing bodily sensations, typically tingling and hot or cold feelings, usually associated with substances such as petrol, paint, nail varnish remover and many toxic chemicals. In 1978 Doty *et al.* observed a systematic relationship between trigeminal stimulation and perceptual scales of odour intensity, pleasantness, coolness/warmth and presumed safety. Most odours have some trigeminal element to them; this is what makes some people's eyes water when peeling onions, or causes people to sneeze when smelling pepper (Herz 2006: 193). Some substances possess odours that are detectable only through the trigeminal nerve, such as a number of air pollutants.

Once an odour is detected, identifying it can be problematic as the brain assesses it for familiarity and attempts to recall previous encounters in trying to identify the source. However, as Engen (1982: 102–103) suggests, the naming of odours is a more complex task than merely recognising familiarity. Desor and Beauchamp (1974) highlight that when asked to identify the source of a common odour using the sense of smell alone, even an individual with normal olfactory performance has only a forty to fifty per cent chance of doing so successfully.

Once odours have been detected and identified, sometimes without involving any conscious thought processes, the body adapts and habituates to those smells with detection decreasing for the remainder of exposure on that occasion. Although they are frequently confused, odour adaptation and habituation are two different responses that take place following smell detection. Engen (1991: 25) explains: 'While adaptation is caused by the fatigue of the receptors, habituation is an adjustment to an odour based on an unconscious judgement that it is of no significance and can be ignored'. Adaptation therefore occurs following initial exposure to an odour as a result of the reduced ability of receptors to detect an odour over time, usually occurring over approximately twenty minutes. Unless an odour is toxic and able to damage the olfactory receptors on a permanent basis, the sense of smell will fully recover from receptor fatigue following a short break away from the odour, sometimes of only a few minutes. Perfumers famously sniff at coffee beans or their own skin in an attempt to clear their nose of odours in between the mixing of different ingredients or accords. Habituation, on the other hand, often leads to people no longer consciously registering an odour when entering environments where it is present, due to it being an extremely familiar smell that does not pose any potential threat. This would include, for example, the smell of people's own homes or, in the case of smokers, the smell of smoke on their clothes, which although not registered by themselves, will usually be detected by others.

3.2 Olfactory performance

Previous studies on olfactory performance have broadly focused on two distinct areas: odour detection and odour identification. The ability to detect an odour and the way the odour is perceived can vary according to the characteristics of the smell, the characteristics of the individual detecting it and the environment; these sources of variation are summarised in Figure 3.1. The characteristics of a smell can vary in a number of important ways, each of which interacts with human detection and perception. These include: *odour concentration*, with some odours being detectable at much lower concentrations than others and even favourite odours being experienced as repulsive at very high levels of concentration; *trigeminal stimulation*, whereby odours that tickle our trigeminal nerves are generally less preferable than non-trigeminal odours,

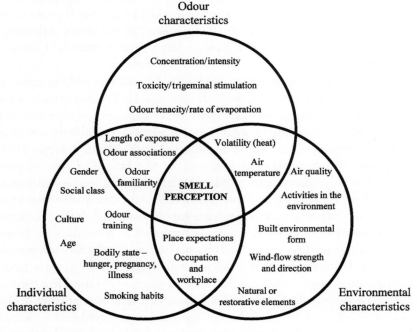

Figure 3.1 Smell perception – summary of influencing factors

although this varies from individual to individual; *odour tenacity*, the rate at which an odour evaporates from a surface, a widely-used term in the perfume industry; and the *qualities of the odour* itself (floral, spicy and so on), which has associations with our familiarity with an odour and our past individual, social and cultural experiences. This will be discussed further under odour perception.

3.2.1 Individual factors

Our different personal characteristics also affect our ability to smell the world around us. In the largest survey on smell ever conducted, including 1.5 million respondents, women were found able to smell more acutely than men (Synnott 1991). Females are documented in numerous studies as displaying higher olfactory performance than males, including detection (Keller *et al.* 2012), identification and recollection of an odour (Doty *et al.* 1985) and detection through repeated exposure (Diamond *et al.* 2005), although not when exposed to an odour on a single occasion (*ibid.*). Although these differences are frequently attributed to hormonal changes linked with the menstrual cycle (Winter 1976, Schenker 2001), it has also been suggested that differences in identification might be explained through better verbal recollection and/or odour familiarity in females, with difficulties in the ability to retrieve information through memory being a limiting factor for males (Cain 1982: 140). Furthermore, Cain (1982) also found that some odours were associated with specific genders, such as the smell of cigar butts, beer and machine oil with males, and soap, baby powder and nail-varnish remover with females.

Prior to commencing 'smellwalks', outlined further in the next chapter, I asked people to rate their own sense of smell in their own words. I found significant differences according to participant gender, with sixty-five per cent of female participants rating their sense of smell highly as compared to only twenty-eight per cent of male participants (see Chart 3.1).

Some male participants went as far as suggesting that the study would benefit from interviewing named female relatives rather than themselves, due to these individuals' more sensitive odour detection abilities. Once out on-site, however, there appeared to be few significant differences in odour detection performance according to gender, although female participants did express more disgust in response to some odours detected, such as those of vomit, urine or body odour, thus displaying increased 'sensitivity'.

Age is known to have a major limiting influence upon smell performance, with fifty per cent of people exhibiting a major loss in olfactory function over the age of sixty-five (Kivity *et al.* 2009: 241). A study carried out in Sweden by Larssona *et al.* (2000) found that the ability to detect and identify odours both reduced with age. Similar to gender, the recollection and retrieval of olfactory information in older people also appears to cause particular barriers

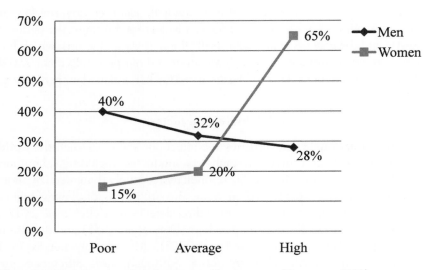

Chart 3.1 Participant smell performance self-assessments (Doncaster, 2009)

in performance (Schemper *et al.* 1981). Many neuropsychiatric diseases linked with ageing such as Alzheimer's disease and Parkinson's disease, along with others that are less age-specific such as schizophrenia, directly influence olfactory performance (Schiffman *et al.* 2002). Indeed, olfactory performance is noted by Strous and Shoenfeld (2006) as a potential early indicator of such diseases. A recent study by Keller *et al.* (2012) also reported that body size plays an influence in olfactory detection, with those people who rated their body size as either under- or overweight having lower olfactory acuity than those with a self-reported normal body weight.

The bodily state of individuals also plays an important role, as I have found in my own research; this is particularly noticeable in the case of food odours. Hungry participants are consistently more likely to perceive food smells as positive, whereas pregnant participants or those suffering from an illness more often than not also reported changed smell performance, becoming more or less sensitive to odours depending upon the nature of the illness. These findings complement existing literature which notes pregnancy (Schenker 2001) and general health (Schiffman *et al.* 2002, Strous and Shoenfeld 2006) as important factors in smell performance.

A person's smoking habits also have an influence; in a study in Germany involving more than 1,300 participants, smoking significantly increased the risk of reduced smell performance (Vennemann *et al.* 2008). For the majority of the general population impaired performance is experienced on a temporary basis at some point, with almost two in three people having suffered a temporary loss of smell (Synnott 1991). Around one per cent of the general population is anosmic, having no sense of smell at all (*ibid.*), with causes ranging from nose surgery or illness to exposure to toxic substances (see Herz 2006: 192–193).

However, the vast majority of people have the potential to improve their ability to discriminate between odours through nose training. Li *et al.* (2008) found that people could be trained to identify the difference between two very similar 'grassy' odours. A larger study carried out at the University of Philadelphia investigated smell and taste function and performance in a visually impaired population, including three test groups in the study design. One of the groups included thirty-nine blind people, another contained fifty-four sighted people with a normal sense of smell, and the last group contained twenty-three sighted people who had been trained in odour assessment relating to water quality. The study found that those with a trained nose outperformed both of the other groups in terms of odour detection and discrimination (Smith *et al.* 1993).

Those undertaking training or using their sense of smell as part of their job, such as city officials in environmental health, are therefore likely to experience enhanced olfactory performance. Similarly, those exposed to specific odours within the workplace, such as people who work in waste-water plants or abattoirs, are likely to become habituated to those odours to some degree. Alongside people's individual characteristics, there are therefore a range of environmental factors impacting upon olfactory performance and perceptions; these will be discussed below.

3.2.2 Environmental factors

Data from the National Geographic Smell Survey carried out in the mid 1980s, involving 712,000 respondents aged between twenty and seventy-nine years, indicated that those who had been exposed to a factory environment over a prolonged period had an increased risk of impairment or total loss of olfactory performance (Corwin *et al.* 1995). This risk was found to be higher in men, and was frequently associated with workplace incidents such as head injuries and exposure to chemicals.

As I discuss further in Chapter 9, the form and content of the built environment also has a significant impact on odour detection and identification. Studies such as those carried out by Cochran (2004), Nikolopoulou (2003, 2004), Penwarden and Wise (1975) and Tahbaz (2010) have examined wind flow for its thermal and haptic (touch) characteristics, but few studies have examined the role of the built environment in influencing odour, such as its role in encouraging odour distribution or dispersal. The importance of these factors becomes apparent when we examine the distances across which smells can travel. The sense of smell is widely described as a proximate sense, concerned largely with stimulation at close quarters (Porteous 1990: 7, Kostner 2002), as compared with auditory and visual stimuli which are believed to be detectable over much larger distances. Although this model holds true in many circumstances, it is not always the case. There are numerous examples where unidentified odours have travelled large distances and covered vast areas. In 2008 an unidentified odour, said to originate from mainland Europe, was detected across the south of England over a couple of days, even travelling as far north as Liverpool (BBC 2008a), and in 2010 the sulphurous smell of the Icelandic volcano was detected many hundreds of miles away in Scotland (Booth and Carrell 2010).

In terms of cities, New York appears to be particularly prone to large-scale mystery smell incidents. In October 2005 the New York Times reported a sweet, syrupy odour being detected overnight right across the city, starting in Lower Manhattan in the evening and travelling uptown before spreading out into neighbouring boroughs (DePalma 2005). Although the smell was one traditionally associated with pleasant products such as maple syrup and caramel, the incident led to hundreds of calls to the city's emergency services. As reporter Anthony DePalma elaborated, 'The aroma not only revived memories of childhood, but in a city scared by terrorism, it raised vague worries about an attack deviously cloaked in the smell of grandma's kitchen' (*ibid.*). In January 2007 the city experienced a similar incident across large areas of Manhattan and eastern New Jersey, but this time the qualities of the smell itself were less pleasant. The odour was described as pungent, sulphurous and gas-like, and was detected between nine and eleven o'clock on a busy Monday morning, leading to an emergency response across the city with some schools, offices and a subway station being closed in response to fears of a gas leak (BBC 2007b, Chan 2007). In both cases city officials used monitoring equipment to determine that the odours were not toxic, but they were unable to identify the source of the odours which dissipated as quickly as they had appeared.

Given the grid layout of New York City, intended by its commissioners to encourage the flow of air and maximise the benefits of freshening westerly winds, such large-scale collective odour experiences across vast populations and areas of the city might be considered somewhat ironic. However, the city's form is likely to have played a contributory role. Patrick Kinney, an Associate Professor of Environmental Science at Columbia University, observed of the incident in 2005 that the cold January night-time air would have been trapped under a lid of warm air over the city, which, given the three-mile-an-hour wind recorded on the evening in question, meant that any odour would have been kept low to the ground. As a result the odour might have slipped between buildings to work its way uptown towards the other boroughs (DePalma 2005).

Individuals are therefore frequently able to detect odours from sources that cannot be seen, with scents carried on the wind over long distances providing information to the individual that cannot be detected through other senses.

Such long-distance detection is highly temporal, dependent on specific weather conditions, wind patterns and seasonal waves of activity, with air temperature directly influencing odour strength and volatility by encouraging the evaporation of odorous volatile molecules from the source. Furthermore, olfactory performance is further influenced in the city by the built environmental form which has the ability to influence wind flow and temperature.

3.3 Smell and memory

Dove (2008: 17) describes the sense of smell as '…the pathway to the memory of a person', given its widely celebrated relationship with memory and its ability to transport people back through space and time to previous encounters with that odour. Compared with memories gained through other senses, odour experiences can be more frequently recalled after many years, even several decades after they were last experienced – hence Marcel Proust's famous recollections of his childhood madeleines (Proust 2006, first published in 1927). In an investigation into differences between memory retrieval from visual and olfactory stimuli, Engen (1977, in Engen 1982) identified that although participants were far more likely to recall and identify visual images in the short term, particularly within the first two months after initial exposure, odour recollection and identification was much more consistent over time. He found that odours were correctly recalled and identified even twelve months after exposure, highlighting that once we have formulated memories of odours, we are very likely to retain them.

The ability of smell to summon nostalgic memories of places, events and people is argued by King (2008) to have immense power and meaning. Nostalgia is described by Davis (1979) as '…a positively toned evocation of a lived past', and odours that prompt nostalgic feelings, frequently recalled from childhood, can vary significantly according to the geographical location and time in which people grew up. In a study by Hirsch (2006), interviews carried out with a thousand randomly selected people found that eighty-five per cent experienced odour-induced nostalgic memories and emotions. The odours that invoked nostalgic feelings changed according to the decade within which participants were born. Those born between the 1920s and 1940s mentioned more naturally-occurring odours such as flowers, grass, sea, manure and hay. Those born in later decades, from the 1950s to 1970s, mentioned food and artificial odours often associated with brands, such as Play Doh, Crayola, parents' perfumes, suntan lotion and cleaning products (Hirsch 2006).

This recollection characteristic is indiscriminate, however, and odour can trigger negative memories, emotional attachments and associations just as it can cause feelings that are more positive and nostalgic. Odour-induced memories are frequently linked to post-traumatic stress disorder, potentially triggering panic attacks (Hinton *et al.* 2006). A survivor of Thailand's tsunami of 2006 was reported in the Guardian a year after the event as having '…a daily intrusion of smells, sensations and inexplicable panics' whenever she encountered the smell of water (Linklater 2007). The sense of smell thus facilitates access to significant memories of odour experiences both good and bad (Schleidt *et al.* 1988), rather than being limited to first encounters with odour.

3.4 Smell perception

Smell perception enables people to make sense of odours and gain insights into the physical and socially constructed environment by attaching meaning through association. Rodaway (1994: 10–13) notes that sensory perception is widely defined according to two different meanings: perception as the detection of information through the senses, and perception as mental insight made up of sensory information combined with memories and expectations. He suggests that a geographical, and thus (within the context of the current enquiry) an urban understanding of perception, must recognise both dimensions, outlining perception as 'sensation' including environmental stimuli detected and mediated by the senses, and perception as 'cognition', a mental process involving memory recollection, recognition, association and other thinking processes, all of which he describes as culturally mediated. It is this understanding of perception as both detection and a mental process that I use within this book.

Engen (1991) suggests that odour perception serves two main purposes: first as a sensor for self-preservation against potentially harmful substances, and second as an hedonic agent relating to enjoyment. He observes that '…anything toxic makes one sick and naturally becomes unpleasant. Anything good or neutral could go either way, depending on individual – often idiosyncratic – experiences with it, which remain in the memory for future use' (*ibid.*: 3). As outlined earlier, odour detection allows the body to note and potentially identify smells, often on an unconscious basis. This mechanism allows the body to recognise whether an odour is familiar or not, with unfamiliar smells being treated suspiciously, more likely to be interpreted as posing a potential threat and therefore be judged as unpleasant (Porteous 1990: 24). Not only does this rule apply to the smells of things, but also of people. Schleidt *et al.* (1988) found that although people described their recollections of the odours of family and friends in positive terms, they described the odours of unfamiliar people in very negative terms. According to Engen (1991), when familiar odours are detected the mind draws on memories of previous experiences and associations with that smell to determine whether it is a threat. However, our memories are individually, socially and culturally situated, varying significantly from person to person (Gilbert and Wysocki 1987, Schleidt *et al.* 1988). Themed preferences therefore emerge among specific groups according to factors such as age (Hirsch 2006), nationality (Schleidt *et al.* 1988, Damhuis 2006) or gender (Wysocki and Pelchat 1993, Wysocki 2005).

On the basis that people consider unfamiliar odours in more negative terms than known odours, then contextual information such as that gained from a familiar environment has the potential to shape smell preference. Differences in various types of places or the components of towns and cities provide place-specific exposure to odorous substances or unique combinations of smells that could not be experienced in nature in other places. That is not to say that the different smell ingredients that combine to form an urban smellscape are themselves necessarily unique to only one place, or one type of place, but that the mix of odours in different proportions has the potential to create a unique olfactory pattern: a smell genetics of place. Ironically, although such an olfactory combination might be considered positive by its indigenous population due to their respective familiarity with the particular local smellscape and its various odorous components, it might also remain unnoticed by them, being more likely to be noticed by visitors to the area.

The hedonic value or enjoyment of smells is therefore a complex issue to understand, and can stimulate both avoidance and pleasure-seeking behaviours. The very foundation on which odour enjoyment is formulated can be further situated within individual, social and cultural experiences and norms if we appreciate that few if any odour preferences are innate (Engen 1982). As Herz (2006: 202) concludes, '...nothing stinks, but thinking makes it so.' Following research at the Monell Chemical Senses Centre in Philadelphia, commissioned by the US Government to investigate negatively perceived odours that might trigger crowd dispersal in any culture, the smell of excrement was identified as that most likely to gain this response (Trivedi 2002). However, as Engen (1982, 1991) and Stein *et al.* (1958) note, babies like odours of excrement and sweat because such smells are familiar to them. Researchers testing odour preferences around the world have therefore failed to identify any odour that is consistently judged as repellent (Herz 2006: 196). Instead, a combination of odours is judged by Monell psychologist Pamela Dalton to 'last[s] longer and provide[s] more of a punch' (in Trivedi 2002).

Schleidt *et al.* (1988) investigated the impact of culture upon odour preference in a study using German and Japanese participants. They found that although there were some cultural and individual differences, most odours were generally assessed in similar ways – for example, the odours of plants were rated as pleasant and the odours of rotten items were unpleasant. Between 2009 and 2010, I carried out my own small-scale study with one hundred people aged from ten to seventy years from across Europe using email and social networking sites, asking people to list their five most and five least favourite smells. Although this was only a small study, the results made for an interesting read with participants mentioning a wide variety of odours. These ranged from environmental, people- and animal-related smells, foods, beverages, herbs and spices, and man-made odours such as perfumes and those odours associated with specific products. I collated the most popular smells into a list of the sixty-one favourite odour types and the least popular into a list of seventy-one least favourite odour types, and I was able to observe marked trends as a result. The list of the most favoured odour types was dominated by food- and beverage-related odours. Chart 3.2 illustrates those smells that were listed by more than ten per cent of the participants as one of their five most favourite. In contrast, the range of least favourite odour types was dominated by odours associated with decomposition, pollution and waste; see Chart 3.3 for a depiction of those odours listed by more than ten per cent of the participants as among their five least favourite. What was perhaps most surprising was the amount of odours that featured in both lists; Chart 3.4 shows those odours that were mentioned by more than ten per cent of the participants as one of their most or least favourite odours, and which were also mentioned by other participants as a contrasting preference.

Although such studies provide useful insights regarding smell preferences and cultural ideals, an inherent weakness is their detachment from environmental context and the impression that odours themselves are perceived as positive or negative. As Engen (1991: 86) comments, '…odour perception is situational, contextual, and ecological', and thus the perception of any one

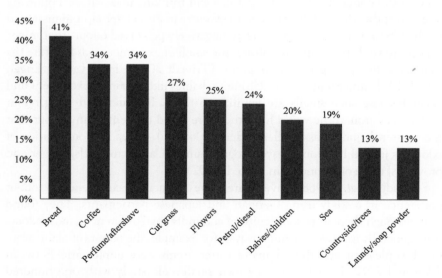

Chart 3.2 MOST favourite odours of one hundred participants

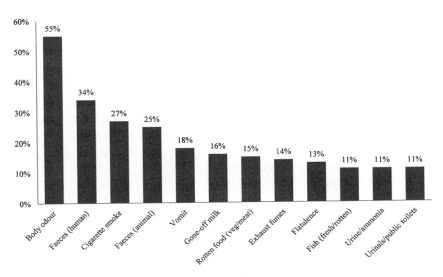

Chart 3.3 LEAST favourite odours of one hundred participants

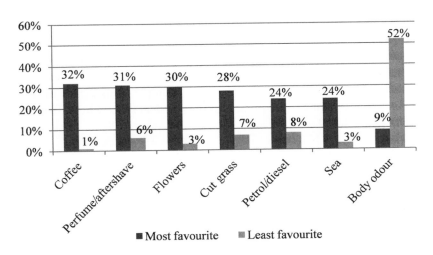

Chart 3.4 Contrasting ratings of MOST and LEAST liked odours of one hundred participants

odour has the potential to change from place to place according to context and expectations. In considering the hedonistic role of odour within the context of an investigation of urban smellscapes, smell therefore has the potential to interact with place enjoyment, potentially having an impact on wider place perception and experience.

3.5 Place perception and odour

The fact is, some cities stink, and odour affects the image of a place. Some communities have worked hard to get rid of the smells and turn their image around. Tacoma, Washington, for example, is a great success story. Others, like Gary, are still struggling. Still others, like Denver (which has an inversion problem that traps air pollution near the ground), are victims of geography. But even when cities make great strides, it's hard to shake image problems associated with odour. (Knopper 2003)

Tuan (1975) describes place as a centre of meaning that can range in size from a piece of furniture to an entire region or a country. He suggests that place can be experienced through different modes including the cognitive, described as active, or the sensory, with smell (and touch) described as passive. King (2008) considers the notion of place as situated both in a physical geographic area – a point in space – and also as a point in time captured within our memories:

What if the place that we are in the midst of is different from the physical space that we currently inhabit? What if the things we yearn for are located elsewhere... We may remember only elements or impressions of it: there may be certain objects, smells, a smile or expression, particular acts or occasions, a word, all of which come out in a manner that we cannot control or understand. Yet any of these elements or impressions makes us feel 'at home' in a way that we cannot find in the physical space where we are now stuck. (King 2008)

Notions of place as both geographical areas and situations in time are captured by Knopper (2003) in his article on 'cities that smell', with descriptions of the smellscapes of Tacoma and Denver in the US. For Knopper, odour links the history of a city to the present through memory associations, creating an image of the city that combines the past with the present. To progress this line of thought further, olfactory perception of place can therefore be understood as similar to olfactory perception as a whole, combining information collected and mediated by the sense of smell (along with information gained through the other senses) with information gained from memories, odour recognition and association. Olfactory perceptions of place are similarly informed by social and cultural factors, including prior understandings of that place gained from representations made by others.

In 2006 the Italian architects Barbara and Perliss (2006: 198–200) suggested that the relationship between smell and place could be considered from two fundamental positions: the search for the authentic smell of a place with an emphasis on the 'true' nature of experiences; and in relation to the emotional marketing of place driven by the tourism industry which seeks '...a memorable and extraordinary experience'. Dann and Jacobsen (2003) pick up on this position in their investigation into the use of prevailing smell perceptions in accounts of towns and cities as tourist destinations. This is conducted via a literature review of classical and contemporary texts and includes writings by independent travel journalists. Dann and Jacobsen found urban smellscapes to be portrayed far more negatively in these texts than were rural smellscapes, with fifty-six per cent of all urban accounts judged to be negative compared with twenty-five per cent of all rural accounts. Furthermore, urban accounts varied according to the period in which they were written, with the most negative accounts produced during the modern period. Contrary to the tourist experience gained from the air-conditioned tour-bus, as outlined by Urry (1990) in his writings on the tourist gaze, Dann and Jacobsen (2002) conclude that odour is an important part of a tourist's perception of place. They go on to suggest that towns and cities should retain, or recreate as authentically as possible, their historical physical infrastructure whilst attempting to remove all negatively perceived odours, introducing new more pleasant varieties instead (*ibid.*: 19–20). I will go on to explore the potential implications of Dann and Jacobsen's writings in further detail in Chapter 10.

A further position that I would also like to add to that introduced by Barbara and Perliss (2006: 125), and which is of relevance to the work of many smell artists and perfumers, is that of a search for the 'essence' of place. This position relates to the recreation of place-related odours, and can be thought of as an abstracted or partial representation of the olfactory identity of a point in space and/or time. As such, the essence of a particular place might potentially draw from different aspects, activities, histories and representations of that place and reflect the views of one person, or many.

Wider olfactory perceptions of place are therefore formed through a combination of experiences, memories and associations with the parts and mixes of odours within an urban smellscape, and are further informed by representations, experiences and expectations of that place.

3.6 Odour sensitivity

The sensitivity of an individual to odour is an important additional factor to consider in exploring the interaction between humans and the smell environment, and it is an issue that has presented me with great dilemmas in my work designing urban smellscapes. The term 'sensitivity' is used in different ways by authors who write on human perceptions of smell. Psychologists such as Engen (1991) use the term to refer to odour detection and therefore consider sensitivity to be part of smell performance. More broadly, the term is used to refer to individual responses (physiological, psychological and behavioural) following the perception (detection and cognition) of smell, and in relation to both positive and negative effects. However, it is important to note that in prior investigations and discussions about conditions of smell hyper-sensitivity (e.g. chemical and environmental sensitivities), sensitivity is generally considered in only negative terms; for example, see the work of Fletcher (2006) and Nordin *et al.* (2004).

It is beyond doubt that concentrated odours are able to influence the physiological bodily state of the individual, particularly as a result of trigeminal stimulation which can lead to coughing, sneezing and other physical effects (Herz 2006: 193). A number of studies report effects on mood via the use of scents (for example, see Baron 1997), although the mere suggestion that a scent has been introduced into an environment can also have similar positive effects (Fox 2006: 4), implying that expectation has an important role to play. Others have suggested that odours can influence decision making, for example when evaluating people (Baron 1983, Wrzesniewski *et al.* 1999), objects and brands (Lindstrom 2005a), or places and environments (Spangenberg *et al.* 1996, Wrzesniewski 1999). Takasago, Japan's largest fragrance company, reported behavioural changes in work efficiency and production following a range of tests they carried out (in Damian and Damian 2006: 152–153). Moss and Oliver (2012) similarly report improved cognitive performance when exposed to the smell of rosemary. Hirsch (1995) observed a forty-five per cent increase in gambling rates, and Knasko (1995) found an increase in store dwell time, all through the introduction of scent into the ambient environment. Such behavioural changes are frequently explained in these studies using a stimulus-organism-response approach like that adopted by Mehrabian and Russell (1974), who suggest that an environmental stimulus produces an approach or avoidance response as a result of changes in individual emotional states.

However, given the influence of individual, social and cultural factors on odour preferences, it is very difficult to predict the response to an odour that any one individual might have. As a result, Fitzgerald Bone and Scholder-Ellen (1999) conclude in their review of empirical odour research in retailing that '…predicting specific odour effects (i.e., specific moods, thoughts, attitudes or behaviours) [is] a risky business'. Individual differences in the perception of odour also play an important role in studies investigating people's response to environmental stress and annoyance, such as those by Evans and Cohen (1987) and Steinheider *et al.* (1998). Definitions of annoyance vary, but all include consideration of the negative evaluation of environmental conditions, negative emotions, fear of harm and potential interference with activities (Guski and Felscher-Suhr 1999). Drawing from a guidance document for local authorities in England (DEFRA 2010: 14–15), influential factors in odour annoyance are summarised as follows:

- *Perceived health status* – Individuals with health complaints have a higher likelihood of experiencing nuisance/annoyance than healthier people at the same exposure level
- *Anxiety* – People who worry that odour has related health risks are more likely to experience odour annoyance
- *Coping strategy* – People who take actions to reduce an odour by making complaints or shutting windows etc. are more likely to experience odour annoyance/nuisance than those who try to change their emotional response to an odour
- *Economic dependence* – People with an economic interest in the activity associated with the source of the odour are less likely to experience annoyance
- *Personality* – Individuals who feel they have the focus of control over their environment may in some circumstances be more likely to experience annoyance/nuisance
- *Age* – the probability of experiencing odour-induced annoyance/ nuisance decreases with age
- *Residential satisfaction* – The more satisfied someone is with where they live, the lower the likelihood of experiencing odour induced annoyance/ nuisance
- *History of exposure and annoyance* – people with a history of odour-induced annoyance/nuisance have heightened sensitivity for up to three years after significant abatements are in place

At the extreme end of people's responses to odours are chemical or environmental sensitivities, with these terms sometimes used interchangeably. Fletcher (2005) describes such conditions as 'the quasi-legitimate medical condition' of environmental sensitivities, outlining this as a '...profoundly dystoposthetic (abnormal place experience) illness' and the feeling of '...being out of place in ways that most people aren't'. Fletcher suggests that this illness is characterised by a variety of reactions to a wide range of environmental triggers, many of which are olfactory (*ibid.*: 380). Individuals suffering from this illness experience reactions to environmental stimuli that would be insignificant to most people. These include physical reactions normally associated with highly concentrated odours, such as headaches, nausea and respiratory problems. However, environmental sensitivities have a much lower profile in some countries, although 'sick-building syndrome' (see Wargocki *et al.* 1999) is more widely recognised. Outbreaks of environmental sensitivities are focused in particular areas, including Nova Scotia, Canada and parts of the

US where social action has led to restrictions in the use of fragrances in work and public places (Sardar 2000).

Studies investigating the impact of individual characteristics on such illnesses have had interesting results. A state-wide survey of over four thousand residents in California found that chemical sensitivity (self-reported and medically diagnosed) was not associated with employment, educational level, marital status, income or geographic location (Kreutzer *et al.* 1999). However, Nordin *et al.* (2004), carried out a population-based study in Sweden using a Chemical Sensitivity Scale similar to that used to measure reactions to noise (see Weinstein 1978) and found that females and older people were more likely to change their behaviour in response to odour detection.

A person's sensitivity to a particular smell or a category of smells is therefore related to their physiological and psychological (emotional) response to them, whether it is positive, negative or neutral, rather than their actual detection of an odour. Some people are more likely than others to experience high levels of sensitivity in negative terms. e.g. experiencing annoyance as a result of odour perception, either as a result of their personal characteristics and coping strategies or because of their current or past relationship with an odour. However, what is perhaps most challenging here is the dilemma of how we might respond to these increasing levels of hyper-sensitivities when we think about designing urban smellscapes. At a macro level, might such hyper-sensitivities be an inevitable response to the increasing olfactory sterility of modern cities and buildings? Are we so unused to experiencing odours in our everyday lives that we experience extreme physiological or psychological reactions when we do encounter them? Or on the contrary, are we filling our air with more and more chemicals that are inducing this response?

3.7 Conclusion

The sense of smell clearly offers many potential challenges and opportunities when we consider the implications of its characteristics when designing and managing urban smell environments. Ranging from the close association between the sense of smell and long-term memory, which combine to create collective images of a city, through to individual differences in how we detect and think of smell, it is important that our approach should be sophisticated and nuanced; based on local knowledge and understanding. To achieve this requires a more detailed awareness of the urban smellscapes of cities today, but little has so far been written about what smells exist in cities today, how these are perceived, and the ethical issues that emerge in the context of increases in environmental sensitivities. It is therefore important that we explore these issues in further detail, and consolidate them with insights provided in other exploratory studies such as those by Balez (2002), Low (2009) and Diaconu *et al.* (2011).

To better understand human experiences of urban smellscapes, it is essential that we attempt to get inside the minds of people as best we can so that we can gain insights into how we might accommodate individual, social and cultural factors. We do so not by looking inwards – researching within the confines of a laboratory by testing people's responses to odours as though odour and environment are experienced separately, as so many have attempted to do in the past – but by venturing out into the urban world and using methods such as 'smellwalking', described in detail in the next chapter.

4

Smellwalking and representing urban smellscapes

Smellwalking is a form of sensewalking which Adams and Askins (2009) describe as a varied method by which we might '…investigate and analyse how we understand, experience and utilise space', and which usually involves focusing on sensory information gained through one or more of the senses. Since its introduction in the 1960s, sensewalking has been used by a range of disciplines in different ways for research, educational or documentation purposes. One of the earliest recorded examples of a sensewalk was that undertaken by Southworth (1969) with a focus on the sonic environments of cities while also investigating interactions between the senses (primarily vision and hearing). Southworth led individuals and groups along a set route through the centre of Boston, USA, and while undertaking the walk he deprived some participants of the use of one or more of their senses by placing them in wheelchairs, blindfolding them or covering their ears with headphones. In doing so, Southworth observed that participants were more likely to pick up on auditory and olfactory information when deprived of their vision. Blindfolded walks were also carried out more recently in Lisbon, Portugal, with groups of people wearing eye-masks being led around the city by a visually-impaired person in order to experience the city through their non-visual senses alone. These examples of sensewalks provide useful insights about non-visual aspects of the environment and the way people use their senses to perceive the environment around them, but they do not replicate the experience of a deaf or blind person. For a more detailed account of the influence of blindness in particular on environmental perception, see the work of Sacks (2005). Devlieger (2011) also draws from projects involving blind people and architecture students in Leuven, Belgium, arguing in favour of a 'mindful dialogue' between disabled and non-disabled people and highlighting an alternative tourist guide and walk that was developed in the town for people with sensory impairments.

Rather than being centred on sensory deprivation, however, sensewalks more frequently focus on everyday experiences of the environment gained through one sensory mode. Soundwalks are the most common form of sensewalking, introduced by Schafer at Simon Fraser University during his work on the World Soundscapes Project in the 1970s. In his research, Schafer and his colleagues used soundwalks to record and identify soundscapes in

Vancouver and five European villages, placing emphasis on 'listening' as a means of educating people about the soundscape, which was classified broadly by Schafer (1994:7) as '...any acoustic field of study'. More recently, Thibaud (2002, 2003) and his colleagues at the CRESSON laboratory at the Graduate School of Architecture of Grenoble, France have similarly used commentated walks in exploring people's responses and feelings to sensory information in urban space, particularly those responses relating to sound environments and broader urban ambiance.

This focusing of attention on information gained through one specific sensory mode is a key reason why I believe sensory walks work well in general, and for researching urban smellscapes in particular. Throughout our entire lives we necessarily breathe in and out, and it is therefore important that we do not consciously register every smell we detect; to do so would leave little scope for processing other necessary information about our environments and lives. Instead, our sense of smell filters odours according to habituation (where we no longer consciously register a familiar smell) and adaptation (where our smell receptors become fatigued following exposure to a smell and are therefore unable to detect odours over prolonged periods), with smells only being brought to our conscious attention if they present a potential threat or a source of pleasure (see Chapter 3). However, at the risk of delving too deeply into psychological theory, it is important to dispel an implied suggestion that individuals maintain a constant state of readiness to detect and process odours. This is not the case. As I outlined in Chapter 3, bodily state, whether it is related to hunger, illness or individual factors, has a significant influence on our ability to detect smells in the air around us; the same is true of our ability to process them, and this we term our 'perceptual state'.

In research on acoustic communication, Truax (1984) observed three distinct listening states in individual soundscape perception: *listening in search*, when an individual undertakes focused listening and actively seeks out auditory stimuli; *listening in readiness*, when an individual is ready to receive sensory information but attention is focused elsewhere; and *background listening*, when an individual is distracted, engaged in another activity such as talking on a mobile telephone. The same is true of smell perception; when we ask people to focus primarily on their experiences of smell we ask them to switch their perceptual state from being one which is generally passive in nature to a receptive state of 'smelling in search'. Smell perception therefore operates differently during a smellwalk than in normal everyday experiences of odour, as these smellwalking participants observed:

> It's [a smell] intrusive but normally I'm just walking by... now I've stood here I can smell it, so I must have smelled it travelling past before, but not registered it. (D50)

...you don't think about smelling things unless you can smell something
that was really nice or really horrible... because you can't see it. (D42)

This does not invalidate the findings of sensory walks, or in the specific case of
my work, urban smellwalks, as this method allows us to gain insights into what
odours people can detect in the environment and what they think of them,
which would otherwise be very difficult if not impossible to access. That said,
it remains important to acknowledge this difference since it does have some
potential implications for the research findings that I will highlight in later
chapters.

In 2004 and 2005, sensory walks were undertaken by researchers from the
University of Salford and University College London, UK as part of the
Vivacity2020 Project, a large project supported by the Engineering and
Physical Sciences Research Council (EPSRC) investigating urban
environmental quality and the sustainable design of twenty-four-hour cities
(Cooper *et al.* 2009). The walks were carried out individually with eighty-two
residents of the three English cities of Sheffield, Manchester and Clerkenwell
in central London, and they were supplemented by photographs taken by the
residents prior to the walks. Residents were asked to select a route of their
choice prior to the walk, and to describe their sensory experiences of city living
in post-walk interviews with each sense considered in turn. Experiences and
perceptions of odours were discussed as a small part of the interviews, with
responses being analysed by the Vivacity2020 project team as part of a wider
analysis of urban sensory experiences and perceptions (see Adams *et al.* 2009).
As a late arrival on the Vivacity2020 project team in 2008, I was extremely
lucky to be allowed access to the dataset of 154 odour-related quotations,
many of which I drew from in developing my ideas, formulating my plan for
further detailed research and informing the arguments to be found in later
chapters. Some of these quotations are included in this book, coded to protect
the identity of participants according to the first letter of the city in which the
participant lived (i.e. 'L' for London, 'M' for Manchester and 'S' for Sheffield;
also D for Doncaster, see below), and a number representing the order in
which the interviews occurred (e.g. L01, L02, L03 and so on). In a limited
number of cases more than one person participated in the interviews, and in
these cases participants are differentiated according to gender (e.g. L01 female
and L01 male).

Prior to commencing my own research on urban smellscapes, I found few
documented examples of walks with a specific focus on ambient smell
experiences in the city. One interesting previous example was that involving
artist Caitlin Berrigan in Brooklyn, New York as part of Conflux, a
psychogeography conference that took place in 2006. Berrigan and her
colleague Michael McBean organised a smellwalk as one component of a

project called 'The Smelling Committee', named after the Fifteenth Ward Smelling Committee of 1891 that discovered oil refinery pollution by following their noses to the source of the stench (http://smellingcommittee.org/). The smellwalk served an artistic and educational function, with the group of participants actively detecting and mapping smells. In 2007, Berrigan and McBean went on to develop downloadable audio clips (still available online) recorded at selected points of a walk around the Nolita (North of Little Italy) neighbourhood in Manhattan (http://smellingcommittee.org/mapit/index. html). More recently other smellwalks have emerged; Natalie Bouchard at the University of Montreal, Canada has introduced a commentated smellwalk in the city exploring and mapping people's memories of odours as they walk along a set route (see Figure 4.1). The route passes through a variety of areas in Montreal ranging from a trendy multicultural district, a busy retail street and road, a residential area and a public park. Bouchard's work seeks to reveal the temporal patterns provoked by smell and to explore how olfactory memory alters perception of space-time in the city (Bouchard 2013).

Sensewalking therefore offers a valuable but as yet under-utilised method of drawing from and gaining understanding of people's everyday olfactory experiences and memories of geographic space and place. However, with few examples carried out specifically relating to smell, little has been written about the suitability of the method and related issues that might arise as part of such an endeavour.

Since 2008 I have led smellwalks in numerous towns and cities across the United Kingdom, mainland Europe, the United States and Canada. I undertook a small number of these smellwalks by myself with the aim of documenting the smells of specific urban environments, in an approach similar to that adopted by Schafer and colleagues as part of the World Soundscapes project. More frequently, I have undertaken the smellwalks with other participants, either individuals or groups, and with the primary purpose of exploring the smells that people can detect, what they think about them, how these change between places and how the built environmental form and component parts influence the urban smell experience. As with some of the early soundwalks, the smellwalks also serve an educational purpose, raising the participants' awareness of the role and potential for smell in the city, and perhaps most relevantly within the context of this book, with the aim of educating built environment professionals such as urban designers, architects, planners and city managers.

I draw from all of these studies in the content of the following chapters, but there are two detailed empirical sensewalking studies that contribute more substantially than any others. The first comprises the data collected with eighty-two participants in English cities via the Vivacity2020 project outlined above. The second empirical study was devised and implemented myself,

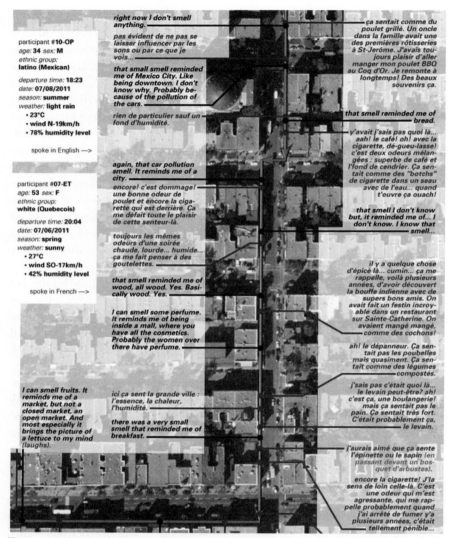

Figure 4.1 Section from commentated smellwalk in Montreal. Montreal 2011 ©natalieb

adapted in particular from methods used by my colleagues at the University of Salford in the Positive Soundscapes Project (Davies *et al.* 2007), which included the use of stopping points and on-site interviews while undertaking sensory walks. It will be useful for me to outline the format and content of my detailed empirical smellwalking study here, both to provide contextual information for later chapters, but also to highlight the practical issues and decisions that I faced when planning the smellwalks with the intention of providing guidance for those attempting to embark on such endeavours in the future.

4.1 Smellwalk case study: Doncaster, England

Doncaster is a large town in Northern England in South Yorkshire's ex-coalfields area, serving a population of almost three hundred thousand residents and situated within the Sheffield city region. I selected the town as the site for the study both due to its suitability for purpose and because it is a town that I know well, having worked as a built environment professional in its regeneration sector for some years.

After gaining access to the Vivacity2020 Project data on urban smellscapes in 2008, I organised and analysed the corpus according to frequently occurring themes across the urban areas included in the project. These themes included odours emitted by food outlets (markets, take-aways and restaurants), smoking, the evening economy (alcohol and street urination), scenting and pollution. The layout and characteristics of Doncaster meant that the town lent itself easily to the further research and exploration of these pre-identified themes, as well as providing opportunities for other odour themes to emerge. Doncaster is home to one of the largest markets in the north of England, it includes a thriving evening economy, and it also contains an area monitored by local authorities as a result of its poor air quality. The town therefore provided ample sites for inclusion in the study as well as an opportunity to compare the experiences of urban smellscapes in a town with that of the three much larger cities of Sheffield, Manchester and Clerkenwell, London.

The Doncaster study had three specific goals: to document and investigate the various meanings of odours experienced in the urban environment; to investigate relationships between urban smellscapes and urban place experience and perception; and to identify ways that smell might more appropriately be considered in urban design decision-making processes and practice. In order to achieve these three diverse and ambitious goals, it was imperative that a wide range of people be included in the study, particularly since wide differences would likely occur between participant perceptions. I therefore set a target to include fifty people and to consider individual characteristics such as gender, age and ethnicity as part of the recruitment process. In the end, fifty-two people participated in the study, one of whom was anosmic, which provided an additional unique and extremely useful perspective. I was also keen to understand different points of view regarding odour control practices and design, and therefore another factor considered in the recruitment of participants was their professional discipline. Local residents, politicians, market traders and retailers, pub and club licensees, restaurateurs and built environment professionals were all included in the study, with the latter group including city managers, planners, architects, urban designers, engineers and environmental health officers.

The targeting of these professionals did, however, result in a bias towards male participation (sixty-two per cent of the total) as compared to females (thirty-eight per cent), and older participants rather than younger, with all but one being aged twenty years or over, and sixty-one per cent being aged forty or over. Participant ethnicity was dominated by white British groups (eighty-eight per cent) with an additional four per cent of white non-British origin, four per cent Pakistani, two per cent Chinese and two per cent of African origin. I highlight these participant demographics because of the influential role that these characteristics can play on both the detection and the association of odours.

Participant recruitment can on occasions present difficulties, particularly in cases such as the Doncaster smellwalks where I had a number of target profiles in mind. As a result I adopted a range of methods to recruit participants, including approaching some of the business people at their places of work to ask whether they would be happy to be involved. Participants from the built environment community were recruited through different professional and special interest groups, and I approached local authority representatives such as those in environmental health, planning and engineering directly. A small number of additional participants were recruited through existing participants or via third parties. Other methods that I have found useful in recruiting participants in subsequent smellwalks in other towns and cities are by developing project blog-sites, using social media such as Twitter or Facebook, and by organising smellwalks with partner organisations with an interest in the built environment, such as the collaborative group smellwalk I led in September 2012 with Studio X at the University of Columbia, New York.

I decided early in the planning process to undertake the walks with people on an individual basis, rather than in groups. Although I have since led many group smellwalks, they present significantly different challenges and opportunities from those undertaken with people on a one-to-one basis. Some of these differences are similar to those between office-based interviews with individuals and focus groups: the interactions between individuals on group smellwalks influences discussions since some people are less likely to voice their own opinion when others are present, or they may be swayed by the comments of others. This offers opportunities if one wishes to encourage discussion between people with different perspectives whilst out on site, but it presents limitations when attempting to understand a wide range of different factors of influence in smell perception and experience, such as I was keen to explore within the Doncaster study.

The recording of people's views can also present difficulties if undertaking a sensory walk with a group of people. On a one-to-one basis I usually carry with me a handheld audio recorder which I use to record participants comments, responses and my own notes to myself where relevant. I later transcribe and analyse the comments using the recording. In contrast, during group walks I find it more effective to record discussions using a video camera when undertaking detailed research, as it is otherwise impossible to discern who said what. However, this requires a colleague to undertake the recording since it would be difficult if not impossible to lead the walk, ask questions and use a video recorder at the same time. With large groups, people also often chat among themselves about the smells they detect, and they may be outside the recording area so it is easy to miss extremely valuable data if one is not careful. Video recording brings its own ethical issues, however, since some people prefer not to be recorded in this way and it is therefore important to ensure that reassurances of confidentiality are given and permission to film is sought from participants prior to starting the walk. This is also important when using handheld audio recording equipment.

Depending on the purpose of the walk, it might not be necessary to record what people say. For example, if the aim is to educate people about the smell environment and to identify the location of different smells in a particular area, this can easily be achieved by providing participants with a paper map and pen, and asking them to mark the smells on the plan and return these to you at the end of the walk; see for example the downloadable do-it-yourself smellwalking maps available on the Smell and the City blog-site (http:// smellandthecity.wordpress.com).

4.1.1 Route-planning

Unlike the walks in Sheffield, Manchester and Clerkenwell, where participants were asked to identify and lead the researcher on a walking route in their area, the smellwalks in Doncaster followed a pre-planned set route. This was focused primarily on the potential of the route to provide exposure to a range of different smellscapes, and it accommodated consideration of additional factors including practical issues such as the layout, terrain, site access and the personal safety of the researcher and participants. The importance of the decisions made at this planning and preparation stage of a sensory walk should not be underestimated; the characteristics of the physical space through which a sensory walk travels determines much about the experiences that can be investigated during the walk, the data collected and the resulting insights gained (Henshaw *et al.* 2009).

I included a number of stopping points in the pre-set route for the Doncaster smellwalks, illustrated in Figure 4.2, with the areas named as: (1.) Priory Walk – a privately-owned mixed-use development; (2.) Colonnades – a secondary outdoor shopping precinct; (3.) Silver Street – a strip of evening economy businesses on a busy bus route; (4.) Copley Road – an ethnically diverse residential and business neighbourhood; (5.) Doncaster Markets – a large, historic market area; and (6.) Frenchgate – a primary shopping street and public space. In encouraging all participants to undertake the smellwalk following the same route and stopping points, a multitude of perspectives were gained regarding odour experience in a number of locations in the town. This facilitated the identification and exploration of differences and similarities in people's experiences and the related judgements they made, and of themes regarding the influence of temporal factors such as the time of day, day of the week, weather, temperature and changing flows of activity and movement. I spent time after each smellwalk recording the weather and temperature and noting the time and the activities taking place in the town on those days.

The first interviews and walks were implemented between January and early March 2009, incorporating periods of cold weather (including snow) and temperatures of –1°C. A second set of walks were carried out between the end of April and July 2009, including much warmer weather of up to 24°C. In contrast to average British weather patterns, it rained during only one of all the walks. Smellwalks were carried out on weekdays and weekends and at different times of the day, with the earliest commencing at 7.30am and the latest finishing at 8pm.

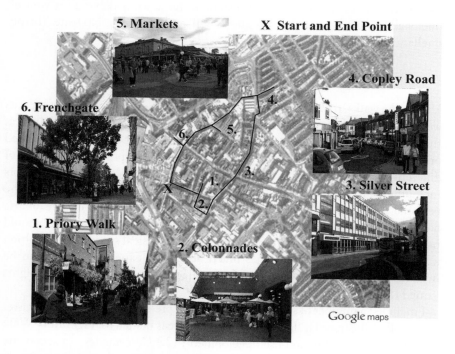

Figure 4.2 Doncaster smellwalking route and stopping points

4.1.2 The mobile interview

Prior to starting the Doncaster smellwalks, I asked participants to complete a short form regarding their individual characteristics such as age, gender, ethnicity and smoking habits. I also asked people about their expectations and perceptions of urban smellscapes, and their relationship with the town. Once out on the smellwalk, participants focused on the smells they could detect until we reached each of the stopping point areas along the planned route. When we were in each of the stopping point areas I asked a range of questions regarding the smells that the participants detected in the area and others they had detected since the previous stop. I encouraged participants to reflect on their smell expectations and their prior experiences of the stopping-point sites and the areas walked through. As part of this process, participants rated how much they liked or disliked the area in which they were standing, and how much they liked or disliked its smellscape. The rating was based on a five-point scale ranging from 1, a place or smellscape that was very much disliked, and 5, a place or smellscape that was very much liked. Such five-point scales are common practice in sound and vibration research; see for example DEFRA (2007b: 18) and Grimwood *et al.* (2002). However, in contrast to those studies, which investigate annoyance or disturbance from sensory stimuli, these questions were also aimed at identifying positive perceptions of places and their respective smellscapes.

After completing the smellwalks, I asked the participants about their experiences of undertaking the walk. Most said that they had enjoyed the walk and it had opened their minds to the many odours present in the town and the roles that the sense of smell can play. I asked additional questions according to each participant's background and experience, with the intention of exploring key issues in further detail. For example, I asked pub or club licensees about the adaptation of their premises following the implementation of recent UK smoking legislation, and I asked built environment professionals about their views on the current and future consideration of smell within odour management, design and policy.

4.1.3 Place and smellscape liking ratings (Doncaster)

After completing all of the Doncaster smellwalks I explored the relationships between the scale rating data on place and smellscape liking collected at each of the stopping point sites. This analysis revealed a strong positive correlation between place and smellscape liking when all of the ratings in all of the stopping point sites were considered (R^2 = 0.34 with a 95% confidence interval of 0.24–0.44). The correlation between place and smellscape liking was also examined according to each of the stopping point sites, with a significant relationship being identified in Copley Road and the Markets areas but not in Priory Walk, Colonnades, Silver Street or Frenchgate. However, this may be a result of the low number of datasets available in each individual area. Chart 4.1 illustrates the average place and smellscape liking ratings in each of the areas.

Despite this statistical correlation between the overall ratings of place and smellscape liking, it is important to point out that there are other factors that might explain this relationship without it necessarily being illustrative of a connection between place and odour liking. It might, for example, be a product of people being unfamiliar and thus potentially uncomfortable with assessing and rating smellscapes. Certainly in several cases participants rated all of the area smellscapes with the same or very similar scores as they rated their liking of the different areas. Furthermore, peoples' liking of different smells, or different smellscapes, changed according to the area in which they were detected – e.g. a participant might rate their liking of a smellscape where no odour was detected as a '3' in one area and a '5' in another.

A number of participants voiced concern that they were rating the smellscape liking 'accurately', and took some time explaining their rationale behind each rating. In such cases, variations in smellscape liking ratings between sites according to the actual odours detected was directly related to the expectations of the individuals themselves. If an area was expected to smell in a certain way and it did not meet that expectation, then this was reflected in the smellscape liking rating. Hence differences occurred in the ratings of the same odour(s) in different places. In practice, this meant that in some areas a lack of odour was perceived to be incongruent with expectations, and therefore it was out of place. Likewise in other areas people did not expect to detect any specific odours and non-detection of odours was more positively

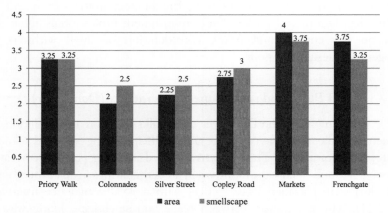

Chart 4.1 Place and smellscape liking rating – averages per area (1: very much disliked, 5: very much liked)

perceived. The scale ratings therefore imply a correlation between odour and place liking, but a more detailed investigation of other factors at play in the perception of urban smellscapes is required in order to develop a deeper understanding of different odour types and the behaviours that people display in response to odour perception.

4.1.4 What smells were detected?

In undertaking the Doncaster case study, one of the original goals of the smellwalks was to document those odours present in the urban environment, since few empirical studies have done so in the past. A range of different odours were detected while undertaking the walks, which I went on to group into a classification of odour types such as people-related odours and industrial odours. I then placed these categorisations into a model. I later tested these odour groupings by seeking the views of built environment colleagues in other universities and countries, and supplemented the content of the model by drawing from people's smell experiences on smellwalks in other cities across the UK, the US, Europe and Canada. The results are outlined in Figure 4.3.

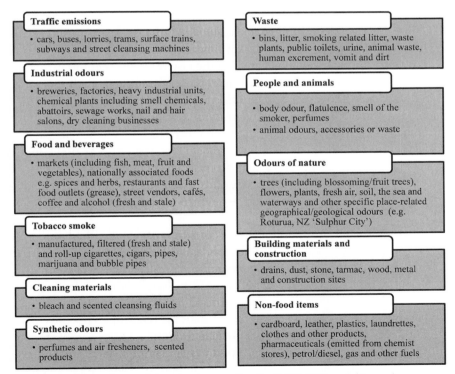

Traffic emissions

• cars, buses, lorries, trams, surface trains, subways and street cleansing machines

Industrial odours

• breweries, factories, heavy industrial units, chemical plants including smell chemicals, abattoirs, sewage works, nail and hair salons, dry cleaning businesses

Food and beverages

• markets (including fish, meat, fruit and vegetables), nationally associated foods e.g. spices and herbs, restaurants and fast food outlets (grease), street vendors, cafés, coffee and alcohol (fresh and stale)

Tobacco smoke

• manufactured, filtered (fresh and stale) and roll-up cigarettes, cigars, pipes, marijuana and bubble pipes

Cleaning materials

• bleach and scented cleansing fluids

Synthetic odours

• perfumes and air fresheners, scented products

Waste

• bins, litter, smoking related litter, waste plants, public toilets, urine, animal waste, human excrement, vomit and dirt

People and animals

• body odour, flatulence, smell of the smoker, perfumes
• animal odours, accessories or waste

Odours of nature

• trees (including blossoming/fruit trees), flowers, plants, fresh air, soil, the sea and waterways and other specific place-related geographical/geological odours (e.g. Roturua, NZ 'Sulphur City')

Building materials and construction

• drains, dust, stone, tarmac, wood, metal and construction sites

Non-food items

• cardboard, leather, plastics, laundrettes, clothes and other products, pharmaceuticals (emitted from chemist stores), petrol/diesel, gas and other fuels

Figure 4.3 Odours detected during urban smellwalks (UK/US/Canada/Europe)

Although representative of the range of different odours detected and reported in many Western cities, this model is not comprehensive of all urban odours and all urban smellscapes. Cities in parts of the world with extreme climates or high humidity, or those within a warzone, would all be expected to include odours not identified in this model. However, most smell groups highlighted in the model would be present in the vast majority of towns and cities, although these would vary according to local customs and environment. After all, where there are people, there will always be food, waste and materials.

4.2 The mapping and representation of urban smellscapes

One final important aspect of smellwalking that I must describe is that of the mapping and representation of the smells detected in a given area. In this book, I use text, models and illustrations as a way of analysing and representing the odours detected within the urban environment. However, as I outlined in Chapter 3, the recording of odour in the environment is notoriously problematic for many different reasons, although technologies are assisting in working towards overcoming this issue. Within the context of developing a more proactive approach to smell in architecture and urban design, this difficulty presents something of an issue, which I will go on to discuss in further detail in Chapter 10 in relation to sensory notation tools. One means of conveying information about smell in the environment that has increased in sophistication over the past decade is the technique of smell mapping. Smell maps bring together spatial information with details of the various smells that can or could be detected in an area, and occasionally incorporate other factors such as topography and wind flow. They are created at one end of the spectrum as an aid to encourage and document environmental odours, and at the other to represent or recreate urban smellscapes in sophisticated artistic and material representations. These types of smell map are not mutually exclusive since they can be used to inform and work with each other.

Some smell maps are simply maps of an area with smells highlighted on them, used as a practical tool to guide a smellwalk. For example, see the downloadable do-it-yourself Manchester smell map that I developed in 2012 with artist and cartographer Kate McLean (http://smellandthecity.wordpress.com/2012/04/03/diy-manchester-smellwalk-2/). Many smell maps use modern mapping technologies and crowd-sourcing techniques to collect and present data on the smells in a given area. The simplest examples of this are online maps where participants place pins to highlight the smells that can be detected in a specific place or area. Examples of these include those highlighted on the Japanese site nioi-bu (meaning smell club), which documents smells from across the world in the Japanese language (http://www.nioibu.com/), and a map developed on the smells of Toronto (http://www.bikely.com/maps/bike-path/Smells-of-Toronto). Such online maps can provide a valuable, cost-effective and relatively simple way of documenting or communicating the smells present at different spatial levels – from very specific sites through to whole cities – and therefore they can be used for a range of different purposes.

At the other end of the scale, smell-mapping has been used by designers and artists as a way of exploring the associations between odours and environments using a variety of media. In 2010, Nicola Twilley at Studio X at the University of Columbia, New York created a scratch-and-sniff smell-map of people's perceptions of the smellscape of New York City, using stickers impregnated with smells that were mixed by perfumers (Twilley 2010). Whilst at college, graphic designer Esther Wu mapped her experiences of the odours emitted by her local donut store on her way home every evening. Her map considered the weather conditions, temperature and proximity to source, but although it was beautifully illustrated, sadly the map was inconclusive in its findings (http://estherwu.com/#whiff).

Designer and cartographer Kate McLean has similarly produced maps of a variety of cities including Glasgow and Edinburgh in Scotland, Amsterdam in the Netherlands and Newport in the US. The majority of McLean's maps are developed with input from local people, sometimes through the use of group smellwalks, as she identifies the key smells of the specific cities she is investigating. An integral part of her work is the creation of smells that accompany the maps when they are exhibited. What is particularly fascinating about McLean's work is that unlike most smell artists, she recreates many of the odours by using everyday ingredients rather than perfuming essences or accords, including sea water, vinegar and fermented squid juice. In doing so she produces creative representations of smells such as that of the penguin enclosure at Edinburgh Zoo, or birds' nests in Newport. In developing a virtual dérive smell map of Paris, France in 2010, McLean created a range of smells that could be detected in the city, and asked people to sniff them and then write their associations with that specific odour on notes and attach them to the map (see Figure 4.4). In doing so McLean found that people have emotional attachments with odours, and the locations they associated these with could be either very much place-specific or far more general (McLean 2012).

Smell mapping can therefore be used in conjunction with smellwalking as an effective means of investigating human perception of smells in an environment, both in recording and communicating the smells that can be detected in an area, and in accessing the meaning that people attach to these.

Figure 4.4 Smellmap, Paris 2011. Kate McLean, Sensory Maps

4.3 Conclusion

Despite the various roles that odour might play in creating new, memorable and enjoyable places or preserving existing ones, a key challenge faced by researchers is the difficulty of identifying, recording and legitimising something that cannot be seen or heard. As a result, new ways of exploring the urban smell environment are required. Smellwalking is a varied method that can be used to identify local perceptions and the meaning of urban smellscapes, with the findings of these walks easily communicated through the use of illustrative tools such as smell maps. However, given the complex interface between the materiality of the body, the environment, the odour itself and individual, social and cultural factors, it will be useful to examine in detail the perceptions of some common urban odours detected in contemporary smellscapes, and highlight issues such as the temporal nature of odour detection in the city.

In Part II we will explore smellscape perceptions according to odour source, drawing from the empirical studies implemented in Doncaster and in Manchester, Sheffield and Clerkenwell, London. In focusing on these cities, I intend to highlight how perceptions of smell in the city are situated within social, cultural and political ideologies, and to reveal some of the strategies at play in the design and control of contemporary urban smellscapes.

Part II

SMELL SOURCES
IN THE CITY

5

Air quality, pollution and smell

In the mid 1990s, air quality monitoring equipment was introduced into the African megacity of Lagos, Nigeria. In a study by Nigerian, German and British collaborators, scientists observed that in those areas of the city with the highest levels of pollution, the majority being highly congested places where people congregated such as markets, bus stops and street selling stands, air pollution could be detected without equipment by its malodour and the eye irritation it caused (Baumbach et al. 1995). At around the same time but on a different continent, a study of residents in the megacity of Calcutta (Kolkata), India identified that seventy-eight per cent were aware of the presence of air pollution in their locality, with a large proportion of people perceiving air pollution as a malodour problem (Mukherjee 1993). In the twenty years since these studies, Lagos has expanded to become the largest city in the sub-Sahara with a population of eighteen million people and growing. Its air is now so heavily polluted from vehicular and other emissions that the city experienced Nigeria's first ever smog in 2006, catapulting environmental issues high onto the country's political agenda (Taiwo 2009). Calcutta too is now home to an urban agglomeration of fourteen million people, who suffer the highest rates of lung cancer in India (Sen et al. 2002). Air quality is of such a poor standard that in 2007 the BBC World News reported that police officers were issued with oxygen to breathe following eight-hour shifts on city streets, in an attempt to counteract some of the negative health effects of chemicals and particulates in the air (Bhaumik 2007).

These cities of the global south are typical examples of air quality at its worst, but experiences of pollution are not limited only to the developing world. In the working class neighbourhood of East Harlem, New York, air quality levels are only just below federal limits with asthma hospitalisation rates being some of the highest in all of the US (Rivera 2006). One of the main reasons for this poor air quality is the concentration of six of Manhattan's seven bus depots in the area, a factor reported in the New York Times in 2006 as causing increasing local concern. As one resident was reported to comment: 'If I don't keep those windows closed, that smell rises up and comes in, a smell like diesel, a nasty stench' (ibid.). Despite reductions in the UK's industrial and traffic emissions achieved in recent years (DEFRA 2007a), a significant threat remains to the post-industrial urban environment in the form of what Porteous (1990: 31) describes as 'omnipresent vehicle odours'.

In Chapter 2 I identified existing legislation relating to odour as dominated by the consideration of air pollution. As the examples of Lagos, Calcutta and East Harlem illustrate, it is very difficult, if not impossible, to separate air pollutants from odours. Indeed, following a review of air pollution perception literature in 2001, Bickerstaff and Walker found the sense of smell to be one of the key sensory tools used by people to assess the quality of the air around them, and as a consequence to allow them to become aware of poor air quality episodes.

It is useful at this point to clarify the differences between air pollutants, odours and odorants. Air pollutants are defined in international guidelines as chemicals that, when released into the air, pose potential harm to human and environmental health or that of the atmosphere. These chemicals may or may not be detected through the human senses. Odorants, on the other hand, are chemicals that can be detected at certain concentrations by the sense of smell, with odours being what is perceived (detected and processed) (see McGinley *et al.* 2000). Some air pollutants have odours, such as benzene, a highly flammable chemical associated with a range of cancers, which has a sickly sweet odour and therefore can be detected and potentially identified through the sense of smell. Others, such as carbon monoxide, cannot be detected through the sense of smell and therefore have no odour. To confuse matters slightly, some air pollutants cannot be detected through the smell receptors but they can be detected through the trigeminal nerve (see Chapter 3); these would be judged by most people or organisations to fall outside the traditional definition of an odour.

The situation becomes even more problematic when we consider legislation relating to 'nuisance' odours, a classification that can be applied to any odours if they are judged to cause annoyance in those that perceive them. The anthropologist Mary Douglas famously described pollution as the perception of matter as 'out of place', and it is perhaps this description which assists us most in seeking to understand the development of local perceptions of air pollution and related legislation and policy. In this chapter I will examine the relationship between local understandings of air and odour pollution over time, and within the context of place.

5.1 Doncaster's historical pollution

Air pollution is a key concern in the Yorkshire and Humberside region where Doncaster is located, in relation to local and regional air quality, the levels of regional emissions produced and their impact on national air quality. Yorkshire and Humberside produces fifteen per cent of the total nitrogen dioxide emissions in England, twenty per cent of the total sulphur dioxide emissions, and twelve per cent of all PM_{10}s (GOYH 2009: 4). Regional monitoring sites indicate an increased number of days where moderate or higher levels of air pollution are experienced and higher levels of ozone recorded, although PM_{10} levels are shown to have decreased in recent years (GOYH 2009: 11). Air quality in Doncaster is generally of a high standard, although pockets of poor air quality exist in and around the town (DMBC 2005: 3). These areas have all been declared as Air Quality Management Areas (AQMAs) due to high concentrations of nitrogen dioxide, the sole source of which is traffic (DMBC 2005: 9).

Doncaster has for many years benefited from its central mainland location. The settlement was originally founded as a Roman fort towards the end of the first century due to its strategic positioning on Roman routes between Lincoln and York. These links later influenced the routing of new road and rail lines, with the town being located on the Great North Road, a coaching route connecting London and Edinburgh. The route was later upgraded to become a modern road serving motorised vehicles (now known as the A1), which ran through the town centre until 1961, when the amount of traffic led to the construction of a new fifteen-mile road bypassing the town. Since the founding of the Roman fort, sensory experiences of Doncaster have been influenced by the town's connectivity, including those produced by people, animals and vehicles travelling through the town – the sounds and odours of animals herded through the streets and smoke from the coal-fired steam engines. Goods that travellers carried with them, many of which went on to be sold on Doncaster's market (chartered in 1248) also contributed to the town's sensory experience, as did the services that were established to feed and water travellers, with many inns and notable buildings built along the original route of the road.

With the introduction of motorised vehicles in the early twentieth century, experiences and perceptions of the town quickly became dominated by traffic:

> …when the old A1 used to come through the middle of town, it used to be blocked up constantly all day long… that was really bad. Now the town is a hundred per cent better… I don't think it's too bad for smells in Doncaster. (D08)

The resulting environment was described as 'Bedlam' (D53), with police required to assist pedestrians in crossing from one side of the road to the other. One participant recalled: '…diesel's never a nice smell, if you'd got a lot of traffic it was awful, and you used to get that 'cos at one point Doncaster just used to be full of chugging traffic' (D09). The impact on air quality and olfactory experience was exacerbated by poor vehicle design and maintenance:

I think it was just a bad smell because if you got buses where they were stationary and they just chugged away … they belched out smoke 'cos they didn't check them for emissions and there was no MOT … so you got some pretty sick engines. (D09)

The re-routing of the road was significant in changing sensory experiences of the town, diverting some traffic away from the centre and providing opportunities for future pedestrianisation. However, this re-routing also prompted the building of a network of new roads circling the town, aimed at connecting local townships to the centre and facilitating access into the wider road infrastructure. A key trunk road developed in the town centre during this period proved to be one of the most damaging changes, reducing the quality of pedestrian experience and town connectivity and exacerbating issues of air quality. The road separated Doncaster's waterfront area, railway station and most significant historical building, St George's Minster, from the rest of the town (see Figure 5.1). The road and its immediate surrounding environment have since become overloaded with traffic, forming the main route of one of the town's Air Quality Monitoring Areas.

Traffic odours were not the only air pollutants detected in Doncaster's recent historical environment. The town is situated in the heart of a large coal mining area with coal burnt widely in the past both in industry and the home. Accounts of this featured frequently in environmental recollections and place perceptions. An immigrant to the area described her first encounter with these odours when she arrived in the UK in the early Sixties:

Figure 5.1 Doncaster town centre circular road (an AQMA)

I still remember the smell of this train ride from London because it was a smell that I had never come across before, it was so strange... as you get nearer to Doncaster you have the industrial smells... that was very interesting, and that smell I will never forget. (D21)

Following the introduction of the Clean Air Act in 1956 and subsequent reductions in coal usage, Doncaster was declared 'Smokeless' in 1994 (Walsh 2002).

Another traditional polluter of Doncaster's smellscape was the town's sewage works, built in 1873 and situated to the north-west of the town centre. Smells from the plant were detected for many years in the town centre: '...on certain days when the wind was blowing we used to get it ... it used to smell terrible ... in the centre of town' (D52). The intensity of the odours emitted from the plant has been reduced significantly in past decades following the enforcement of legislation and assisted by modern technological innovations. However, development activity on the outskirts of the town today threatens to increase nuisance odour reports from the site as residential properties creep ever closer to the works.

5.1.1 Meat rendering plant

A number of additional industrial, manufacturing and processing smells were also detectable in Doncaster's historical smellscape, the most notable being from a meat rendering plant on the town's outskirts. The plant opened in Doncaster in 1926, contributing towards the town's smellscape for many years: '...go back to when I were a child, and the town used to just smell of rotting flesh and that's all it were ... but the smell's a lot better controlled than what it used to be' (D20). The odour was often accompanied by visual stimuli:

...it was the first thing you'd notice whenever you came in by train, you'd pass their factory and you used to see carcasses just laid out in the yard, there'd be like dead cows and things, the smell was horrendous. (D20)

Odours were particularly strong in warmer months and were influenced by wind flow direction:

Certainly in summer, when it was still or when there was a north-easterly wind ... it would blow that into the town centre, and particularly in the summer of '76 when it was really, really hot for weeks, the town centre stunk. (D06)

Control over the plant gradually increased during the latter half of the twentieth century as the local authority enforced tighter regulation:

It was putrid and people were, it almost made them sick … they were trying to shut the windows and keep it out and then, this must have been in the '60s … it got better, and less objectionable and you could ring them up if you were getting great belts of it and say 'it's terribly smelly' and they'd say 'oh right ok' and they sort of went away and turned it down to number six or something. (D09)

Consequently these odours reduced in the town: '…well they had to change didn't they … because it was getting really bad and people were complaining' (D52). Today, odours from the plant are rarely detected. However, when temperature and wind conditions are right, these historically situated odours do occasionally leak into the town centre once again, serving as a reminder of past lived experiences: '…it tends to be in the summer … if the wind's in a particular direction' (D11).

The plant's reputation continues to affect it today. In early 2009, the company applied for permission to build a new anaerobic digestion plant on the site, harnessing energy created by the decomposition of up to forty-five thousand tonnes of waste food per year (Invest in Doncaster, 2009). Neighbouring residents were fearful that odours might be produced as a result. A representative of the area's Tenants and Residents Association commented in the local paper: 'We are the people who live adjacent to the site, we are the ones who have to live with it 24 hours a day, 7 days a week and 365 days of the year' (Mason 2009). A local councillor added, 'We have got enough of [rendering plant] sites here at the present time and we have put up with [rendering plant] smells for the past fifty years' (*ibid.*). The application was delayed while the local planning committee visited the site following receipt of a petition expressing residents' concerns, but the plant was granted planning permission in February 2009 and has since been constructed on site.

5.1.2 Sweet factories

Close to the meat rendering plant in the north-east of Doncaster were a number of factories including some manufacturing sweets. Descriptions of odours from these factories were recalled nostalgically as mainly pleasant experiences: 'when I were a lad, the Nuthall Mintoes factory was in Holmes Market, that was a good Doncaster smell … as opposed to the [rendering plant] which was the bad smell, and they weren't that far apart' (D09). Another resident recalled online: 'In those days they had the doors open to let the fumes out, and we would wander up and they invited us in to look round. The smell of the mint was so strong your eyes would be streaming' (Rouse 2003).

Another sweet factory across the road manufactured butterscotch. One participant described how she lived in the neighbourhood as a young woman and worked in the butterscotch factory before the Second World War, until she was laid off when the warmer weather came and the toffee would not set. She recalled the odours in less positive terms than other participants: '…the smells were abominable really … sweet, sweet smells' (D52). Memories of these odours were recalled and associated differently by this participant who experienced them on a daily basis. This illustrates the impact that the ability to exercise control over odour exposure or concentration has on how an odour is perceived. Stallen (1999) observed lack of control to have an influence on people's level of annoyance in response to environmental noise, and Nikolopoulou (2003) found the same effect with respect to thermal comfort. Starr (1969) concluded that people are far more accepting of environmental risks when exposure is voluntary, or when the benefits of exposure to the environmental stimuli are believed to outweigh any related risks.

5.1.3 Breweries

Another common industrial odour source mentioned in accounts of urban smellscapes in Doncaster, Sheffield, Manchester and Clerkenwell, London was breweries. The smell of brewing was once commonplace in the urban environment, but rising land values and global forces have driven many breweries out of business with those remaining often being taken over by larger companies and relocated away from town centres. Although the physical marks of the brewing trade frequently remain as a legacy in terms of buildings, the olfactory experience accompanying the brewing process has increasingly diminished:

> I can remember going to see Sheffield United play and you could smell beer being made in Ward's Brewery because it was only down the road, and now of course it's sort of city apartment living with no brewery, so that smell's gone. (D40)

One resident of the once industrial, now gentrified waterway in the city of Leeds, England lived close to the celebrated Tetley's brewery which closed in June 2011 following its purchase by Danish brewery company Carlsberg (Sibun 2008). Until the closure, smell experiences as a result of the brewing process remained a highly temporal part of daily life:

> …through the week they often have different brews, so there's different smells … I've often wondered whether it means that all my clothes smell of malt … they have a fantastic, really good smell and it kind of defines that area … the whole Tetley's site along the river there … that differs throughout the seasons because the wind direction actually changes and I've been surprised to find that you can smell Tetley's from right the other side of the city. (D27)

However, the detection of brewing odours isn't always described in such positive terms. The relocation of one of Manchester's breweries away from the city centre was described as a positive move by this resident: '...now Boddingtons has gone, you don't get the smell of the brewery ... you used to get the horrible smell of that ... it used to sort of pollute the air quite badly as well, especially with the yeast' (M16). Similarly, a licensee recalled: '...twice a week ... Hull used to absolutely stink of Molton Hops, like Horlicks, 'cos there was a brewery right in the centre, when I first lived there, but after I'd been there a year it closed down' (D34). All accounts, good and bad, highlight brewing odours as having a dominating effect on the surrounding smellscapes. They also illustrate a strong association between odour recollection, place perception, identity and belonging, occurring in association with the branded products they produce: Ward's in Sheffield, Tetley's in Leeds and Boddingtons in Manchester.

Another factor that is influential in the case of breweries is location; for practical reasons the majority were sited on waterways or in poorer areas of towns next to undesirable neighbours such as other odour-producing sources. During an interview I gave on a radio show in Perth, Australia, one local resident phoned in and described how he had worked as a prison guard in both Perth and Manchester, and in both locations the prisons were situated next to breweries. He explained how the brewing smells used to be detected by the inmates and this created frustration because they were unable to consume the products they could smell. Doncaster also has a large prison adjacent to its town centre, and although there is not a brewery in the area the prison is proximate to the meat rendering and anaerobic digestion plant, all next to some of Doncaster's most deprived communities.

5.1.4 Localised air pollution sources – hair and nail salons

Although most industrial producers of potentially toxic odour emissions have been regulated and re-located out of the centres of Western cities, some small-scale producers do remain. Odours from hairdressing salons, barbers and nail bars were detected whilst undertaking the smellwalks. The smells emitted were perceived fairly negatively, and an environmental health officer reported: '...we do get, quite often, complaints about smells from ... nail bars, you know, smells from acetone and things like that' (D44). The strength and other qualities of the odours, including trigeminal stimulation as a result of the salon smells, were highlighted as reasons for negative perceptions and reported complaint levels. In the US, nail bars have been scrutinised due to the high levels of toxic agents they release and the related risks to workers. Nail bars are frequently concentrated in international districts, and in the US they are staffed by a high proportion of black minority ethnic females (California Healthy Nail Salon Collaborative 2010). Following a campaign by a number of women's groups on behalf of the rights of workers in such premises, the US Environmental Protection Agency (2004) published guidelines highlighting the numerous potentially harmful chemicals used in nail salons. These guidelines advised about the storage, staff welfare and potential side effects from such chemicals. In the UK, nail salons are regulated under the Control of Substances Hazardous to Health (COSHH) regulations enforced by the Health and Safety Executive.

Hairdressing salons have similarly been found to emit high levels of gases such as ethanol whilst undertaking chemical processes like dyeing, bleaching, perming, and spraying aerosol hairsprays, posing a significant health risk to workers (Leino 1999). A study carried out by Muiswinkel *et al.* (1997) in the Netherlands, as part of a wider study on reproductive disorders among hairdressers and their offspring, found that air quality varied between hair salons and was highly temporal. The ventilation of hair and nail salons is therefore important in reducing indoor chemical concentrations, but as a result, related emissions are likely to be detected out in the street.

5.1.5 Air quality and changing odour expectations

A theme that is apparent in descriptions of the historical urban smellscapes of Western cities is that experiences of air quality were quite different in the past than they are today. The release of manufacturing and industrially generated odours that are now considered to constitute a nuisance was commonplace in the past; indeed, they were frequently released at ground level where they were likely to be detected by large numbers of people. Odours released from industrial sources into city air were often more concentrated in the past due to less advanced technological knowledge, regulation and control. They were also more varied as large numbers of small factories were situated within, or proximate to, town and city cores.

The very way that regulatory authorities judged air quality in the past, focusing on the visual characteristics of emissions rather than their potential to harm or create discomfort, was generally different to that of today. Increased awareness of invisible pollutants, combined with technological improvements and enhanced measurement and control, have undoubtedly made some positive contributions to air quality in the Western world. Sites such as Doncaster's meat rendering plant are now far less likely to be detected through the sense of smell despite, in this particular case, the plant continuing to operate on its original site, working on a much larger scale and incorporating additional activities. Such technological enhancements, changes and controls have combined with trends for the relocation of manufacturing operations to out-of-town sites, with the result that opportunities for the detection of some of the more positively perceived industrial odours, such as those of the sweet factories, have also reduced. These changes have been accompanied by shifting social expectations of the urban smellscape: 'You got smells from factories as well ... I think that was the norm, but you accepted it then, didn't you? Nowadays if you got it you'd think it was different, wouldn't you?' (D52).

This reduction in the release of many historical industrial emissions does not suggest that potentially harmful smells are no longer present in urban air. Indeed, although some historical emissions were harmful, such as those emitted through the burning of fossil fuels, many were nuisance odours rather than being directly harmful to health. Rather, large-scale historical sources have been replaced with other kinds of air pollutants. Hairdressing salons and nail bars, for example, release potentially toxic emissions at a micro level within contemporary urban smellscapes. Moreover, vehicular traffic continues to pose a serious threat to urban air quality and has a wide-ranging and complex relationship with urban smellscape experiences and perceptions.

5.2 Traffic odours – a trade-off for city life

The smell of traffic fumes is one of the odours that people most frequently associate with urban environments, and it was highlighted as one of the most disliked smells in my smell preference survey of one hundred people, forming fourteen per cent of responses for least favourite odours (see Chapter 4). Just as Taylor (2003) observed a dominating impact of traffic on overall sensory experiences of the city, traffic odours feature as a key aspect of people's perceptions, expectations and experiences of urban smellscapes. Traffic smells often provide the background odour of city life and their detection impacts on individual assessments of air quality: 'I think the city smells ... because of the amount of traffic ... the UK just smells of traffic to me ... I think the air quality is quite bad' (M31). In Sheffield, Manchester and Clerkenwell, London, residents displayed both an acceptance of traffic odours and a resignation that they would experience them as part of their daily routine:

> ...it's just something that you accept, you're so used to smelling it. And it is right outside the building that I live in, and you just get used to that as soon as you walk outside ... it's everywhere that you walk. (M27)

However, people also acknowledged the important function that vehicles play in servicing the city, and therefore accepted the presence of traffic odours as an inevitable consequence of city life to be traded against the benefits of living in the city: 'you can't really avoid traffic in those places ... bringing people into town, we actually need those, but it's a bit of a double-edged sword because along with that you do get the pollution' (D17). See Adams *et al.* (2007) for a detailed discussion of sensory conflict and trade-offs in twenty-four-hour cities.

Doncaster's air quality is superior to that of Sheffield, Manchester and Clerkenwell, London as measured by air quality monitoring stations across the UK (see http://uk-air.defra.gov.uk/), although pockets of poor air quality do remain in heavily trafficked areas. The entire city centre areas of Sheffield, Manchester and London are identified as Air Quality Monitoring Areas with air quality being generally poorer across the entire city than in Doncaster. Despite this difference, the same resignation to the presence and smells of traffic pollution was displayed in Doncaster as in the larger cities: '...it's just what you expect, it's normal and you don't even think about it ... obviously if it's particularly strong ... but normal levels of town traffic I don't think pose me a problem' (D18). However, this same participant later went on to describe petrol fumes as one of her least liked odours: 'I don't like industrial smells, sort of metally, enginey smells or petrol fumes, or petrol stations, the smell of petrol and things like that'. Clearly this participant's level of discomfort was dependent on contextual information as well as odour concentration.

Much of Doncaster's town centre core is pedestrianised and therefore experiences of traffic odours are localised, detected when proximate to vehicular routes through the town. Occasionally traffic fumes were detected within Doncaster's pedestrian zones when commercial activities were accompanied by a vehicle or generator, or when small service vehicles such as street sweeping or pavement gritting machines were around. In these cases people were less accepting of these fumes as the activities themselves were considered non-essential.

Buses were identified as the worst smelling vehicles in all of the English cities studied, releasing diesel fumes and adding significantly to pollution levels: 'it's the sound and the smell for me with buses, I just find it so intrusive' (D05). Participants were generally supportive of public transport, however:

> People go on about the pollution of buses, but a bus carries between sixty and ninety people, it's entitled to put out four times more pollution than say a car and you're still winning ... it's the cars that are the problem. (L16)

This reduced the associated annoyance:

> ...it can sometimes become overpowering, but I don't mind the smell. I specifically don't mind it because I think it's essential that we keep a traffic flow and I think that if we move much more of the traffic over to public transport, we wouldn't get all the car fumes that are adding to a bad environment ... you can put up with things if you know that it adds to a better environment as a whole. (D21)

Investment in cleaner, less polluting buses was highlighted as an important factor by built environmental professionals in Doncaster (architects, planners, urban designers, engineers and city managers), although not in comments from other groups in Doncaster nor from residents in Sheffield, Manchester or Clerkenwell, London. This need for investment influenced acceptance of bus emissions and odours, rendering them no longer an inevitable consequence of public transport, but representing instead the failure of companies to invest in their fleet. Older buses were perceived by those with knowledge of emission monitoring, statistical information and policy as more damaging to health. In a study of environmental quality assessment by different stakeholders, Bonnes *et al.* (2007) found differences between inhabitants' and experts' air quality assessments which highlighted that laypersons and experts do not always share the same criteria when evaluating and forming perceptions of the environment. One Doncaster participant had a degree of direct control over investment in the local bus fleet, and this was reflected in his perception of the town's air quality:

> …there are far less of the buses going around spewing out the exhausts than there used to be, and they're much healthier, so yes, I thought today was, I would have thought, for a town centre, was probably good. (D13)

The perception and acceptance of traffic odours are therefore deeply embedded within wider beliefs, informed by individual and professional position, access to information and the ability to control or influence odours:

> …the diesel smell of buses is really obnoxious … there's no reason why buses shouldn't be operating on ethanol or electricity … everything's caught up in your own political views and your own kind of, what's right and what isn't, and what you're prepared to accept and what you aren't prepared to accept. (D27)

The design and layout of city streets also impacted on traffic smell experiences. Anywhere vehicles had to stop and wait was identified as a potential traffic odour hot-spot. This included traffic lights, bus stops, taxi ranks, businesses where commercial vehicles drop off and pick up goods, or places where cars pull up and wait with idling engines. Two factors contributed towards this: the first being vehicles having to stop and start for a specific reason, and the second being vehicles standing waiting for customers, companions or goods to arrive. Efforts to either maintain vehicular movement or encourage drivers to switch off engines while their vehicles were stationary were judged to be important in reducing emission levels: '…we've had issues in the past with traffic drivers just sitting idling and we've said you shouldn't be doing that, or idle in one, if you've got a long time to wait' (D11).

A Sheffield resident explained: '...there's the obvious smell of the [supermarket] lorry downstairs when it's delivering. For some reason they leave the engine on and it's the smell from that, I get fumes, it's really, really unpleasant' (S32). The resident had complained to drivers in the past, but the drivers were different every morning so she felt no control in preventing the odours from entering her home through the window. In the UK, powers enabling local authorities to penalise drivers for keeping engines running are limited, but this is not the case everywhere. The city of Montreal, Canada, for example, introduced a by-law in 1978 stating:

> No one may keep running for more than four minutes the motor of a vehicle parked outdoors, save when the motor is used to carry out work outside the vehicle, or when the outside temperature is lower than −10 degrees Centigrade. (City of Montreal 1978, in Zardini 2005: 277)

The location of bus stops also played a role in experiences of traffic odours. Bus stops that were situated directly in front of residential blocks increased the likelihood and concentration of traffic odours in nearby homes, counteracting to some degree the benefits of convenient access to public transport for the residents. Although this was not as serious an issue in Doncaster due to its flat town centre topology, roads situated on a gradient also caused increased emissions, such as those in parts of London and Sheffield:

> ...you can smell the traffic and I thought you could particularly smell it on St John Street, which is a slight incline with traffic lights, so the buses ... do have to really put their foot down to get up that. (L24)

5.2.1 Description, detection and meanings of air pollution odours

Prior to undertaking the Doncaster smellwalks, I asked participants to describe their preconceptions of urban smellscapes. Of the forty-three participants that answered this question, over sixty per cent spontaneously associated odours of air pollution with urban areas, while forty-four percent specifically attributed these to traffic. Industrial and manufacturing odours were less frequently associated with urban areas (mentioned by only nine per cent of the participants). In Sheffield, Manchester and Clerkenwell, London, when they were asked about the smell of the area in which they lived, twenty-five of the eighty-two residents (thirty per cent) gave detailed descriptions of detecting traffic odours in their local environment. Residents described the smells as 'acrid', 'metallic' or 'sulphurous', with some describing the odour of their area using the same terminology but without identifying the source as traffic: 'The smell ... it smells like metal all the time. Yeah, that's the feeling that I get ... I don't know where it's from ... but there's this sort of metallic smell that I pick up' (L31). Doncaster participants also described 'chemical' and 'acid' characteristics of traffic odours, with an environmental health professional likening the detection of some air pollutants to what he termed the 'lemon-sherbet effect':

> You know, when you get a bit of lemon sherbet in the back of your throat and you get that tingling feeling, other people might describe it as something different ... I don't think they would describe it as a smell, they'd say there's something there, it's tickling my throat. (D50)

These sensations can be explained by such odours being detected via the trigeminal nerve (see Chapter 3). In an examination of terms used to describe odours detected via trigeminal stimulation, 'petrol' was highlighted in a study by Laing *et al.* (2003). Such traffic-induced trigeminal experiences were generally described by participants in negative terms, often likened to the feeling of burning: '...you can catch that kind of throat-burning diesel fumes, petrol fumes' (D39); '...to stand crossing the road there, you could almost feel it going in your nostrils ... it literally burnt your nostrils' (L14). The strong association between smell and taste also provided dual-sensory experiences:

> ...traffic fumes, it's the taste of it with people, and they can feel it, breathing it in. (D43)

> Sometimes the fumes from cars can get up your nose and they get into your throat and you think agh, and you feel like you just want to sort of spit in the gutter and to get out the smell. (L23)

Unlike sounds from traffic, which are occasionally described in positive terms by participants in soundscape research (e.g. Davies *et al.* 2007: 5), in this study the participants' experiences of traffic odours were notable in being described in predominantly negative terms; they were occasionally neutral, but only on one occasion was the description positive. In this case, the participant recalled these odours as part of her memory of Soho, London, an area she really liked, but she disliked the same odours when she experienced them in Doncaster. When they were asked to elaborate further on why the smell of traffic was perceived as a widely negative contributor to overall environmental experience, participant responses fell into two broad categories: the qualities of the odours themselves, and health concerns resulting from a perceived embodiment of pollutants through inhalation. Several participants used words describing the traffic odours in negative terms, judging them as 'bad' and 'sickly'. As well as the characteristics of the odours themselves (i.e. sulphurous, metallic and chemical), odour strength was also problematic, overpowering the sense of smell and creating unwanted bodily responses: 'It's not blowing away, it's there in your face … especially if you're trying to cross and that, and you're stood there and it's flirting out fumes … it can get up your nose and sort of keep sneezing' (D38). As a result, some participants described these experiences as '…quite choking' (D05).

In those identifying the qualities of traffic odours as the reasons they disliked them, strength of odour was highly influential in whether the smell of traffic was judged as acceptable or not:

> I don't mind them up to a point … and then there's a certain point where, and it's either, it's too strong or it isn't, there's no kind of in-between … over that, it's too much and hits the back of your throat. (D27)

In contrast, those highlighting health concerns as key factors frequently considered weak odours of pollutants in negative terms:

> …it feels like it's bad for you, it doesn't smell as strong … it's more a kind of a health kind of thing … it doesn't feel healthy to be by a road. (D29)

> I think it's because you associate the smell with polluting you in some sort of way, so you don't think of it as being a nice smell because you think of it filling your lungs with the diesel fumes. (D25)

Health concerns were particularly pronounced in participants suffering from respiratory illnesses: 'You sort of expect it when you're near a busy road, but it's not a pleasant smell … I'm asthmatic anyway, so if I am stood around where there's a lot of traffic I do feel it' (D36). A London resident explained:

> …because I'm asthmatic … you pick up on the air quality. There might be some mornings where I'll be alright. Other mornings I go out and I'm feeling breathless … wholly due to the traffic pollution because we're on a major road … I mean it's sitting there not moving. The amount of pollution that's pumping out … I'm asthmatic so it's ten times worse for me. (L4)

Poor air quality is known to impact disproportionately on those with existing medical complaints, particularly lung disease or heart conditions (DEFRA 2002:7). An environmental health officer explained the related response at a local level:

> If there is an event where [air pollution levels] go from … medium to high, we will then contact the [Primary Care Trust] and say look, this is now potentially going to affect people who do suffer from respiratory

diseases, you know, a more healthy person wouldn't probably notice a difference. (D50)

Day (2007) highlights that in addition to suffering disproportionately from poor air quality episodes, those with existing respiratory illnesses are also more likely to rate local air quality in negative terms.

The length of time that people are exposed to traffic odours also influences their judgements regarding their potential to cause harm: '...exhaust fumes, that's horrible ... it doesn't smell nice ... if it were there all day then you would worry about the health side of it, but just getting the odd whiff in the morning, no you don't' (D20). The perceived health effects of long-term exposure were traded off against more positive aspects of city life:

> ...the older I get, the more I feel annoyed that possibly I'm going to be like more ill and more wrinkly and more whatever quicker than my colleagues in the countryside, but you know, you kind of feel that the advantages of living in the middle of a city outweigh that. (L18)

5.2.2 Odours of pollution and behaviour

People adopted a range of behaviours with the intention of limiting inhalation or ameliorating the effects of breathing in traffic fumes and other sources of air pollution. These varied according to the odour source and the normal background air quality of the areas where pollutants were detected. In Doncaster, where experiences with traffic fumes are generally brief and localised, such as when they are emitted from a passing vehicle or while walking past stationary traffic at traffic lights, bus stops or taxi ranks, individuals frequently held their breath with the aim of preventing the fumes from entering their bodies: 'It's pretty bad for you and you try and hold your breath and not smell them whenever you can ... you don't really want to breathe in a load of it' (D03). In the centre of the larger cities as well as on some of Doncaster's main traffic routes, where odours of traffic sometimes dominate much larger areas, these short-term responses were impractical. Avoidance behaviour therefore changed, with individuals planning their walking and cycling routes to avoid areas where fumes were concentrated: '...it's pretty dense usually. You can smell the fumes so I try and take back routes' (L10).

Similarly, residents in Sheffield, Manchester and Clerkenwell, London frequently closed their windows in attempts to shut out traffic odours:

> ...we can't open the windows in the summertime ... if it is busy for buses you have to close them after a while because the fumes are too much, you can smell, you know, like I'm coughing, I can't breathe. (M15)

City centre residents often relied on medication to control the effects: 'I've got asthma. It's not particularly bad, I take my inhaler and it's fine. But it does make you think, what am I doing to myself, living here?' (M14).

Some city residents undertook physical activity with the aim of counteracting the effects of air pollution. Just as the presence of pollutants was judged to be a negative aspect of city life traded against the benefits, health was also considered a factor where positive efforts could remediate the negative impacts of pollution: 'I kind of try to compensate consciously by, you know, getting myself to the countryside and going on walks in the park and cycling instead of taking a tube' (L18). The idea of countering the effects of pollution through accessing what are often referred to as the 'more natural odours of the countryside' was mentioned by a quarter of the residents of the three cities, a fact that is examined in further detail in Chapter 9.

5.2.3 Presence of additional sensory stimuli

I remember last summer I was walking down Euston Road in London … that was just horrendous … it was a really hot, really humid day and the traffic was just crazy and I was finding it quite hard to breathe and every breath I could actually taste the fumes. I thought, this is real pollution. (D43)

Both the detection of traffic odours and the judgements made about them varied when accompanied by other related sensory stimuli. Such additional stimuli, including the tastes, sights, sounds or feel of traffic pollution, led to encounters being described in more negative terms than when odours were detected in isolation. As such, when information received from two or more of the senses was aligned (i.e. where air pollution was detected through both the eyes and the nose, or through the mouth and the nose) then information may become more convincing; see Burr and Alais (2006) for a more detailed discussion of the integration of multi-sensory information. One Manchester resident observed:

I suppose it's about layering, isn't it? … layers of senses. If you look at something it might please or displease you on the eye, and then you smell it and that gives you a different level of understanding of whatever you're looking at, and sound is obviously on top of that. (M29)

Despite its current reduced status in comparison with vision and hearing within design theory and practice, smell clearly functions as one in a range of sensory tools available to the individual for use in assessing, gaining meaning from and understanding the world:

I think [the air quality] is quite good. I'm not feeling it or smelling it or tasting it. Again it's not summer, it's not hot, when you notice it more … there isn't a huge amount of traffic in the centre that we see, apart from that busy road, no, I think it's good. Better than I think people would imagine. (D43)

The frequently invisible nature of air pollution, often detected through the sense of smell without other sensory stimuli, makes it easier for people to dismiss. In a society where belief systems and the design of the built environment are based upon a predominantly visual paradigm, pollution that can be seen with the eyes might also be perceived as more legitimate in warranting concern and attention than that detected through smell alone. An environmental health officer identified this as an issue he faced in his work trying to increase awareness of air quality issues:

…pollution now has gone from visible, bonfires etc., to invisible … they [the people] can't see it, and if you can't see it, it's out of sight, out of mind literally, apart from the very few who might have a respiratory problem … the pollution we are now dealing with doesn't stain houses black, green, yellow, blue and so on. If you look round you don't get the old smoke-coloured buildings anymore, once they're cleaned up they stay cleaned up. (D50)

The smogs that occurred historically in Western cities, reappearing to some degree as a haze in warmer weather, are associated with higher, more harmful levels of air pollutants (Quality of Urban Air Review Group 1996: 146). Similarly, traffic pollution seen in the form of smoke is associated with more highly polluting vehicles than with those that produce non-visible emissions: '…when a really old banger goes past and you can see the black, that really does frustrate me … you can physically see the damage it's doing, to your own lungs as much as to the environment' (D23). People clearly found visible experiences of emissions harder to ignore: '…you don't mind a hint of it, but I think when you actually see the fumes it's, you know, you'd rather avoid it or walk away' (D31).

5.3 Air pollution and the sense of smell

At the outset of this chapter, I highlighted some key differences between odours and pollutants and observed that an odour is the perception of an odorant through the sense of smell. To detect a smell it is essential that we have three elements: first, the sensing body, human or animal, with a functioning sense of smell; second, the odour source that emits the volatile odorous compounds or molecules; and third, the air that acts as the medium for carrying the smell, with air temperature playing a role in the volatility of the odorous compounds. The release of different chemicals into the air, even those that have no odour themselves, can influence different parts of this mix and therefore the relationship between air pollution and the urban smellscape experience is complex.

As we have already established, the presence of some chemicals in the air poses significant risks to human and environmental health. What is less widely recognised is the impact that many chemicals have on human olfactory performance, affecting people's ability to smell the world around them on either a permanent or a temporary basis. Hudson *et al.* (2006) compared the olfactory performance of long-term residents of Mexico City, an environment with high levels of air pollution of both vehicular and industrial origin, with that of residents of the Mexican state of Tlaxcala, a region geographically similar to Mexico City but with comparatively low air pollution levels. The study identified significant differences in overall olfactory performance between the populations, concluding that air pollution in Mexico City appeared to have a substantial impact on olfactory function. Not only did this influence residents' olfactory function for the period during which they lived in Mexico City, but it also had the potential to affect it on a permanent basis.

An environmental scientist that I interviewed had worked on several sites contaminated with pollutants in the past. She explained:

> …my previous job has definitely affected my sense of smell … the different pollutants and particles we were exposed to in the line of work … I think it's permanently been reduced to a certain extent, but certainly at that time it was more reduced, temporarily … I just lost that smell, smell-ability and was congested all the time … it was just awful. (D14)

Air pollution can also affect individuals with an otherwise fully functioning sense of smell on a temporary site-related basis, limiting the detection of other odours that may be present. This is a consequence of some odours masking others, a process used for many years in hiding negatively perceived smells in indoor environments by the application of air fresheners. Odours of traffic pollution in particular have been argued by Landry (2006: 63) to overlay and mask more subtle odours of place such as those of local flora, rendering them difficult and sometimes impossible to detect. Descriptions of such effects threaded throughout participants' comments in all of the studied areas, including those that were less polluted: 'I think in my experience, they are more pungent, they are stronger, the pollution smells … they must block out all the other more subtle smells' (D27). Historical pollutants also had this masking quality. One participant described the detection of odours from a sweet factory in her home town: 'I suppose I actually smell it more now than I did when I was young because the smoke was so overwhelming' (D43). The masking effects of traffic emissions have therefore replaced those of previous industrial or manufacturing odours in some areas.

Although some people recognised traffic pollution as reducing their detection of more positively perceived odours, the majority accepted and were resigned to this factor, just as they were of the presence and smell of air pollution. The loss of other more positively perceived odours was accepted as an inevitable consequence of traffic:

> I think it's mainly because of the pollution that you can't smell most of the things ... We love the country but wouldn't want to live there ... whatever smells are around ... it seems the pollution seems to take over from that ... it blocks. (L14)

Air pollutants also have the capacity to reduce the presence of other odours in the air. McFrederick *et al.* (2008) identified air pollutants as dramatically reducing the ability of floral scent trails to travel through the air from source, resulting in detection difficulties by pollinators. Air pollution was found to degrade phytogenic hydrocarbon chemical signals produced by plant sources through an increase in the chemical reactions occurring in air parcels carrying scents away from source. As a result, the distances at which pollinators are able to detect floral scents has reduced significantly since pre-industrial times. These findings have important implications for humans and environmental sustainability, potentially contributing towards recent trends in reduced pollinator numbers with serious implications for agricultural production and biodiversity.

5.4 Pedestrianisation, air pollution and judgements of place

Pedestrianisation offers a popular means of improving environmental quality in central urban areas and reducing encounters between pedestrians and vehicles. Following the re-routing of traffic onto Doncaster's bypass road in the 1960s, the local authority delivered a number of projects aimed at limiting vehicular access and creating new public spaces in the town. Some of these areas closed access to most forms of traffic during core daytime trading hours (10am to 4pm Monday to Saturday). Others delivered re-designed streets combining traffic and pedestrians, but which were designed to reduce and slow down vehicular movement.

Despite initial reservations expressed by local business people that pedestrianisation might adversely affect trade, many of those participating in the study reported increased investment, customer footfall and spending since the scheme's implementation. Participants were widely positive about the impact of pedestrianisation on sensory experiences of the town: '...there was only one place where we noticed the smell of vehicles and then the rest of the walk was certainly, it was near enough traffic-free, and it was improved because of that' (D01). Another participant commented, 'Doncaster has benefited from being quite largely pedestrianised in its core ... if you went to other places that were similar but didn't have that, I just don't think they would be as nice' (D05). In a study in the city of Chester, UK, Chiquetto and Mackett (1995) identified that the pedestrianisation of some city streets significantly improved air quality in those streets, reducing levels of all key traffic emissions. However, pedestrianisation was also found to increase emission levels in those streets and roads surrounding pedestrianised areas because of traffic re-distribution. In effect, pedestrianisation created greater differentiation in air quality between the pedestrianised areas and those immediately outside it. Differences in olfactory experiences of traffic in Doncaster's pedestrianised and non-pedestrianised areas were similarly pronounced, and participants described the 'localised', 'concentrated' and 'overpowering' odours of traffic in those streets surrounding pedestrianised zones:

> ...it's nearly all pedestrianised now so you haven't got the traffic fumes, unless you're on the side-streets where the buses frequent, that's not always very pleasant because the smell of fumes can be quite strong, but right in the centre where it's all pedestrianised, you don't really have that problem. (D25)

Overall, pedestrianisation was perceived to offer more varied and pleasurable urban smellscapes than trafficked areas: '...it's a lot more pleasant, it's safer for people to walk about ... you've not got that unpleasant smell from the car fumes ... you're not looking for vehicles' (D22). Of the six stopping points included in the Doncaster smellwalks, the top three most liked areas, both for overall place and smellscape liking ratings, were pedestrianised with very few pollutants detected in those areas. Of the three least liked areas, again in relation to both criteria, two were open to traffic with related odours frequently detected on-site. Paradoxically, however, the least liked area overall, a publically owned and outdated outdoor shopping precinct (Colonnades), is also pedestrianised (see Figure 5.2). This area's smellscape was rated as poorly by participants as that of the most heavily trafficked road (Silver Street). Despite being closed to traffic, participants expected Colonnades to smell of traffic because it is located close to a bus drop-off, pick-up and standing point, with buses frequently seen and/or heard by participants at this location. Despite this expectation, traffic odours were not detected in the area by any of the fifty-two participants. They frequently explained this anomaly by referring to temporal factors such as the wind and cold:

> I'm expecting that the smell isn't going to be as clean or as fresh for me ... on a bad day and a bad wind, you could get quite a lot of car fumes into here which wouldn't be able to escape easily given the way it's designed, so on some days it could be really horrible here and maybe we've caught it on a good day. (D05)

Across all the studied towns and cities, traffic odours were associated with a lack of cleanliness: '...it might be to do with the buses and the streets and a certain sense of grubbiness, I think' (D04). In Colonnades, traffic emissions were expected, reinforcing links between the senses and highlighting an anticipated congruence between sensory stimuli, impacting in turn on the overall place perception. Similarly, in another unpopular stopping point which had relatively high levels of traffic, the traffic odours contributed towards a negative place perception: '...it just kind of highlights what the area's like ... you can smell it ... lots of traffic going past, that kind of thing ... it's just a bit of an unpleasant, a dirty smell, that's the perception that you get ... it's then perceived as not being a very clean place' (D24).

Figure 5.2 Colonnades, Doncaster

In contrast, smell experiences of the more popular stopping point areas were noted for their lack of traffic odours: 'The smells are quite satisfying because it's a characteristic of the area ... there's no traffic fumes, that's a big bonus' (D14). Odours of traffic were therefore connected with various judgements of sites, feeding into notions of area cleanliness and incorporated into overall place perception.

5.5 Air pollution and the design and control of urban smellscapes

Modern legislative and policy understandings of air quality frequently include the consideration of pollutants as having the potential to cause direct harm or discomfort, thus indirectly reducing quality of life through increased stress and annoyance. In examining accounts of industrial, manufacturing or traffic-related odours we can appreciate that the situation is more complex than legislative categorisations might initially suggest. Many odours are categorised as pollutants due to their potential to cause discomfort; however, some of these odours, such as those from sweet factories or breweries, are identified by some people as a positive aspect of urban experience and local place identity. Today these odours are increasingly rare components of urban smellscapes in Western cities as a result of globalisation, legislation and modernist-inspired practices that segregate and centralise manufacturing operations.

In cases where odours are seen as creating a nuisance, local authorities are able to place restrictions on the odour sources with the aim of controlling odour concentration and periods of exposure. However, existing practice does not accommodate the possibility that odours might be experienced differently by different people, depending on whether they are residents, workers or visitors to the town, or specific segments of the community. Indeed, previous studies such as those undertaken by Bickerstaff and Walker (2001), Brody *et al.* (2004), Bonnes *et al.* (2007) and Day (2007) have all found that general perceptions of local air pollution are influenced by environmental and individual context. Pressure for new urban developments has increased the likelihood of dwellings being built next to odour-emitting sources, with the complaints of new residents leading to the further control, relocation or closure of long-established plants. Existing legislative and policy frameworks might therefore perpetuate the reduction and limitation of certain types of odour in the environment, although these are being replaced by other odours such as those of nail and hair salons and traffic.

In recent history, urban air quality in Western cities was of a poor standard in comparison with today, polluted predominantly by the release of sulphur dioxide into the air through the burning of coal. Despite the highly visible nature of such pollutants, known to impact significantly upon human health, it was not until people started to die in large numbers that public dissatisfaction grew to a point where environmental concerns were prioritised over economic growth. Many of those who lived and worked in towns and cities did so through economic necessity and poverty, accepting air pollution as a trade-off against the positive benefits of city life. Sadly, as we highlighted at the start of this chapter, the same is now true not only of many of those who live in cities in the developing world, such as Lagos and Calcutta, but also in poorer communities in Western megacities such as New York.

Traffic pollution is not only harmful to health; it also has the ability to impact on urban experiences, perceptions and judgements of place in many complex ways in cities on all sides of the world. Despite these negative impacts and perceptions, however, the participants in this study displayed resignation to the presence and effects of these pollutants in a similar way to the feelings reported by previous generations. Such ambivalence can be interpreted in several ways. First, it may signify the competing factors considered in people's decision-making processes when selecting areas to live. Although urban air usually contains higher levels of pollutants with the potential to cause damage or discomfort than air in the countryside, this negative factor is weighed up against more positive aspects of city life, such as access to jobs, services and urban lifestyles. Second, people may experience a sense of powerlessness (Carolan 2008: 1244–1245). As Reynolds (2008: 71) observes, 'Ultimately, public space is neglected because most of us have passed responsibility on to someone else'. It is only in cases where individuals have access to further knowledge, or the perceived health or discomfort impacts of pollution become severe (Bickerstaff 2004), that annoyance levels rise and prompt people to take action. Examples have been identified where perceived health impacts or discomfort following the detection of air pollution odours became sufficiently great to stimulate action. The requests of a Sheffield resident to lorry-drivers to turn off their idling engines when parked below her window, and complaints made about odours released from Doncaster's meat rendering plant, are both examples of situations where a tipping point was reached and odour levels were no longer judged to be acceptable.

Third, this resignation to the odours of pollutants in cities can be understood as cultural, a consequence of the ocular-centricity on the basis of which contemporary society comes to consciously know and understand the world. Thus, threats or discomfort presented by odours of pollutants, whether they are from industrial or vehicular sources, are greater if they are experienced alongside other sensory stimuli. In part this might relate to the sub-conscious nature of the processing of odours, with additional sensory stimuli serving as means of bringing odour perception to the forefront of the conscious mind.

Some key lessons can be taken from these findings for further exploration in later chapters. Interactions between sensory stimuli are clearly of importance in how pollution is experienced, judged and even anticipated, offering opportunities and threats for creating enjoyable and successful places. The invisible nature of many pollutants, and their respective odours, has an influence on the public acceptance of their presence. In cases where city authorities are committed to raising public awareness, efforts might therefore be made to use additional sensory stimuli as a means of communicating pollution levels. These could range from very obvious, digital visual displays illustrating air pollution levels, through to more subtle design measures using specific sounds or materials that change colour according to the pollutants present. Urban designers might also consider the use of restorative aspects of urban smellscape design, such as the introduction of greenery and planting in attempts to enhance smellscape experience and place perception, as discussed further in Chapter 9.

A range of additional factors were also associated with olfactory experiences of pollution, including pedestrianisation schemes, the existing topography of a city, temperature and wind conditions, and spatial layout. Urban designers have the ability to consider such issues when selecting future city locations, master-planning, land allocation and building or street layout, as considered in further detail in Chapter 9.

5.6 Conclusion

Contemporary urban design and management approaches to air pollution, underpinned by much of the existing legislation and policy, are too simplistic, only taking into account negative experiences reflected in the complaints made by members of the public against odour-producing sources. Some historical industrial and manufacturing odours are experienced by some people as positive aspects of the urban environment, contributing towards place identity. However, through the combined effects of globalisation, separation and control, many of these odours are becoming increasingly rare experiences. Other, more negatively perceived historical polluters are similarly less likely to be experienced in town and city centres today as a result of separation, technological improvements and control. By adapting legislation, policy and design practices to include wider consideration of odour experiences and meaning, city authorities would be in a better position to respond to the wider needs of local stakeholders, enhancing environmental experience and place attachment.

Odours of traffic pollution have in Western cities replaced those produced by industrial and manufacturing sources, and these are impacting on urban smell experience in many complex ways. As a result, these odours are dominating urban smellscapes, but people frequently feel powerless about their presence and assign responsibility for controlling pollution and its effects to built environment professionals. However, given the visual domination of the practice of these professionals, opportunities are being missed. In the following chapter we will go on to explore experiences of food sources in the city, and in doing so we will begin to gain a more detailed understanding of the role of culture and built environmental form in urban smellscape perception.

6

Food and smell

Food plays a tremendously important role in people's everyday life, and no matter what part of the world one is in, it is likely to form a main component of city smellscapes. Unlike traffic fumes, which is one of the least liked smells to be found in urban environments, food odours have the potential to both delight and disgust, with the meanings that are attached to them being changeable and invoking different emotions at different times, in different places and in different people. Food is socially situated, described by Pottier (2005, in Furniss 2008: 3) as '…the most powerful instrument for expressing and shaping interactions between humans … the primary gift and a repository of condensed social meanings … Food derives its 'power' from the web of interrelations it evokes'. In this chapter we will investigate relationships between food and the city with reference to four different components of everyday city life: markets, international districts, ventilation, and fast food restaurants. Before discussing these four aspects, it is first useful to outline the relationships that exist between bodily state and food odour perception, and to expand upon the impact of context on wider smell perception.

Given the physiological function of food to provide fuel and nourishment, individual bodily state and hunger in particular have the potential to impact significantly on food odour perception, as do specific dietary habits such as vegetarianism. Interactions between the different senses, and specifically those of taste and smell, occur every time we eat or drink, with levels of each increasing the gustatory intensity of the other. Odour therefore has an important role to play in eating. Similarly, odour has a role to play in perceptions of food, in a symbiotic relationship where meanings associated with food also contribute towards its odour perception. The associations that people have between the smelling, tasting and consumption of food, where the food becomes part of (or in the case of sickness is rejected by) the body, also mean that any pleasant or unpleasant memories and associations people have with respective food odours are likely to be significant.

In my own study of one hundred people's odour preferences, outlined in Chapter 4, over a third of all responses given for favourite smells were food- or beverage-related, with bread and coffee being the two most frequently mentioned favourite smells overall (mentioned by forty-one per cent and thirty-four per cent of all respondents respectively). Furthermore, eighteen per cent of the responses in relation to least favourite odours were also food- or beverage-related. When investigating the reasons for this, I found that many odours were associated with past negative experiences, such as one participant who named the smell of a specific branded biscuit. He explained that as a child he ate one of the biscuits, which had a wasp on it that stung his mouth. He recalled the painful incident alongside the taste of the wasp's blood and the smell and taste of the biscuit. In such cases, individual memory associations with specific food odours serve as warnings to steer clear from that source. From this perspective, we would be forgiven for assuming that such negative associations would prevent these individuals from experiencing any pleasure from the odours, suggesting a correlation between self-preservation and enjoyment (hedonism) when considering responses to food smells. However, as this chapter will go on to illustrate, this is not necessarily the case; the site in which an odour is detected has the potential to impact on an individual's attraction or repulsion towards a food odour, as well as their ability to enjoy the site itself.

As a result of the nature of the smell preference study, most of the odours listed by respondents were included without a reference to context. However, some favoured food odours were positioned within specific points in space and time, such as 'Sunday lunch/cakes cooked by my mum'. One respondent identified curry as a favourite smell, but stated that her perception of the smell '…would change depending on circumstance, as I would like to smell curry when walking home but wouldn't want my hair to smell of it'. If the context within which an odour is detected is incongruent with expectations, this also has the potential to impact negatively on the enjoyment of that odour. We will therefore go on to examine relationships between environmental context and odour perception with respect to one of the staple components of cities: markets.

6.1 Markets

Like many markets in the UK, Doncaster Market has suffered periods of decline over the past forty years, although there has been growth in recent years with increased visitor numbers and the market being awarded the title of Best Street/Outdoor Market in the UK in 2011 by the National Association of British Market Authorities. Doncaster Market is one of the largest markets in the north of England. It incorporates different specialist markets including a large fish market, a meat market and an indoor food hall, as well as an outdoor fruit and vegetable market and other specialist markets at different times of the week and month. The important role that the market plays in the town's economy was highlighted unexpectedly in the mid-1990s when a fire caused the temporary closure of some of its buildings while refurbishment took place. During this period pedestrian footfall across the town as a whole declined, with a wider impact on trading across the town. One local authority official recalled: '…because the market wasn't open the rest of the town suffered considerably … I think the council, before then, had an idea that the market was really not that important … perhaps it was a bit old fashioned and had had its day' (D28). As a result of the fire, Doncaster Market was revealed to serve a dual role: operating as a retail establishment in its own right, and attracting people to the wider town. These two roles were reflected on numerous occasions in participant comments about Doncaster Market, but also in comments made about markets in Sheffield, Manchester and Clerkenwell, London.

Doncaster's market area is one of the most liked places in the town, providing an important historical feature (see Figure 6.1). It was frequently recalled in participants' memories of growing up in the area, and was highlighted to have a significant role in local sense of place, identity and belonging. Odour occasionally featured in people's descriptions of the area: '…it's funny when you think about it, how much the smell does, in my mind, form part of my image of the place … I kind of associate those spaces with those smells … not unique smells but within the context of where they are I think they're quite strong' (D04). The musky and highly temporal odour of the markets area, and of the fish market in particular, were identified as the only relatively unique smell in the town. This uniqueness was attributed to the strength of the smell of the fish market rather than its source, a product of the size of the markets and their spatial concentration. The perceived strength of stimulation equally applied to the other senses:

> …there's a very delicate balance between turning a market environment into a shopping centre environment, and going the other way and making it a shabby, stinky mess, because markets can so easily fall into that trap … yes they're mucky, yes they're messy, yes they're shambolic, they're noisy, they're loud, they're all those things, but that's what gives them their character. (D39)

Experiences of the markets were therefore enjoyable in spite of the strength and variety of sensory stimulation, combining food and non-food odours, traditionally pleasant odours with those that were less pleasant, and linking memory and place association.

> …it just seems attractive, not because of the built environment but because of the activity and the noise and the, I suppose, the smells and the interaction … that's the kind of place that I find interesting to go to, and the places that I remember … that kind of real cluster of energy … buzz and atmosphere. (D31)

Figure 6.1 Doncaster Markets

6.1.1 The Fish Market

Odours of fresh fish and seafood from the fish market were detected and identified by most participants while undertaking the smellwalks through Doncaster, both in the markets area itself and in the surrounding streets. Doncaster's fish market is located within the markets buildings and under a roof, but with a frontage opening directly out onto the street (see Figure 6.2). Only three participants did not detect any odours of fish in the markets area; one of these was an anosmic individual who is unable to detect any odours but who does experience some trigeminal smell detection sensations, another was a fishmonger who had worked on the market for the past thirty years – 'I don't smell it … probably everybody else can but I can't' (D20), and the third was the fishmonger's daughter, who had also worked on her father's stall. Their inability to detect these odours was a clear illustration of habituation, outlined in Chapter 3.

Odours of fish and seafood were described as strong, pungent and dominating with perceptions varying from extremely positive – '…now I have a splendid smell of fish' (D13) – to more negative – 'It's not very nice, I'm a vegetarian, it's got very negative associations' (D29). Whether participants liked or disliked the odour itself, the majority expressed pleasure in detecting the odour in the markets area, with half of the Doncaster participants commenting that the smell enhanced the experience of being in the market: 'It's not a particularly nice smell but it does kind of remind you of sort of really nice fish, and it's quite

Figure 6.2 Doncaster Fish Market

well-known, Doncaster, for its fish market, it's quite a big one' (D17). Another participant reflected:

> ...it's quite a strong smell ... I think it all adds to the sense of place and around here you do expect to smell quite strong smells ... the fish market is probably one of the only parts of the town where a lot of people that live here can recognise or associate that smell ... it's a defining smell of this place. (D04)

Odours of fish were therefore expected and widely accepted as part of the overall experience of being in the markets area, and when participants didn't immediately detect them, they frequently sought them out: 'I wanted to smell fish and I can't smell fish … can we go closer? … That's alright, I like smelling the fish market, in fact I love it' (D34). Even those people that generally perceived odours of fish in negative terms thought that these odours increased their enjoyment of being in the markets area.

The area was heavily associated with past memories, particularly from childhood:

> I used to come down here with my granddad when I was visiting him in Doncaster and get some mussels from the fish market … a nostalgic thing but I still do, I'm quite tempted now to go over and get some. (D34)

Smells of fish were also frequently associated with nostalgic recollections of the sea:

> …it has sort of connotations of where I grew up … I spent my summers on the beach where they were catching mackerel … so those smells were fairly familiar, so it has that sort of … memory association … maybe that influences the way I think about this place as well. (D10)

The sight of the fish and the live shellfish, the feel of the cold of the iced stalls, the bustling crowds and the loud and varied sounds of the wider markets area, all combined with the odours of the fish market to deliver an experience of a place that nearly everyone, with the exception of only one of the fifty-two Doncaster participants, saw as an enjoyable place to be and a positive contributor to the town.

6.1.2 The Meat Market

Doncaster's meat market is located next to the fish market, within the enclosed Corn Exchange building. The meat market opens into the fish market, which in turn opens out on to the street. Whether by accident or design, odours of the meat market are therefore generally contained within the building and do not filter into the street. The odours from the meat market were perceived in less positive terms than those of the fish market, with far fewer positive memory associations described. In the case of fish, some vegetarian participants had commented that they liked and/or were able to enjoy the odours, whether they ate fish or not. This was not the case with the meat market: 'I actually like the smell of the fish market, not that keen on the smell of the meat market … it's not such a pleasant smell, I don't think' (D18). Some vegetarians explained this interlinked with visual stimuli: '...if I see a butcher's it's like psychological I think, that I'm not going to like the smell of it' (D36); '...the look and smell of meat as well, I really avoid it at all costs' (D29). Unlike the fish, which are often presented whole on the fish stalls, the meat products in the market are largely prepared for display so although there are some hanging carcasses, the meat is generally laid out in smaller chunks and pieces. The redness of the meat provides vivid visual stimuli, impacting on odour perception. One meat-eating participant talked of his experiences of the odours of meat and blood: 'I used to live quite close to an abattoir ... It's not a horrible smell. The whole thing about blood in particular is it's very, very sickly sweet and it's only when you know what it is that you think it's horrible ... smell, it's very, very subjective' (D11).

In Clerkenwell, London, some participants lived close to the celebrated Smithfield meat market, which, similar to Doncaster's fish market, is partially enclosed inside a building although it is well ventilated (see Figure 6.3). Odours and other sensory stimuli from the market were generally described by London participants in much the same way as those of Doncaster's fish market:

(L1 female): ...if we walk down there ... that does smell of meat... very strongly ... I don't really mind that, but sometimes it's alarming to see a carcass being bundled in front of you.

(L1 male): But, that of course is one of the advantages ... we are meat eaters, and there are two or three extremely good butchers, you know, around, associated with the market ... that's very nice indeed.

Figure 6.3 Smithfield Market, London

As with the participants' experiences of Doncaster's fish market, although the odour qualities were not always liked, the odours of Smithfield were enjoyed as part of the wider place experience with the benefits of the market outweighing negative associations:

> …if you go late in the day when they've washed the market, there's still this raw meat smell that's like quite cloying and unusual … I like them, because to me, if I'm going through the meat market, I kind of expect it and it means that the meat market is functioning … but the smell … it is abrasive to the nostrils 'cos the body's kind of saying – warning, raw, raw meat, germs … so you do get a physical response to it, but mentally you kind of turn it into a positive thing. (L18)

In Doncaster and Smithfield meat markets, which have operated for over 750 and 800 years respectively, live animals were originally sold and slaughtered on site. In the late 1830s Charles Dickens described the highly sensory environment of Smithfield meat market in 'Oliver Twist':

> The ground was covered nearly ankle deep with filth and mire; and a thick steam perpetually rising from the reeking bodies of the cattle … the hideous and discordant din that resounded from every corner of the market; and the unwashed, unshaven, squalid, and dirty figures constantly running to and fro… (Dickens 1837–39)

In the mid 1800s, in response to increasing concerns regarding public hygiene and the treatment of cattle, Smithfield market ceased trading livestock (Dodd 1856) with animals being slaughtered off-site instead and their carcasses transported to the market for sale. In Doncaster market, livestock continued to be traded within living memory. However, Doncaster's 'Cattle Market', as it was known, was relocated in the 1960s to make way for the town's new dual carriageway, positioned at the other side of the town's main circular road, in close proximity to the meat rendering plant. This relocation of the sale of livestock changed the odour experiences in the town centre:

> …you used to get the smell of cattle and horses … every market day, and pigs and all that … it's a smell that you expect in that type of area … it wasn't the best smell in the world … that's disappeared altogether … you don't get much animal smell in town now. (D08)

This changed smellscape is perhaps an inevitable consequence of competing demands for space and rising land values in the town. Such relocation is also representative of much wider trends for spatial separation and the concentration of activities. But does it also indicate changing odour expectations in society? One participant in her eighties considered this issue when asked whether people today would mind the smells of livestock in the town:

> I'm sure they would, and they'd say 'pooh, what's that pong!' I'm sure nowadays if they smelt it, they'd be complaining ... but I mean it was part of our life and was something that you took for granted ... you knew you couldn't expect anything else. (D52)

Differing odour expectations therefore played a role in their acceptance over time.

A key point noted from this observation, identified through analysis of the participants' experiences of Doncaster's fish market and London's Smithfield market, is that odour expectation and acceptance are related to place experience and enjoyment. In the past, the sale of livestock was seen as normal practice in towns or cities, with most people having little power, and perhaps little desire, to change that practice. Accompanying odours provided part of the anticipated smellscape of that area, and were both expected and accepted, effectively freeing people to go on and experience the odours as part of a potentially pleasurable overall sensory experience.

6.2 International food and cultural districts

Many city centres today combine a heady mix of Italian, Chinese, Thai, Indian, Caribbean, Japanese and Mexican restaurants, since minority groups often gain economic presence through opening restaurants, takeaways and food stores selling non-indigenous foods. In addition to introducing new gustatory experiences, these businesses frequently bring with them unfamiliar odours, impacting on the sensory experiences of the streets and neighbourhoods in which they are located. The concentration of minority communities in particular (often deprived) locations in the city has in many cases resulted in nationally associated food businesses grouping together in one geographical area. In some cities, distinct efforts have been made to develop and promote international and cultural quarters as part of what Evans (2003) terms the hard branding of the cultural city, responding to the demands of global tourism markets for new and authentic experiences (Urry 2003). However, such areas can act as sites of contention where sections of the community struggle for resources and space, with this tension often manifesting in complaints about sensory environmental characteristics (Degen 2008, Low 2009).

In this section we will examine experiences of odour in two very different international districts and their relationships with wider place perceptions:

first, Doncaster's Copley Road area, positioned in the heart of a deprived and highly transient town centre peripheral residential community; and second, Manchester's long-established Chinatown.

6.2.1 Copley Road, Doncaster

Copley Road, Doncaster is not dissimilar in its built form to many streets found in towns and cities across the UK, and in its use it is similar to areas found in towns and cities across the world (see Figure 6.4). Located just outside the town centre core within a highly deprived and ethnically diverse neighbourhood, it includes an eclectic mix of independent businesses such as music stores, sex shops and other specialist outlets as well as a range of health and outreach services. The major commercial component of the street's activity is food-based, featuring an array of international cuisines. These range from well-known international food providers such as Indian, Chinese, French and Italian restaurants through to the more recently established Afghan, Nepalese, Caribbean and Vietnamese restaurants, takeaways and cafés: '…you can start your way at one end and eat your way around the world' (D09).

The impact of these businesses is not limited to the fascias and building interiors within which they operate, but is felt much further afield, influencing sensory experiences, use and perceptions of the street by a range of stakeholders. Some of the food businesses are well established, having had a presence in the street for years, although the neighbourhood in which Copley Road is located has altered:

Figure 6.4 Copley Road, Doncaster

I've lived up here for almost six years and this street has changed as successive waves of migration come to Doncaster. (D11)

...there's more shops now, more ethnicity, that's clearly true, I mean there always was but it's even more so. (D40)

The concentration of a varied immigrant community in one specific area contrasts with the area's wider demographics. In the 2011 Office for National Statistics (ONS) Census, 95.2% of Doncaster's population was identified as White British, while 3.7% of the population was identified as Black Minority Ethnic (BME), compared to a national average of 11.9% (ONS 2012). Recent immigration into the town is significant with the area hosting an official immigration removal centre (DMBC 2008: 6). Many immigrants in the town reside within the Copley Road area.

The neighbourhood's smell environment was perceived by participants to have a very 'different' quality when compared to that of the wider town. This difference contrasts with the physical structure and format of the street, which has not changed significantly since it was built over a hundred years ago. Traditional terraced housing remains throughout the area, but it is the street's activities and inhabitants that have diversified. Conversely, the new businesses fit well with established local traditions of small independently owned and run enterprises: '...it is almost a traditional shopping street, apart from the fact that so many of the things in it are basically foreign ... the fact that it's got Asian and eastern European' (D13). Whether they were positively or negatively perceived, descriptions of the 'foreign' nature of the odours detected in the area threaded throughout participant comments. Perceptions of these odours were highly variable, divided between two concepts that were firmly grounded in individual and political positions: the street as a multi-cultural, cosmopolitan asset to the town, and the street as a site of conflict and discord.

The independent nature of the Copley Road businesses was liked by several Doncaster participants because it was thought to provide a welcome contrast to the homogenised appearance and use of the High Street:

These are my favourite sort of streets in towns ... you normally get that whole mix of a place, you can find out about its ethnic populations, you can find out the quirky side of a place, you normally have specialist shops that you can't find anywhere else. (D43)

Similarly, those businesses established and run by immigrants were frequently described as complementary to existing businesses:

...it's got this really nice mix of shops and uses ... it does sort of represent something that's a bit Bohemian for a place like Doncaster ... it's got a lot of really nice restaurants, ethnic restaurants ... ethnic shops which are really appealing in a sort of informal sense. (D06)

Smell expectations featured as part of this perspective: 'Lots of different smells, lots of different activities and lots of different interests, I think that's what a town centre should be' (D26). This linked into place perception: '...there's a hint of eastern cooking in the air somewhere, which is quite nice ... It has a sort of cosmopolitan feel about it but whether that's my sense of smell not speaking its name, I don't know' (D39).

The international food odours were usually described in gustatory terms such as spicy, tangy, sweet, and above all else, strong. Those who liked and felt comfortable in the area, approximately a quarter of the Doncaster participants, usually also liked the international food odours and felt they contributed towards the overall experience and identity of the street:

I only associate this [odour] with a lot of the food places, especially the international cuisine type thing, so this is the sort of smell I would expect, which I enjoy, because it's a good smell. (D48)

...I think it's good, it's continental isn't it, like being on holiday. (D51)

In these cases odours met expectations, and through prior associations they linked with other points in space and time. They provided experiences that combined recollections and idealised notions of others with lived experiences of being in Copley Road.

Copley Road was simultaneously experienced very differently by some: 'I don't like the area ... all these shops, bloody ali shops, whatever they are, and takeaways, restaurants' (D45). In this and similar comments from the eight Doncaster participants who described the area in negative terms, Copley Road was described as a site of conflict where minority groups were viewed as threatening the established culture and order: '...the number of immigrants in Doncaster, the asylum seekers ... have destroyed Doncaster. Now I know a lot of people say it's bringing a different culture, but most people in Doncaster don't want a different culture' (D08). Unlike those people who perceived the international food odours as a positive multicultural experience to be savoured, these participants perceived them in an equally negative manner:

I don't like Indian food ... It's some foreign foods, the smell that I don't like. (D30)

...my partner's father ... a very intelligent, clever man, he wouldn't touch curry ... to save his life, because it's 'foreign muck' ... you're looking at the whole cultural vibration. (D10)

In these cases the odours were seen as out of place, and although they were identifiable and even expected in Copley Road, they were not accepted due to associations with their source.

The concentration of immigrants in the area had an additional impact on place perception, with safety and cleanliness featuring heavily in these descriptions. Some participants, including those with generally positive area perceptions, described how non-indigenous food odours combined with the sounds of different languages and the sight of groups of immigrants, with the area perceived to be less safe as a result:

It's quite an undercurrent of being quite edgy ... it's very multicultural ... I don't know whether that brings an element of, you know, feeling threatened ... but I guess you get that with a mixture of like the places that we've got now, and a kind of multicultural society. (D03)

The degree to which people felt threatened or not was highly individual, situated within personal experience and linked to belonging. One long-term White British restaurateur commented: 'I feel more comfortable with the ethnic people really ... they're not threatening in any way, whereas we get a lot of violence through drunkenness sometimes you know ... I feel safer with them than I've ever felt' (D32).

Those living in the area appeared to be more concerned with doorstep issues such as waste and litter, associating these with the neighbourhood's food businesses. Participants contrasted front-of-house operations, the official face of the business, with activities at the back:

...one of 'em had been burning their cardboard ... and there was tins and that ... the back alley has been full of black bags and you couldn't get down it, it was completely full of 'em ... all they're interested in is the front and it's about time that the environmental health brought that area down. (D08)

Doncaster's Copley Road area can be understood through these odour experiences as an area in the midst of transition, with much of the town's immigrant community being concentrated in one specific neighbourhood in contrast with the wider demographic of the town. Odour experiences in the area are framed within the socio-economic contexts of individual positions on the wider issues of immigration, and clear divisions arise in odour interpretation and enjoyment. It will be useful to examine experiences of international food odours within the longer established community of Manchester's Chinatown before going on to explore key themes and contrasts emerging within and between these two neighbourhoods.

6.2.2 Manchester's Chinatown

Manchester Metropolitan District is home to over 13,500 Chinese people, forming 2.7% of the local population (ONS 2012), and many of the city's Chinese businesses, services and cultural activities are focused within its centrally-located Chinatown. The area is the third largest Chinatown in Europe (Christiansen 2003), and it has gone from strength to strength since the 1970s when many of the district's well-known restaurants first opened their doors (BBC 2004), boosted by a doubling of Manchester's Chinese population over the past decade. Today Manchester's Chinatown includes numerous Chinese, Cantonese and Thai food-based businesses, including restaurants, takeaways, bakeries and supermarkets as well as community services, facilities and attractions such as the Chinese Arts Centre, the Chinese Women's Centre and a casino. Most are situated in the area's old cotton warehouses, thereby maintaining the historic built environmental form. The area has its own distinct identity, and with it a concentration of sights, sounds, tastes, textures and odours that cannot be found to the same intensity in any other area of the city (see Figure 6.5). Despite differences in area size and the concentration of a limited number of national groups rather than many, the range of smells that were detected in the area include some also found in Doncaster's Copley Road. Similar to a number of the Doncaster comments, many Manchester residents described the food odours as a positive aspect of city life:

> In the city what I like best is the variety of food smells … I prefer a kind of a smell that I associate with a lot of different things going on, a lot of different cultures, a lot of different kinds of food … and events happening. (M26)

In contrast to Doncaster, the vast majority of perceptions of Manchester's Chinatown were positive and none appeared to be stimulated by competition for resources or underlying racial tensions. Similarly, Chinatown's smellscape, which is dominated by the smell of Chinese food, was seen as a positive aspect of the area experience and a significant contributor to the wider city: '…it's good walking through Chinatown because over there it does smell of Chinese food, especially as they've got a lot of Chinese bakeries … they're constantly making food and things like that, so that's really, really nice' (M31). The highly concentrated nature

Figure 6.5 Manchester's Chinatown

of the odours also presented some issues, serving as a positive 'smellmark' for the area whilst also stimulating behavioural responses, both attracting and repelling: 'I think Chinatown's always quite funny with the smells of Chinese food. Always, no matter what time of day or night, it's there ... depending on your mood it's either quite sort of, umm, I fancy a Chinese, or go ugh' (M7). A smellmark is a term originally coined by Porteous (1990: 27) to be the olfactory equivalent of a landmark, similar to the idea of a 'soundmark' as explored by Schafer (1994) and referring here to an odour of some distinction to a place, neighbourhood or city.

Several Manchester residents commented they would not want to live 'on top of the smell' due to its strength. Given the leaky nature of odours, the inability to contain them within Chinatown does occasionally present issues for closely proximate residents in the surrounding area: '...if you open wide this window ... sometimes it's not particularly nice ... I like Chinese food ... they start cooking probably about three and four o'clock ... in the afternoon. But then in the evening, the smell just starts ... melting into each other and mixing' (M30).

Cultural and international districts such as Manchester's Chinatown are increasingly common in large cities. Although these sites frequently act as social and commercial hubs for minority groups, in this case the Chinese community, these areas can also be understood as what Shaw *et al.* (2004)

describe as 'reimagined districts and exoticised landscapes', where ethnoscapes feature as a spectacle. Manchester Chinatown's sensory landscape is promoted by city authorities with the aim of attracting visitors into the city. Existing residents and city inhabitants go about their daily routines alongside tourists: '...you feel as if you're living a bit in a kind of tourist attraction, people do come in coach loads to visit Chinatown, take photographs of it, including the Chinese which I always find odd' (M2). Manchester's Chinatown therefore presents a different scenario to that of Doncaster's Copley Road, because the Chinese population gain a majority presence through the concentration of people and activities in one area. As a result, and as with Copley Road, the district is marked by its difference, communicated and detected through sensory information including the various components of the area's smellscape.

6.2.3 International districts – discussion

In Manchester's Chinatown, where the Chinese community and other ethnic minority groups are well established, racial antipathy appears low and the presence of immigrant communities is considered an authentic and positive aspect of city life and experience:

> ...you do really get a sense of a variety of different cultures ... and not just different cultures in terms of, oh, we have a lot of different kinds of restaurants, but like Chinatown where you get a feeling of a community. (M26)

Here, related odours are perceived in generally positive terms, considered part of a unique experience that is marketed as such – a means of attracting visitors and potential customers into the area and the city as a whole.

In contrast, Doncaster's Copley Road neighbourhood, where many minority groups are recent immigrants, is in the midst of change. Although the smell environment is considered by some as representative of an authentic community, and the international food odours therefore perceived in positive terms, it is simultaneously experienced very differently by others who consider these odours foreign and unwelcome. In Chapter 3 unfamiliar odours were highlighted as more likely to be judged negatively than familiar odours. This phenomenon has important implications in relation to 'othering', where unfamiliar odours are used as an expression of ethnic antipathy and difference (Classen *et al.* 1994: 165–169, Low 2006, 2009, Degen 2008). In both Doncaster's Copley Road and Manchester's Chinatown, international food odours contrasted with the wider smellscapes of the town, with this contrast itself perceived differently by people. As Low (2009: 102) observed in a study of the smellscapes of areas associated with different national groups in

Singapore, 'Racial communities become more pronounced when the olfactory enters the process of judging and likening one either to a "relevant" (we group) or a "non-relevant" (they-group) racial grouping'.

The size and concentration of activity also plays an important role. A participant recalled of London:

> ...if you walk through Chinatown, that's very characteristic ... Italian districts and sort of Asian districts, you'd get all of those as well ... most of what I've described you don't get in other towns or cities except on a micro-level, you know, you get your Chinese restaurant, your Asian restaurant, but you don't get a whole street of them. (D10)

Through sheer numbers and demographic variety, large cities have the scope to separate areas into different national types or themes, contrasting with the options available within smaller urban centres. Although this separation frequently occurs as a result of shared languages, lifestyles, culture and (importantly) economics, especially given that immigrants are some of the most deprived city residents (Tinsley and Jacobs 2006), this trend presents political challenges:

> ...all the Chinese food tends to be in Chinatown and most of the Indian food tends to be in Rusholme ... I like to think about it as being organised into pockets, but I guess you could look at that as being really separated and segregated. (M27)

The establishments of some specific nationalities were less likely to group together in English cities: '...the Italian is just dotted around all over the place, and there are a few Greek restaurants ... they tend to be in different areas even though they're not all that distant from each other' (M27). However, this trend varies between cities and countries according to immigration patterns, with Italian districts being well established in cities such as New York and Tianjin, China, and Greektowns in Detroit, US and Toronto, Canada.

The grouping of similar or different national food businesses into districts creates particular design considerations. In Copley Road, Doncaster and Manchester's Chinatown the built environmental form preceded the activities, but today it is the activities that dominate most aspects of these areas' perceived sensory environments, including their respective smellscapes. This in turn impacts significantly upon lived experience, local place perception and identity. The role of the built environmental form in enclosing or opening up these areas is highly influential in either magnifying and containing or diluting the intensity of the smellscapes.

6.3 Odour extraction and ventilation

Technological advancements have played an important role in controlling the release of odour from source and reducing the likelihood of many smells being emitted directly into city streets. Perhaps the most common mechanisms are extraction systems, used in the majority of the one and a half million restaurants and food outlets in Europe (EUKN 2002). Extraction systems are also commonly used in retail, office and service premises as well as shopping centres, leisure facilities such as gyms, and transport interchanges. They facilitate the capture, redirection and release of emissions into specific parts of the city, generally above first-floor level where they are less likely to be detected, and their redirection towards the back of premises such as alleyways and enclosed private areas. Whenever I take people on smellwalks in Manchester's Chinatown we always venture into the alleyways running at the back of and in between premises, and we usually detect strong and changeable cooking odours combining with odours of waste in the street (see Figure 6.6). Decisions regarding where, and if, these emissions should be released are usually made by city officials such as planners, building control officers and environmental health officers.

The fact that odours can be controlled and manipulated through such systems means that decisions can be made and enacted regarding what odours are to be removed and which will be allowed to remain. Given the highly subjective nature of odour perception, many of the odours that are considered and reported to be a nuisance by some city inhabitants provide positive reactions, even delight, in others, as with the perceptions of international food odours in Doncaster. At an operational level, context is important, as this environmental health officer explained:

> One of the things we've got to do is say who is being affected by [the smell]. And so you or I walking down a street complaining about [odours from a specific restaurant], for example, that wouldn't be classed as a nuisance, possibly, because walking past for a few seconds is different to you being able to sit in your garden and enjoy your garden. If that was your garden then there would definitely be a problem. (D44)

The likelihood of someone being exposed to an odour over repeated or prolonged periods is taken more seriously than reports of brief or limited exposure because the potential for annoyance is increased. However, this approach deals with odour from a position of being a solely negative aspect of environmental experience. It also raises an issue when permission is granted for new residential developments to be built next to long-established odour-emitting sites, sometimes despite the concerns of environmental health officers:

Figure 6.6 Back of house ventilation: Manchester's Chinatown

…that is really where we [environmental health officers] have a difference of opinion with planning … we say, 'well, you're putting that next to something which is going to create, cause a nuisance and we're then going to have to investigate that afterwards; and it's unfair for the business'. (D44)

Officials occasionally fail to consider the cost of buying or renting premises, and indeed the original purchase of the land upon which they sit may be lower due to its close proximity to odour-emitting sources. In other scenarios, however, city officials attempt to accommodate these factors in assessments:

> We've got to … try to draw the line into what is reasonable and what's not. If someone buys a flat above a commercial premises, to then complain about the smell from the take-away or the restaurant below … we've got to say at some point, 'you've chosen to live above this premises, you cannot expect there to be no smell'. (D44)

A consequence of this is that poorer communities and individuals frequently concentrate in the most odorous areas or residences. However, in the alternative scenario where an applicant wishes to build new premises, or change the use of existing premises to one that is odour-emitting, approval is far less likely to be granted if established residential properties are nearby unless the remediation of the emissions can clearly be evidenced through the use of sophisticated modelling tools, as outlined in Chapter 2.

Different food types are usually required to have different types of extraction systems, depending on the odour concentration and amount of grease released. Fish and chip shops, fried chicken outlets and pubs with a high turnover of deep-fried foods create the most highly concentrated odour and grease emissions in the UK, closely followed by restaurants serving national food types such as Chinese, Japanese, Indian and Thai foods (Netcen 2005: 18).

Ventilation systems provide architects and designers with a tool to design indoor smellscapes, potentially even those that are odour-free. Consider the controlled environments of modern enclosed shopping, service and leisure facilities and their reliance on ventilation and air conditioning in controlling odour within wide-open malls and large open-fronted units. As a retail manager explained:

> A shopping centre couldn't get away with allowing strong smells to pervade the malls … maybe some very slight food smells from a distance, but you would have a big problem … if you had that wonderful, heavy curry or Chinese … strong food smells wouldn't do at all. (D39)

As a result, the manager summarised: 'Really, to describe shopping centres as bland is not wrong; they need to be because they have to please all the people all the time, and obviously that homogenised retail experience is what results' (D39).

Such control of odour through ventilation is not restricted to building interiors:

...there's such a concentration these days on getting rid of bad things, that in the course of doing so we're also eliminating what were a lot of nice things, smells of food ... everything's air conditioned, even on the open [market] stalls you've got extractor fans ... those weren't bad smells, they were nice smells. (D41)

With a focus upon potentially negative rather than positive effects of odour, existing control mechanisms and practices are risking an increased homogenisation of ambient odour in the street, threatening existing place associations and urban smellscape experiences. Under less stringent legislation in the past, odour-producing sources were allowed to release emissions directly into the street, with some released at ground level from basements and street-level premises. In the UK, odour-related legislation applies generally only when new premises are created, when a change of building use is required, or when complaints are received. As a result there are many long-established businesses, particularly those cooking and serving food, that continue to release odours into the environment at lower height levels than would be permissible in new builds.

One such basement restaurant operates in Doncaster, releasing odours into the street and acting as a notable smellmark in the town. The odours are liked by some: 'I walk past ... and they use a lot of herbs and different kind of smells ... the smell from the extractor fan just hits you and wow!' (D38). However, they are equally disliked by others:

...one of the smells that I'm most common with, and usually when I walk by I hold my breath, is the fumes coming up from under [restaurant name] on the roadside ... If you'd have asked me one smell in Doncaster that bothers me, it's that. (D18)

The restaurant's emissions are also notable in that they can be detected by their temperature, stimulating generally positive comments:

I couldn't tell you what the smell was, but what you could smell was like the warm ... it smelt nice. (D21)

...there was a really strong smell of the cellar vent from [name of restaurant] which was really, really strong ... it's really nice at night in the cold, me and my sister used to stand there. (D06)

Such warm emissions, whether from extraction or shop heating systems, were usually commented upon in a positive manner right across the town, but these perceptions were limited to the cold winter months when it was easier to differentiate between the emissions and the ambient air temperature; the warm vents provided a welcome respite from the cold. The relocation of ventilation outlets to above-ground and first-floor levels have made such experiences less common, prioritising odour control above that of any pleasure-related thermal or olfactory experiences.

In addition, the multi-sensory nature of ventilation interacted more widely with odour expectation: 'I can hear air conditioning … which is making me imagine then that there's a smell that's going to come' (D05). This occasionally influenced judgements of place: 'you can hear some kind of extract system, so it's not so well controlled as the last area' (D28). The ventilation and displacement of odour is therefore highly influential in overall experiences, but before discussing some of these themes in further detail, we will consider convenience food, fast food restaurants and the relationships between food types and odour values.

6.4 Convenience food, fast food restaurants and odour values

In the small American city of Mountain View, California in 2007, the front page of the local paper featured the headline 'Neighbors dislike smell of KFC' (DeBolt 2007). The paper reported:

> Neighbors packed a small meeting room at City Hall last week to oppose a KFC-A&W fast food restaurant … They expressed concerns about the appearance of a fast food restaurant next to their homes. Some living as close as thirty feet away complained about future exhaust fumes from the drive-through. Vegetarian neighbors balked at the smell of fried chicken potentially wafting through the neighborhood. (DeBolt 2007)

In the same year a blog on the smells of Toronto, Canada observed:

> Every KFC in the city emits the KFC smell. I would presume this would result in a localized reduction in value of residential properties that happen to be very near. I know a woman who while house hunting fell in love with a small house in New Toronto, but could not get over the KFC smell, so did not put in an offer … Same goes with behind every McDonalds. I imagine this is a worldwide issue. (Blackett, 2007)

Fast food businesses have also gained an increasing presence in towns and cities across the UK (Schlosser 2002), impacting on urban environments in many ways (Steel 2008) with the senses playing a central role. Given the worldwide popularity and growth of such businesses, many issues highlighted in Mountain View and Toronto are also raised in English cities. A Doncaster planner described:

> ...if you've got a hot food take-away application comes in and there are houses nearby, they'll all kick off saying they don't want it ... mainly because they're going to get cars coming at all hours or they'll have bikes doing the delivery service ... it'll be the disturbance, not just the food ... or people will come, kids will come and hang out... (D09)

Depending on the location and nature of the restaurant, fast food businesses can attract high volumes of traffic whether as part of a drive-through service, access to customer parking or customers pulling up outside premises to collect food, increasing vehicular fumes in the area. Businesses which encourage the stopping and starting of vehicles and the ticking over of engines, such as fast food and takeaway outlets, are particularly problematic. Fast food premises also generate large amounts of on-street waste and litter (Keep Britain Tidy 2003) with such waste generating its own odours, impacting negatively upon wider place experience and perception.

Fast food restaurants, specifically those producing a high turnover of fried foods, release the most concentrated odour and grease emissions (Netcen 2005: 18) and require more sophisticated and complicated ventilation systems than other restaurant types. The large chain restaurants are well versed in dealing with legal requirements for ventilation, with their formulaic kitchen and restaurant layouts incorporating standard systems. However, many smaller independent businesses need detailed guidance from local officials to ensure compliance with equipment and maintenance requirements. Odours from fast food premises are commonly detected in urban environments, perceived in mixed terms and influenced by associations with brand identity and food types.

In Doncaster, fast food restaurants were frequently associated with rundown areas, and emphasis was placed on the 'greasy' nature of the food:

> The chip fat really isn't nice, it's not a nice smell at all, it's really pungent ... I guess you always relate it back to areas that you know ... where all the kebab shops are and it's all a bit dirty ... it's the area of town that's not been regenerated ... where you end up at the end of a night, really ... it's not the pride of the city kind of smell. (D27)

Greasy fast food odours were frequently associated with the evening economy, drawing from past, drunken experiences of the streets where judgements are less restricted by constraints that might apply while in a more sober bodily state: 'I would expect [fast food restaurant] to smell like what I'm smelling now, which is not appealing one little bit. Whether I would feel the same at half past eleven with a skinful, I don't know' (D39). Values associated with fast foods impacted upon place perception:

> ...this is a street which has gone down the pan because of all these places [fast food businesses] which are part of the night time economy. (D09)

> I actually find this street a bit shabby, yes, it's smelly, it's got that kind of underlying, unclean smell, nasty greasy cheap food and traffic smells that are lingering. (D39)

Not only did participants detect odours and start to transfer odour associations and values to the areas where they were detected, but they also expected to smell fast food odours in those areas that they considered rundown. In Colonnades, the least-liked area included in the Doncaster smellwalk, just as people had expected but failed to detect traffic fumes, they also expected to smell grease:

> ...as I look round all the types of stores that we've got on offer, and then some of the ... clientele that then attracts, and I guess it's just a lower, lower sort of offer ... I mean, you wouldn't get that sort of, I don't know, that freshly ground coffee smell and that garlic type fresh oil cooking ... I would expect ... that sort of greasy spoon café smell. (D47)

In research across England and Scotland, Macdonald *et al.* (2007) highlighted a significant relationship between the location of restaurants owned by the four main fast food chains – Burger King, KFC, Pizza Hut and McDonalds – and neighbourhood deprivation. The concentration of these restaurants in areas of poverty was explained as potentially linked to a higher demand for fast food in such areas, cheaper available land and the easier attainment of planning permission (*ibid.*: 253). However, in an earlier study in Glasgow, Macintyre *et al.* (2005) mapped the location of all restaurants (fast food restaurants, cafés and takeaways) in the city and did not find such a link. In reflection on the differences between the two studies' findings, Macdonald *et al.* (2007) suggest that it is the type of fast food business that differs according to neighbourhood deprivation, with fast food chains other than the main four, as well as independent outlets, not concentrating in deprived areas. This explanation is intriguing when considered in relation to odour. In Doncaster, it was odours from independent fast food outlets, kebab shops in particular, that were associated by participants with more rundown areas, rather than known brands which were considered in a slightly more favourable light. This association related to perceived links between small independent businesses and kebab shops, with the evening economy as described earlier. Fish and chip shops and their smells were perceived more positively than other fast food restaurants, as one participant explained when speaking about fast food odours:

> …it's a different smell to the smell of fish and chips, which I think we've got a love for … it's part of our heritage and our tradition, but that smell was much more kebaby shop really, and it isn't held in high regard. (D27)

The general distaste for greasy odours was reduced in the perceptions of food odours from street vendors in the primary retail and commercial core of the town. Such activities, including a burger van and a hot dog stall, were described as part of the street theatre, and like the odours of candy floss detected in the market place they were associated with past memories of fairgrounds as well as other cities. Street-vending activities were sited occasionally in Frenchgate, the primary retail area in the town, much to the aversion of those who were responsible for street-control:

> The hot dog seller is revolting … if he did not have a peddler's license we would not tolerate it … there was a week before Christmas when we actually had one outside [the shopping centre] … we got inundated with people complaining … the smell was what people were complaining about … [local retail manager] was going apoplectic with it. (D11)

The retail manager's complaints were accredited both to concerns that the odours would deter customers from the store, and the qualities of the odour itself: '…it would drive him mad the smell of rancid fat and onions' (D11). This perception contrasted with comments from the majority of the eight Doncaster participants who discussed the odours from this specific food vendor in detail; six of them perceived them in very positive terms.

In contrast, those same individuals with responsibility for controlling the town's streets also organised specialist street markets in the town, perceiving these very differently as playing an important part in '…making the streets more interesting' (D11). Such street markets were widely liked by participants, although they were described as a little expensive. Perceptions of food odours are therefore significantly linked to food type, and they interrelate with place identity, management and control. Through exploring experiences of fast food odours, the sense of smell is found to provide insights into the social life of cities, being used as an invisible marker in reinforcing socio-economic boundaries.

6.5 Food and smell – discussion

The world can be split into all sorts of halves, haves and have-nots. But here is a new source of division: smell. And we in the rich half are the ones who are the have-nots ... All new or strong smells seem bad or unpleasant ... Smell is now the most striking difference between them and us. (Gill 2005)

In her book discussing fear and happiness in the twenty-first-century city, Minton (2009) investigates relationships between urban policy and trends towards the privatisation, cleanliness and securitisation of public space. She notes the development of business improvement districts, gated communities and residential developments, all concepts imported from the US, as commonplace in the UK's larger towns and cities. Such areas are highlighted by Mean and Tims (2005) as being designed with specific community sectors in mind, namely those with the money and educational background to afford to live, work and consume in those areas. These districts frequently bear little relation to the wider context of the towns, cities and regions in which they are located; this is an ongoing argument resonating with debates about the increasing homogenisation of town and city centres and the resulting creation of clone-towns (New Economics Foundation 2005). Architect Elizabeth Diller describes the process of designing such areas:

...take any air bound badness out of the air: humidity, smells, heat ... We want total control over the environment. It's the kind of control that neutralizes everything into nothing, a flat line condition, a culturally identified comfort zone in which everything is average – a sensory deprivation. (Barbara and Perliss 2006: 134)

Minton notes that such areas exclude large numbers of people including the young, the elderly, the deprived, the homeless and the mentally ill, impacting upon society as a whole: 'The real problem is that because these places are not for everyone, spending too much time in them means people become unaccustomed to – and eventually very frightened of – difference' (Minton 2009: 36). Similarly, in examining lived experiences of two regenerated urban centre sites, one in Castlefield, Manchester and the other in El Ravel, Barcelona, Degen (2008: 196) concludes: '...the interaction of local and global processes is developing new forms of spatial contest that threaten the social cohesion of the city'.

In this chapter, perceptions of odour have been revealed to play, and reflect, important factors in place perception, identity and judgements. Very different food odour expectations were attached to those areas visited during the Doncaster smellwalks, such as the 'cosmopolitan' or 'foreign' odours of Copley

Road and the greasy fast food odours of more rundown or evening economy areas. Likewise, the site of detection influenced odour perception, with those individuals who usually disliked odours of fish being found to enjoy these and even seek them out as part of the wider experience of Doncaster's fish market.

A notable contrast existed between the perceptions of city officials with responsibility for controlling areas of the built environment in comparison with other users of public space. It wasn't until its partial closure following a fire that city leaders recognised the importance of Doncaster Market in local identity, place experience and the town's overall economic success. Similarly, olfactory experiences of on-street food vendors were generally positive, although again they were perceived very differently by those with responsibility for controlling town centre streets. In Degen's study of sensory experiences of regenerated spaces, she observed that the strategies adopted by built environment professionals, underpinned by various urban policy strands and discourses, aimed to fix representations, frame interpretations and control the lived experiences of those areas (Degen 2008: 197). Sensory aspects of place experience, including those of urban smellscapes, clearly play a contributory role towards local place belonging and identity, but they often fall below the radar of officials who frequently perceive the built environment through professional and personal lenses that do not always match those of local people. In turning attention towards the nuances of the sensory environments of cities, including those within urban smellscapes, built environment professionals are able to think about the environment in revealing new ways.

6.6 Conclusion

Through the examination of experiences of food odours in the built environment, smell and place are found to be closely linked with odour, impacting upon place perception, identity and enjoyment. Likewise, the context of the area in which a smell is detected can affect how that odour is perceived, with odour expectation and acceptance both having a role to play. The active role of the individual in odour perception is therefore critical, given the potential for odours to be simultaneously experienced differently by different people.

Perceptions of the physical and socio-economic context of the site interact with factors of odour expectation and acceptance. This is further reinforced by modernist trends for separation, potentially intensifying social divisions and reinforcing difference. Legislation and policy approaches food odours from a primarily negative position, attempting to limit and control their release by considering complaints rather than accommodating any wider positive meanings or local associations. In effect, professional practices work towards achieving physical and social order, but this can be problematic with respect to smell. Odours do not always respect or obey the boundaries imposed, and they can thus be perceived as 'matter out of place' (Douglas 1966). These factors will be further explored in the following chapters investigating a number of recent strands of policy that impact directly and indirectly on urban smellscape experiences.

7

Urban policy and smell

Architect Herve Ellena suggests that the sense of smell, along with the other chemical senses, falls within the '...dark side of architecture', included in the details frequently forgotten as part of everyday design practice with place odours being created unconsciously as a result (in Barbara and Perliss 2006: 98). This chapter explores the direct and indirect impacts that different policies have had on urban smellscape experience. Although this discussion is situated within a UK context, similar policies have been implemented in cities across the Western world.

The chapter is structured into four broad sections: the twenty-four-hour city and odour, including examination of the olfactory impacts of evening economy and café culture initiatives; smoking and odour, exploring experiences of tobacco smoke following the introduction of the English smoking ban in 2007; waste production in the twenty-four-hour city, examining experiences of waste odours including those of smoking-related litter, street urination, vomiting and public toilet provision; and a case study examination of two areas in Doncaster town centre that brings together all the themes from the previous sections.

7.1 The twenty-four-hour city and odour

Following the election of the Labour government in the UK in 1997, a new emphasis was placed on town and city centres as having an important role in addressing outward population migration, failing local economies and social deprivation. The Urban Task Force White Paper 'Our Towns and Cities: the Future – Delivering an Urban Renaissance' (DETR 2000) identified leisure and culture as a means of attracting inward investment and tourism to urban areas and stimulating new residential development. Linking into this rhetoric was the idea of the twenty-four-hour city (Heath 1997), where an idealised notion of the evening and night time economy and café culture were imported from continental Europe to the UK. Bars and pavement cafés were introduced in attempts to re-animate public areas beyond traditional trading hours, and were argued by the Urban Task Force (1999) to encourage public life. Critics were quick to point out the increase in binge drinking and anti-social behaviour that often followed such developments (Tiesdell and Slater 2004), and revised licensing legislation was introduced in the form of the Licensing Act in 2003. The key change introduced by the Act was that local authorities were provided with flexibility to determine the closing hours of premises in their areas, as outlined within their licenses. Doncaster's local authority responded to this new political emphasis by introducing a street café policy allowing those premises licensed to sell food, alcohol and/or other beverages to extend their trading out onto the public highway in areas where sufficient space was deemed available.

Sennett (1994) identifies cafés and bars to have played an important role in the past public life of cities, with cafés such as those in eighteenth century Paris interfacing directly with the street. In contrast, traditional English pubs of the same era encouraged people to talk to one another, but they '...did not relate spatially to the street ... appeared as a refuge space, fragrant inside with the comforting mixed smells of urine, beer and sausage' (*ibid.*: 346). Today, pubs and bars are increasingly opening their frontages onto the highway (see Figure 7.1):

> ...you used to go past a pub and you could smell ... the smell of smoke and the beer in the pub ... the idea of being able to look into a pub and see people drinking, that would have been not allowed by the licensing ... it's changed now. (D09)

Odours from these types of premises were frequently detected during smellwalks, perceived in highly temporal terms despite the legal ventilation requirements placed on premises cooking food. Such restrictions limit the release of cooking odours, but they do not halt them completely, with some odours leaking out

Figure 7.1 Traditional pub and modern bar frontages, Doncaster

particularly in areas where food is served and eaten in pavement cafés. Encounters with the odours of fresh food were perceived by people in generally positive terms, with the exception of some foods that were deemed to be highly greasy, as outlined in Chapter 6. Odours from alcoholic beverages were also detected, with those of 'fresh' alcohol described in positive terms, tempting passers-by: 'I have to say, the last week I've sort of gone, ooh I really fancy a pint of lager and then I think, I don't even drink lager, what's going on there, and it is like, oh, a smell, you know' (D36). In contrast, those odours of alcohol detected in the environment from the night before were usually described using negative terms such as 'stale', 'sour', 'musty', 'bitter' and 'pungent'. Such odours were thought by some participants to be incongruous with pavement cafés: 'I don't like that old beer smell, it's not a pleasant smell at all … just the combinations of people being drunk … it doesn't really go hand in hand with a cultural kind of café like spill-out space' (D17).

Traditional English pubs, with their carpeted floors, wooden and upholstered booths, separate rooms and low, beamed ceilings, smelled very different than the large, well ventilated, open-plan and open-fronted wine bars of today. These differences were sometimes linked to the beverage types sold:

> I think like old-fashioned pubs … when they had sawdust on the floor … first thing in the morning, you have the smell of stale beer, a lot less appealing than the smell that you have later on in the day, sort of like fresh beer … in these new big places where all young people go, it's shorts and whatever, it's a different smell. (D21)

The clientele and activities were also thought to influence odours:

> …it depends on the people that are in there. I think if you went in, for example [name of premises], with the live music and things like that, it sometimes tends to be very stuffy and a little bit sweaty. (D18)

Following the criminalisation of smoking in enclosed public places in the UK in 2007, the odours of licensed premises have changed significantly. Throughout the twentieth century the smell of tobacco was synonymous with public houses, and in particular with the male dominated 'tap-rooms', arguably a cultural hangover from nineteenth century smoking rooms. These were symbolic spaces described by Barbara and Perliss (2006: 67–68) as laden with the values of bourgeois culture. The new smoking legislation effectively removed this culturally specific smell: 'There's been a massive change … bars used to ubiquitously stink of cigarettes … and in fact … if you got cigarette smoke and asked people, 'what does that remind you of', they'll say a pub' (D34). Some participants attached positive value to this odour: 'I associate going into pubs with that sort of heavy, smoky smell and I kind of miss it' (D05).

The cigarette smoke of the pubs of old had a masking effect on a variety of odours: 'I've noticed since the smoking ban you can smell things more outside pubs ... like the smell of like lager and beer seems a lot stronger' (D36). As in Scotland, where the media reported 'noxious odours' soon after that country's smoking ban came into force in 2006 (Grant 2006), a similar effect was found in the pubs, bars and clubs of Doncaster:

> ...you can smell body odour often a lot more now than what you could before because that was masked by the smoke, and I find that a lot more unpleasant than the smoke smell ... I think it's worse in clubs because people are dancing a lot more ... they tend to be a lot sweatier. (D25)

A licensee from a large pub chain described the residual odours:

> We used to have extractors before, so the smoke itself was not that bad. What you do find now is the smoke smell used to cover up a multitude of sins ... we have obviously bottles in a pub so there's bottle skip housings in the pub and that – it now smells of sick that you never noticed before. The toilets, you can smell toilets now. (D35)

As a result, licensees have adopted new strategies for dealing with odour in their premises:

> ...my gaffer's always on at me now, 'your pub stinks'. Yeah, it's bloody BO, but it's not my fault ... you walk into a pub nowadays, especially during the day, it's all a bit different, obviously on a night time with all the hustle and bustle I don't think you're smelling as much ... I've never shaked and vacced so much in my life. (D45)

In addition to cleaning, licensed premises are increasingly using synthetic scents in an attempt to mask less desirable odours. The company Luminar Leisure announced in 2007 that it was going to introduce artificial re-creations of some of the country's favourite smells into two of their nightclub brands (Urban Planet 2007). Similarly, a Doncaster licensee explained: '...you have to clean a little bit more heavily than you would have done before, spend a lot of money on air fresheners' (D35). The smoking ban has therefore impacted significantly on the interior environments of pubs, bars and clubs, removing a culturally significant odour, itself formed of a combination of odours of which smoke was most dominant.

Trends towards twenty-four-hour trading have also influenced experiences of licensed premises in the street:

The smell of pub has been quite a characteristic smell in my life ... walking past pubs in the daytime, where you do get the smell of tobacco and booze and cleaning materials, particularly in the mornings ... I know it's perverse but I quite like the smell, I mean, now that pubs are open almost twenty-four hours a day you tend not to get that impact, but when pubs opened at eleven o'clock in the morning, you'd get an hour before that or a couple of hours before that where they were being cleaned and you'd still get the smell. (D06)

Pubs and clubs today continue to adjust their opening hours and diversify their services, targeting various markets in response to opportunities presented by legislative and policy initiatives. The pub chain JD Wetherspoon now opens as early as seven in the morning in many English cities, attracting an increasingly varied customer base that even extends to parent and toddler groups. Premises such as this emit very different odours to those of more traditional establishments, playing host to varied activities and new forms of social life. Consequently, lines between the evening economy and café culture, as well as those demarking interior and external operations, are blurring.

One key principle of urban design practice is the active frontage, where interior private spaces interact with more public exterior space. This principle features in high profile national guidance documents such as the UK's Urban Design Compendium (Davies 2000), trickling down into city-based initiatives. Cafés and restaurants, along with markets and other retail uses, are suggested as a means for local authorities and private developers to achieve this crossover between indoor and outdoor use. The notion of outdoor cafés providing a positive Continental-style environment that encourages public life is not limited to government rhetoric and documentation. It was also widely propounded by the built environment professionals who participated in smellwalks in Doncaster, and was reflected in their observations about the burgeoning café culture in the town:

...although it is European-ish, it's not quite like Barcelona or places like that, but it is an improvement to what we had before, outside cafés, outside drinking, and more meeting places for people really. (D50)

...this is a nice area ... it's got an open café style, it's quite busy ... it's quite cosmopolitan. (D48)

Odours of coffee are popular; participants in all of the cities associated them with, and expected to detect them in, urban environments. So positively associated is the odour of coffee with the city that a cloud of coffee scent was used to 'perfume the sky' in celebration of the arrival of a new bar in Exchange

Square, Manchester (Milligan 2005). Surprisingly, however, odours of coffee were infrequently detected during smellwalks, even in those areas where the café culture has a presence.

The British weather featured in perceptions of the café culture, believed to play a temporal role in limiting outside dining to the summer months. In Doncaster, permission to extend trading activity onto the public highway is given subject to a number of pre-conditions. There has to be a sufficiently wide pavement area outside premises in order to maintain pedestrian access. Businesses must also be considered to be reputable, with limited previous public disorder issues and compliance with a list of rules, including an agreement to use plastic rather than glass and to cease serving alcohol outdoors after eight o'clock in the evening. For permission to use the public highway, premises pay a nominal fee: 'It's £400 a year, which is peanuts ... some of them have nearly doubled the size of their premises by having an outside area' (D22).

Expansion out onto the public highway creates potentially lucrative opportunities for businesses to expand trade, and is argued by Minton (2009) to be part of the wider trend of privatising public space. However, on a practical level in Doncaster, opportunities to do this are limited by the lack of sufficiently wide pavement areas. In contrast, businesses in some privately-owned areas of the town are able to spill out onto the street without having to apply for local authority licences to do so, although permission from private landlords would almost certainly be required.

7.1.1 Summary of key impacts of the twenty-four-hour city on the urban smellscape

Licensed premises, and the entertainment and leisure sectors overall, have experienced significant changes following the enactment of the English smoking legislation, impacting upon their environments, operations and related indoor and outdoor experiences of odours. Changes in building layout and the development of a burgeoning café culture have increased the permeability and leakage of odours between internal and external environments. Those activities traditionally undertaken inside such premises – eating, smoking and drinking – are now also undertaken outdoors, increasing frequency of encounters with related smells in the street. When fresh, odours of alcohol and food are generally perceived as positive contributors to the overall ambience of an area. However, spillages often lead to staler odours, seen as out of place, olfactory hangovers from the night before. At the same time the shifting of some of these activities – specifically smoking – outside has opened up opportunities for premises to attract new clientele types. However, the removal of the masking smoke odours from internal environments has led to the demise of the historically situated odour of the traditional English pub.

The passing of this smell is mourned by some but welcomed by more, as explored in further detail below.

7.2 Smoking and odour

In 2007 England followed many other European countries in introducing laws preventing the smoking of tobacco in enclosed public places. The new laws were primarily targeted at improving indoor working environments and public health. The most publicised environments targeted were pubs, clubs, cafes and restaurants, although the legislation also extends to most other types of workplace with very few exceptions. The legislation complements public health campaigns aimed at reducing the number of smokers across the UK and it has in this respect been successful, with over four hundred thousand people reported to have given up smoking during the first twelve months of the ban (BBC 2008b). Similar laws were introduced in Ireland in 2004 and in Scotland in 2006, and although each act varies slightly in its legislative detail, the main thrust is much the same, relating to enclosed indoor environments only. In some countries anti-smoking legislation is also applied to outdoor public areas; this is the case in Tokyo, Japan and California, US (BBC 2002, Pocock 2006) and in India, although enforcement varies. In New York City, for example, the smoking of tobacco is prohibited in public parks although it continues unchecked in the city's Chinatown area, where smoking is considered by its inhabitants as a right. The majority of smoking legislation requires smokers to change their behaviours, and this is reflected in people's sensory experiences of the street, changes in their behaviour, and observations of others.

People's reactions and descriptions of the odours from different smoking products vary considerably and are far from clear-cut. The majority of non-smokers in all the cities studied disliked the odours of filtered cigarettes: 'I don't like smoke; that really, really offends me … I don't like the smell … it just hangs around so much … it's like an invasion of your space' (D47). Cigarette smoke was described by participants as having a strong, overpowering, stale and lingering odour, with some people experiencing nausea, breathing difficulties and a burning sensation in the throat following its detection. As with reactions to odours of pollution, the dislike of the odour of filtered cigarette smoke related to both health concerns and negative odour qualities, with the latter mentioned most frequently.

Smokers' perceptions differed in that although few said they liked the odours of cigarette smoke, most were neutral about it, commenting that they 'didn't mind it'. Some smokers did express a dislike of stale smoke odours, specifically when they lingered on clothes and in their homes. However, as one ex-smoker described, '…there's the smell of the smoke and the smell of the actual person who is the smoker' (D10). In this and similar frequent comments made by other people, smokers were identified by their odour as being separate to the non-smoking majority. Indeed, a fear of acquiring a 'smell of the smoker' through close proximity to those smoking reoccurred in descriptions by non-smokers as well as those of smokers: 'I dislike the smell of stale smoke. If I'm with someone and we're smoking, that doesn't bother me but then the cling of the smell of the smoke and the stale smell bothers me' (D18).

Following the introduction of the smoking ban, one dramatic consequence was that a night out no longer led inevitably to the acquisition of the smell of the smoker:

> ...when people smoke, it's in their hair, it's in their clothes, it's in their whole environment, it can't be healthy for any of them and when you used to be able to smoke in pubs and wherever, we never went out because I hated the fact that when you got home after a night out, you had to wash all clothes and you had to wash yourself and your hair as well. (D21)

So significant has this change been that the smoking legislation has had a dramatic impact on the UK's dry cleaning industry (BBC 2008b). The mourning of the traditional pub smell by some was therefore outweighed by the numbers of people who enjoyed the fact that they no longer smelled of smoke after a night on the town.

In contrast to responses to cigarette smoke, odours related to other forms of smoking activity were described in much more positive terms. Cigars, pipe tobacco and odours of marijuana were all detected at various points during the Doncaster smellwalks, although far less frequently than filtered cigarette smoke:

> I quite enjoy that smell [marijuana], and I don't know, there's a thing caught up in your political sensitivities I guess, and I don't have a problem with people smoking it, and I enjoy the smell so actually it's a nice, kind of punctuation mark in your walk. (D27)

When they were detected, odour associations and qualities were frequently used to explain this more positive reaction:

> I don't mind cigar smoke ... it's quite a nice, sort of distinguished smell ... cigar smoke can be there but it doesn't stay on your clothes or, you know, in the air, it's there at the time and then it doesn't linger on. (D24)

Given the infrequent detection of odours of cigars, pipes and marijuana in the street, their presence was unexpected and out of the ordinary:

...when you're in an urban environment, everything's sort of sanitised in some respects, and as a result the overwhelming smell is of there being almost a plateau of nothing particularly to take note of ... there was a bloke ... smoking a pipe ... if you walk past the same coffee shop every day, you get used to it, whereas that pipe tobacco, that was different. (D34)

Judgements regarding the odours of smoke therefore varied, but were generally negative regarding the most common form, filtered cigarette smoke. However, the context within which odours are detected interacts with enjoyment both of the odour itself and of the place where the odour is detected.

The new laws restricting smoking relate to behaviour – specifically the smoking behaviour of individuals and groups, and the physical spaces where society deems it acceptable for smoking to take place. Such views are expressed through legislation and policy, the provision of spaces and facilities, and wider societal attitudes and expectations. The smoking ban has changed this behaviour by shifting the location of smokers, representing changes in societal attitudes towards smoking overall:

...it's relatively recently ... that smoking became socially, not unacceptable, but distasteful, but that made it possible for the legislation ... ten years earlier, you couldn't have dared to try ... because so many of the public would have reared up ... but by the time it came in, there was a social unacceptability to it ... there was a lot of social pressure already building. (D41)

Smokers reported that when socialising, they and their smoking friends are now more likely to stay at home or visit their friend's homes where they are allowed to smoke than go to restaurants and pubs where smoking is now prohibited. However, comments from licensees illustrated the uneven impact of this trend. The manager of a large modern bar belonging to a chain reported: 'To be honest we did alright out of it ... we're taking more money' (D35). In contrast, traditional pubs and working men's clubs were worse hit: 'That killed us, that did ... this is a drinker's pub, you look at the people in here and you can tell by how they look ... you know what class of people they are' (D45).

Those smokers that spend time in offices and leisure and entertainment facilities within the city are now required to go outside to light up. Unlike many places in the US, where smokers must stand at least a certain distance away from the doorways of premises or food establishments, legislation in England has no such provision. In many offices non-smoking policies have been in place for some time, and people are already accustomed to the sights, sounds and smells of a few isolated smokers on pavements and public areas close to the entrances to office buildings. Traditionally pubs, bars, restaurants and cafés offered a separate location for smokers. Because smoking is no longer allowed in these premises a displacement effect has occurred, impacting upon odour experiences in the public realm. As a result, olfactory encounters with filtered cigarette smoke in the street have increased:

> I'm not a smoker so I notice the smell of smoke a lot more, and as soon as people come out now they're sparking up, aren't they? (D51)

> It's not a thing that you used to notice so much in the past because people could smoke wherever they were, and now they have to go outside and when you get into public walkways it's more noticeable, especially to a non-smoker. (D01)

In public areas, smokers are lighting up in the street as they walk from one place to another and clustering in doorways in large groups, producing a new social organisation:

> I suppose it is changing society ... if you're in a group and two of you are smoking and two of you don't, then you end up kind of having gaps in conversation when two people go out and then come back again, so it's a bit strange. (D23)

The separation of smokers outside has led to the formation of a new sub-culture:

> ...suddenly you're forced out into the street ... I met some really interesting people from being a smoker, who I would never normally have met ... because you smoke you talk to each other, so perhaps on the social side of it, it's quite positive. (D43)

Bell (2008) argues this increased solidarity and sociability between smokers has contributed towards the broader public culture of cities. However, many participants (non-smokers and some smokers) perceived the resulting odours very differently:

> I dislike people smoking in the street ... there's nothing social in smoking, it's the most anti-social thing you can do to yourself and then anybody else. (D21)

> I hate it more when I'm walking through the town centre in the daytime than I would have done if I'd been sat in a pub or outside in a café having a drink ... when I'm walking and the idea of smelling it and breathing it in, I really don't like it. (D31)

Some negative perceptions were linked with expectations of urban smellscapes, with the odours of cigarette smoke being rejected as valid parts of the experience. Unlike olfactory experiences of other forms of tobacco, where the unexpected nature of the encounter appeared to enhance positive perceptions, participants frequently didn't expect to detect filtered cigarette smoke in the street and they did not accept or enjoy its presence: '…it's in the street that somehow, sort of bothers me … Like I don't expect to smell it along with all the fresh air' (D07). This can be explained partially by the relatively recent introduction of the legislation; people are still adjusting their perceptions regarding normal and acceptable smoking-related behaviour in the environment. It can also be linked with society's wider preoccupation with controlling and ordering the environment, and boundaries that exist between public and personal space (Degen 2008, Minton 2009).

Experiences of entering a building can be more off-putting as a consequence of smoking on the threshold:

> I think in the doorways there's quite a problem … it's a bit of a barrier and you have to kind of hold your breath just to go into it … it's not much of an advert just going into a space. (D17)

In an attempt to minimise the impact upon corporate image, many businesses are responding by introducing staff smoking rules and thereby displacing the issue further into the street:

> …obviously they've been told not to smoke in their foyer because it looks bad … so they've just moved to the next sort of shop doorways and smoke in there instead … it doesn't look good, all the bank staff stood outside having a cig … we have a similar thing where staff, if they want a cigarette, they have to either take their staff uniform off or put a jacket on in the alleyway. (D35)

Another site that now accommodates street smokers is the pavement café. Under the previously outlined street café legislation, the number of related applications in Doncaster has increased significantly following the smoking ban. In many cases, pubs and restaurants have invested in covered areas by building shelters on private land, introducing canopies over public areas and using patio heaters to ward off the effects of inclement weather. For those licensees who are able to meet the criteria, the benefits can be great. However, one interviewed licensee was unable to gain permission to develop his back yard into an outdoor smoking area since it did not meet requirements, and also unable to extend onto the pavement outside the front of his premises because the public highway was insufficiently wide. As a result he reported losing trade, with his remaining smoking customers gathering to smoke immediately outside the entrance to his premises. The increased demand for outdoor smoking facilities has led to outdoor seating areas intended for eating and drinking being taken over by smoking customers (see Figure 7.2). Although this was considered in negative terms by many participants because it increased the presence of smoke in the street, some built environment professionals perceived it differently:

> It's had some positive effects in many ways in terms of urban design and urban renaissance – it's got a lot of people sitting outside and you go outside all the coffee shops and there's tables and chairs and places for people to sit and it's animating the public realm. (D04)

The 'animation' of such areas with odours of smoke rather than coffee has led to differing perceptions, the most notable difference occurring between smokers and non-smokers. However, this also varies according to the time of day.

Figure 7.2 Smoking in outdoor café areas, Doncaster

7.2.1 Summary of the key impacts of the smoking legislation on urban smellscape experience

The smoking legislation has impacted upon urban smellscapes in a number of ways, first and foremost being an increase in the amount of people smoking in city streets and public spaces. Whether in private outdoor areas outside a venue or in dedicated seating areas on the public highway, the smell of smoke cannot be contained within those places and it is now more likely to be detected in city streets. This is exacerbated by experiences of tobacco from people smoking as they walk from one place to another. However, smoke disperses at a much faster rate outdoors than it does in enclosed indoor environments, quickly reducing the odour to concentrations unlikely to be detected through the sense of smell. Theoretically, tobacco smoke might also be masking other smells in the ambient environment, as was the case in traditional English pubs.

Legislation has also impacted upon everyday experiences of the odour of the smoker. Primarily, this has been achieved through the removal of smoke from inside licensed premises, with odours of smoke no longer impregnating the clothes, skin and hair of non-smoking customers. Indeed, it appears the majority have accepted that the benefits of removing tobacco smoke from enclosed environments outweigh the loss of the historically situated odour of the pub and the related ejection of smokers out into the street. However, smoking legislation, combined with the emergence of the twenty-four-hour city, has also influenced urban smellscapes through increases in the amount of smoking-related waste in the street.

7.3 Waste production in twenty-four-hour cities

7.3.1 Smoking-related litter

In the first year following the English smoking ban, Keep Britain Tidy reported a large increase in smoking-related litter in the urban environment. Cigarette butts, matches, packets and wrappers could be found on the ground in nearly eighty per cent of English streets, representing a forty-three per cent increase in the geographical impact of this type of littering since the ban (Doyle 2008). Today, smoking-related litter is described as England's largest litter problem (Keep Britain Tidy 2009), with cigarette butts being the single most littered item (Keep Britain Tidy 2010). In Doncaster, cigarette butts were detected in corners and cracks in the pavement, tree pits and planted areas: '...you walk past the planters in St Sepulchre Gate and they look like huge ashtrays, until they're cleaned out. I don't think there's a culture of personal responsibility for living space, never mind public space' (D10). Although detected by participants predominantly by sight, some also described an associated stale odour and sometimes fresh tobacco smoke as cigarette ends continued to burn on the floor or in cigarette disposal receptacles. The Chief Executive of Keep Britain Tidy places the blame on smokers: 'The sheer size and scale of the cigarette litter problem is shameful and disgusting. Clearly many smokers have yet to be convinced that their cigarette stubs are litter and they seem happy to drop them everywhere' (Keep Britain Tidy 2009). However, in many towns and cities disposal facilities are limited:

> …you get situations like this guy here, he's obviously not allowed to smoke in his office so he's come out to smoke on the street, but I guarantee you, there'd be no provision for his dog ends. The company who own the building can't allow him to smoke in there, but they don't make provision outside the building to deal with the rubbish that comes from him smoking, and it's not the kind of litter that you can take away with you … what are you going to do with it? (D41)

The disposal of cigarette butts poses a particular issue because prior to the legislation, smokers were discouraged from using litter bins for this type of waste, because of fire concerns. As a result, '…you've got cigarette butts all over the place. You could smell them, where the litter bins were, because some of the cigarettes have been stubbed out on top of the litter bins' (D28). Cigarette ends have formed a component of street litter for many years, but the issue has been magnified by moving smokers outdoors. In Doncaster the local authority has responded to this issue in a number of ways. It has introduced more stringent street cleansing regimes aimed at collecting, removing and washing away any remnants of such waste, and introduced on-the-spot fines of £75 for those caught throwing their cigarette waste onto the ground. The local authority has also adapted the physical infrastructure by modifying or replacing existing bins to accommodate cigarette disposal, designing new public realm schemes with ease of maintenance in mind, and removing elements of the public realm that are perceived to be problematic:

> …we've taken a lot of stuff out, mainly because it was filling up with cigarette waste and doggy waste and stuff like that, but that was almost like a political decision and the members saying … you've tried to make a difference but you've really created us a health problem, let's cut it back. (D11)

In this latter case, increases in smoking-related litter were reported to be used as justification for the removal of some planted areas in the town. However, planting is generally perceived as a positive and potentially restorative aspect of urban smellscapes (see Chapter 9), and something that is considered to be lacking in Doncaster town centre. Its removal therefore has a potentially negative impact upon environmental quality. The local authority has additionally worked with licensees in encouraging them to provide cigarette disposal facilities and to clean the areas immediately outside their premises. This has not been without incident, however:

> I must have gone through, no word of a lie … seven or eight cigarette bins out there … the smack-heads have dragged them open … and I know it sounds stupid, but they're twenty, thirty quid a piece … it's awful and I sweep it up every morning. (D45)

Increased smoking-related litter on the street has impacted directly on experiences of city smellscapes by increasing people's encounters with odours of stale tobacco, and has indirectly contributed towards the removal of more positively perceived planted areas in Doncaster town centre. Furthermore, changes have been introduced to the physical layout and maintenance of public areas in an attempt to manage disposal and thus remove visual and olfactory remnants of smoking from the streets.

7.3.2 Street urination, vomiting and toilet provision

The concept of the twenty-four-hour city, where the inhabitants are serviced around the clock with food, drink and entertainment, has required city authorities to rethink their service provision in response to the issues presented. One issue of particular relevance to urban smellscapes is public toilet provision, which impacts unevenly on certain populations, specifically women, older people, children and the disabled (Greed 2003). The Public Health Act 1936 gave local authorities in the UK powers to provide such facilities if they wished, although doing so is a non-statutory duty. In the context of decreasing budgets, increased governmental demands for efficiency savings and required adaptation costs following the introduction of the Disability Discrimination Act in 1995 (DCLG 2008), many local authorities have chosen to either reduce public toilet provision or consider alternatives for their delivery, such as encouraging private businesses to provide toilets. Provision looks set to reduce further as a result of recent public sector funding cuts (BBC 2011a).

Odours of public toilets featured as one of people's most disliked odours in the study of smell preferences (mentioned by eleven per cent of respondents). Similarly, odours of vomit and urine or ammonia were also listed among the most disliked odours (mentioned by eighteen per cent and eleven per cent of participants respectively). Odours of public toilets were therefore considered by some to impact negatively upon urban smellscapes:

...you used to walk around, it doesn't matter which town or city, all these external toilets did smell – you could smell them from fifty yards away ... they're nearly all indoors now as part of shopping centres and restaurants and cafés. (D01)

Doncaster Council does still maintain public toilet provision in the markets area during the daytime, although the facilities are closed at night. Manchester Council similarly provides one centrally-located public toilet that is free to use and open in the daytime, supplemented by paid-for toilet units in and around the city.

Odours from the public toilets in Doncaster Market were detected during smellwalks, but the odours differed considerably from participants' recollections of those odours more generally associated with public toilets, namely a combination of urine and bleach. In contrast, Doncaster's public toilet block emitted odours of cleaning fluids, which were perceived positively in some cases: 'I got a lemon smell when we went past the toilets ... I think they'd just been cleaning them ... I thought, ooh that's alright, they're cleaning the toilets' (D19). The maintenance and cleaning of public toilets was thought to be key in odour control: '...if they're busy, it doesn't matter how hard you work, it's almost impossible to keep on top of the odour ... that's a constant battle' (D39), with potential impacts on place perception: '...a lot of places, I feel, are judged by how clean the toilets are and how good the toilets are, particularly in public places' (D24).

The odours of urine and bleach that were more generally associated with public toilets were, however, detected when participants were in close proximity to the entrance and exit from an underground car park. Some people incorrectly identified the source:

I can also smell a bit, kind of, a toilet smell. Are there public toilets around here or something? (D14)

...not being far away from the entrance to the car-park, there is quite a waft of smell from there, I don't know whether there's public toilets in there but I just got a whiff. (D18)

As well as being associated with public toilets, mixed odours of urine and bleach are therefore also detected in and associated with car park stairwells:

...they've got that residue of a car park stairwell, it really stinks ... urine mixed up with bleach ... it's absolutely distinct and it isn't just Doncaster that has these smells, all car parks everywhere have that smell as if they spray it on, when they've just finished the last brick they go around and spray 'car park' smell on it. (D31)

In a survey carried out by the national car parking company NCP, this 'usual' smell of car parks was reported to deter as much as a third of potential custom (BBC 2009). Of the two thousand people surveyed, two in three identified stairwells as the worst-smelling areas of car parks, with one in three associating these areas with the odour of urine. As a result, NCP has adopted a similar approach to pubs, clubs and bars in introducing artificial re-creations of more pleasantly perceived odours such as roses, baking bread and cut grass in an attempt to mask the odour of urine (*ibid.*). Whether such contextually out-of-place odours are preferred to combinations of urine and bleach has yet to be determined.

Street urination and vomiting, and the odours they produce, are closely associated with the evening economy, created by a combination of excessive alcohol consumption and the closure of public toilets during the evening (Bichard and Hanson 2009: 88): 'Well, with anti-social behaviour you get the urinating on street corners and urinating in shop doorways, with some people that may well be because of the lack of toilet facilities' (D22). However, those involved in managing and policing Doncaster during the evening disputed whether the lack of toilet provision was a contributory factor:

> I just think that the town centre at night time has got more toilets than anywhere else, there are toilets within the licensed premises … I think if there was a toilet available, the level of person that will use a shop doorway would still use the shop doorway and probably wouldn't use the toilet that was available. (D22)

Odours of urine and vomit were specifically associated with dark corners, doorways and alleyways: '…urine, that's kind of linked to a down and out area, and I get around to thinking of drugs and needles and all that kind of thing' (D14).

Many town and city centres have attempted to address these issues by introducing self-cleaning toilet cubicles and out-of-hours unshielded urinals that rise out of the ground at the start of evening trading hours (see Figure 7.3). Proposals for a pop up urinal were considered in Doncaster as part of a major public realm scheme in the town and were supported by many evening businesses, but were eventually shelved following opposition from daytime retailers and a lack of funding. Street urination and vomiting therefore continue to present an issue in the town, acting as sensory leakage via the detection of residual odours between differing temporal activities carried out during the day and the night.

Figure 7.3 Urilift, a public urinal which lowers into the ground ©Urilift BV

7.3.3 Summary of key issues with waste production, management and odour

Policies introduced with the aim of encouraging the evening economy and café culture have combined with the effects of anti-smoking legislation to increase the levels of waste in city streets. Rather than introducing new and unfamiliar odours, these policies have instead increased the likelihood of encounters with the already familiar odours of urine, vomit and cigarettes in the street. In the next section we will compare the impacts of these policies on the smellscapes of two specific areas visited during the Doncaster smellwalks: Priory Walk and Silver Street. These two areas have been selected as case studies due to their similarities; both are mixed-use areas, including a concentration of pubs, clubs and bars.

7.4 Case study comparison – Doncaster's Priory Walk and Silver Street

Priory Walk was developed in the early 2000s, in a site located just off the primary retail core area. The multi-million pound pedestrian precinct incorporates a mix of refurbished historic properties of up to three storeys tall and new standard block buildings situated on what was previously a surface car park. The area is pedestrianised, adopting a street format and including a mix of cafés, bars, clubs, restaurants, independent and chain retailers and services in units at either side (see Figure 7.4). Although Priory Walk has a public right of way running through it, the site is privately owned by a local company and is not a public highway. The layout, planting, cleansing and maintenance of the site is controlled by the owners along with the general activities undertaken in the street. The area includes planting in the form of trees running down the centre of the street, with flower baskets hanging on entrances into and throughout the site.

Silver Street is sited further from the retail centre, forming the south-easterly boundary of the town's medieval core. Running through it is a road carrying two-way traffic, forming a major bus route through the town (see Figure 7.5). There are pedestrian pavements on either side of the road, with both road and pavements classed as public highways. Properties located on one side of the road back onto the town's markets area, with historic properties and newer buildings interspaced along the street. The facing side of the road includes some historic properties, although a large stretch of buildings were replaced in the 1960s and 1970s by a modern structure featuring entertainment uses at ground level and office accommodation on the three floors above. The street is home to a mix of users including bars, pubs, restaurants, takeaways and independent retail and service units. The area is dominated by the evening economy, forming the main evening leisure site in the town with capacity for up to fifteen thousand people in the licensed premises alone. Silver Street falls

Figure 7.4 Street cafés, Priory Walk, Doncaster

immediately outside the town centre's pedestrianised core, and due to the width of the road running through the site, the pavements are deemed by the local authority to be too narrow to allow pavement cafés to operate. However, the road is closed to traffic on selected evenings throughout the year when town centre numbers are at their highest. The public highway is controlled and maintained by the local authority, with the area under surveillance by the town's main CCTV network operated by the local authority and the police.

Participants were asked to comment on odour detection, place perception and environmental quality in each of the areas visited during the Doncaster smellwalks. In general, Priory Walk was liked more than Silver Street, both in terms of overall area liking ratings and the ratings of the areas' smellscapes (see Chart 7.1).

Participants commented on a wide range of environmental characteristics while they were standing in the two areas, including those without direct relation to odour. These ranged from physical aspects of the environment (the architecture, quality of the public realm, the amount of trees and planting, the degree of enclosure, roads), activities (the evening economy, retail, café culture etc.), sensory stimuli other than odour (road noise, the sight of chewing gum etc.), and assessments of other area perceptions (cleanliness, safety, the level of investment etc.). I analysed these comments according to whether the environmental characteristics were described in positive, negative or mixed/ neutral terms, with the results displayed in Chart 7.2 (Priory Walk) and Chart 7.3 (Silver Street).

Figure 7.5 Silver Street, Doncaster (public highway)

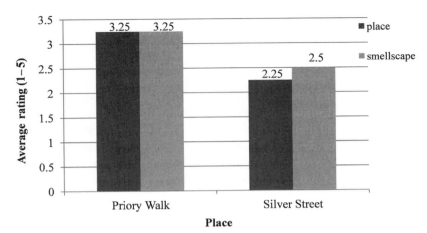

Chart 7.1 Place and smellscape liking – Priory Walk/Silver Street (1: very negative, 5: very positive)

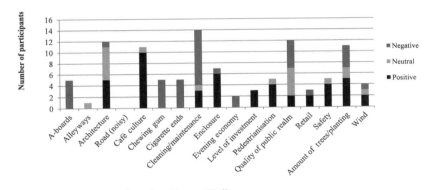

Chart 7.2 Environmental quality: Priory Walk

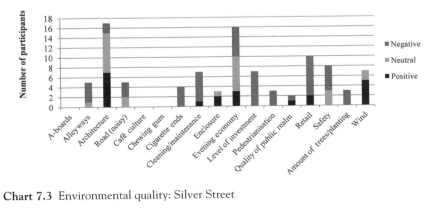

Chart 7.3 Environmental quality: Silver Street

In comparing and contrasting data from both sites it is apparent that the road in Silver Street causes much wider effects on the area's perceived environmental quality and smellscape than its impact on air quality. Pedestrianisation in Priory Walk was mentioned by several participants as having a positive effect on smell: '...there's no car noise, there's no fumes, it's less of a burden kind of thing, if you want to call it that' (D38). In contrast, the layout and use of the road in Silver Street was described negatively: 'It's too dominated by the carriageway and knowing how this street gets used, I think it's an unfair distribution of the built environment and the public realm' (D31). The pedestrianised nature of Priory Walk provided the physical space required for street cafés to flourish, with café culture being the area's most positively perceived characteristic. In contrast, the lack of space available for a similar café culture in Silver Street was seen as a missed opportunity:

> If this area was improved and businesses could spill onto the street it would make a huge difference to the smell in the street ... if it was narrowed it would give fantastically wide pavements, or if it became one-way, you could do it. (D11)

Priory Walk's pedestrian area also provided space for planting with the site being considered safe, again presenting a stark contrast to Silver Street:

> ...for an area that should attract so much sort of pedestrian traffic, it always feels slightly dangerous because everyone's always drunk and they're always wobbling across the street ... this is a hard urban landscape, I can't see a single piece of greenery down here. (D26)

However, the cleaning and maintenance standards in Priory Walk were rated poorly when compared to those in Silver Street, despite the disadvantages faced in Silver Street through associations with traffic emissions, dirt and grime. Chewing gum and cigarette ends were identified more frequently as a problem in Priory Walk than in Silver Street, with some (public sector) participants going as far as suggesting that the private sector owners should collaborate with the public sector in an attempt to improve standards:

> This is typical ... of where you've had environmental improvements, significant investment ... partnership is often an over-used and abused word, nothing wrong with talking to them and getting a fee from it ... you can see in this corner here, it's just a smoking corner isn't it ... but it looks grot, doesn't it? (D40)

Similarly, despite the lack of vehicles in Priory Walk, it was perceived as less controlled than Silver Street with A-boards considered unsightly and acting as barriers to movement. Six of the fifty-two participants described the dominance of the evening economy in Silver Street in negative terms; leading to lower daytime footfall levels, impacting on the sustainability of daytime retailers in the area and generating large crowds in the evenings:

> ...last Saturday ... it was ten o'clock at night when I got the bus back to this area and the bus couldn't get through the centre of town because of all the people ... all the people that were stood around drinking out of bottles and staggering all over the place ... Silver Street, that used to be a very nice street, but now it's nothing but pubs and wine bars. (D52)

I organised and analysed participants' comments on the odours detected in the two areas using the same method as for comments on environmental quality, according to smell type, and whether they were described in positive, negative or mixed/neutral terms; see Chart 7.4 (Priory Walk) and Chart 7.5 (Silver Street). In both areas, smell experiences were dominated by one particular odour, although this was a different odour in the two areas. Silver Street was dominated by traffic fumes (mentioned by twenty participants) which was described in either negative or neutral terms. In Priory Walk, the dominating odour was that of a fast food chain restaurant (mentioned by eighteen participants), which was described in highly mixed terms.

In general, the odours detected in Priory Walk were perceived more positively than those in Silver Street, specifically the food odours of the numerous restaurants, cafés and bars and outdoor seating areas:

> I mean, it's quite nice to have like a different array of food smells as you are walking down, it's a nice place to meet for lunch, you know, and on a night it's totally different, it's transformed on a night, because obviously they don't serve food. (D12)

In contrast, odours of alcohol in both areas were interpreted predominantly as stale odours from the night before, conflicting with daytime usage:

> I don't really like the old beer kind of smells ... if you're trying to promote an area of coffee shops, like an alternative use in the daytime ... and it's not a particularly pleasant place to be in terms of the smells and things. (D17)

Cigarette smoke was detected more frequently in the daytime in Priory Walk than in Silver Street, a combined effect of people smoking in doorways and outdoor seating areas, and the fact that more people were actually present in

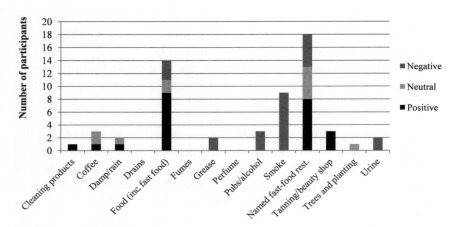

Chart 7.4 Odours detected and perception: Priory Walk

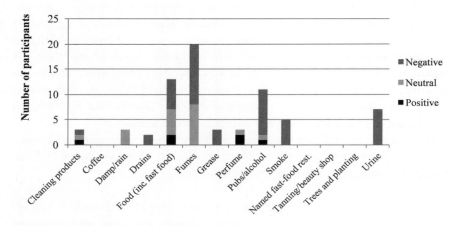

Chart 7.5 Odours detected and perception: Silver Street

Priory Walk in the daytime. In contrast, the smell of urine was detected more frequently in Silver Street, specifically in the alleyway running between two of the buildings (see Figure 7.6): '…it smells of wee all the time and you find stockings and thongs and all sorts down there … and again where people have been throwing up. You know, because people find quiet corners to throw up in' (D42). In Silver Street, the alleyways were considered to be dirty, unhygienic, dark and unsafe places, associated with odours of urine and vomit. In contrast the alleyway cutting through Priory Walk was mentioned by only one participant, spoken of in neutral terms as a functional short-cut to other parts of the town. Similarly, Priory Walk's overall smellscape was perceived more positively than that of Silver Street. The enclosing architecture of Priory Walk was frequently described as a positive characteristic of the area (mentioned by six participants):

> I think the enclosure is quite nice ... you could actually capture smell in this place and I think if I owned [name of fast food restaurant], I'd be pumping out the smell to get my customers in so I would be exploiting smell in this situation. (D05)

In contrast to Priory Walk's positively perceived enclosure, it was wind flow through Silver Street that was perceived in positive terms, described as 'freshening' the air:

> I mean, on a day like this when it's quite windy, it's tending to blow [pollution] away ... it's more to do with psychologically you're realising that you're not breathing fresh air if you're in an enclosed space, whereas if you're out in an open space, and there's an element of breeze that's kind of blowing the smell away, it doesn't seem so bad. (D06)

Environmental form and wider aspects of environmental quality can therefore be understood as interacting with urban smellscape experience and wider place perception.

Figure 7.6 Alleyway, Silver Street, Doncaster

7.5 Discussion

The concept of the twenty-four-hour city, where the city extends its trading hours well into the night and incorporates elements of a European-style café culture, is influencing the lived experiences of Doncaster town centre. This policy, as well as that relating to smoking and the closure of public toilets, are all having an effect on urban smellscape experiences of the town and perceptions of overall environmental quality. However, as identified at the start of this chapter, none of these policies accommodate a consideration of their impact on urban smellscapes.

Pubs and clubs have serviced the town's inhabitants for many years, and therefore the presence of these activities and the release of related odours into the street is not in itself new. What is new is the changing nature of the odours and the places in which they are detected. Changes have occurred in the type and strength of detected odours. Following the introduction of the smoking ban, for example, the traditional odour of the English pub has changed and new cleansing and maintenance regimes have been introduced with the aim of removing or masking those odours that remain. The larger, open-plan, wooden-floored and well ventilated layouts of modern bars, some of which also now spill out onto outdoor pavement café areas, have easily facilitated such odour removal activities. Traditional establishments have found this more difficult with their carpets, wallpaper, lower ceilings and closed frontages. In the past, when smoke combined with other pub-related smells, a distinctive odour was created, recalled fondly by some as enhancing their experiences and being associated with happy memories and other sensory stimuli, such as the sight of smoke combining with the fog produced by dry ice machines. In contrast, the odour of stale smoke clinging to clothing after a night on the town was widely disliked, associated with odours of the smoker rather than of the cigarette itself.

The spatial concentration of certain types of odours has also increased in the city in recent years. In Doncaster, larger pubs, clubs and bars have been established with the majority clustered in particular areas of the town. The grouping of these businesses in specific areas alters the expectations of the types of smells that might be detected there. These included expectations of odours of alcohol, smoke, urine, vomit (fresh during the evening, stale during the daytime), combined with odours of perfumes and aftershaves in the street at night. In the two case study areas, street cleansing and maintenance regimes reduced these odour concentrations in the publically-managed Silver Street (with the exception of the alleyways), whereas maintenance was considered poorer in the privately-owned and maintained Priory Walk precinct. Priory Walk was perceived to have a more favourable daytime smellscape due to the presence of odours of fresh food and beverages, and it benefited from odours emitted from the trees and flowers. In contrast, the pavements and businesses in Silver Street were quiet in the daytime although the road remained busy, with the consequence that traffic-related odours dominated smell experiences in the area.

Although sensory encounters with urine, vomit and tobacco are likely to have been experienced in all historical English towns and cities, there are areas where even in the distant past one would have been more likely to experience some odours rather than others. Contemporary societal norms, whereby odours and activities are separated into specific areas (e.g. the separation of heavy industry from urban centres), and also frequently separated in time (e.g. the evening economy), are reflected in people's perceptions of odours and the environmental context in which they are detected. These associations draw on participants' previous experiences of those particular places and other similar ones: the busy road, the pedestrian precinct, the evening 'strip'. Through such associations, odours become perceived as appropriate to specific places and times, and therefore they are more likely to be identified, expected and accepted in the correctly associated context, or perceived as 'out of place' when they are detected in a non-associated context. For example, the odours of cigarette smoke were regularly more annoying for both smokers and non-smokers when they were detected in the street than when (in the past) they had been encountered in the enclosed environment of a pub. Similarly, odours of vomit and urine were seen as private, belonging to the individual and the personal spaces they inhabit, rather than belonging to the public sphere. Experiences of these odours in the street were therefore perceived in negative terms, symbolic of the anti-social and uncontrolled behaviour of others and also drawing on memories and associations with illnesses. The increased pervasion of the odours of toilets, spilt beer and body odour in pubs and clubs following the introduction of anti-smoking legislation were similarly perceived as out of place, and had to be removed by licensees through the application of varied forms of odour control.

From an urban design and management perspective, odour clearly challenges illusions of temporal and spatial separation. Within the notion of the twenty-four-hour city the built environment is portrayed in many ways as a stage, where one act is played out during the daytime (the café and retail culture) and another in the evening (the drinking culture). Without the application of rigorous odour control processes the separation of these two acts is difficult to maintain, with those smells produced as a by-product of related activities leaking out of the places and times where they belong into the wrong physical, social and temporal space. Odour crosses boundaries between public and private space and represents a potential breakdown in control as odours from one area leak into, and potentially pollute, those from another. Alongside the implementation of more obvious forms of odour control, such as cleaning and maintenance regimes, a number of physical aspects of the built environmental form were identified that can be considered to be part of urban smellscape design. These included the use of enclosure in increasing the strength of more positively perceived odours, the encouragement of wind flow through the built environment to reduce the concentration of negatively perceived odours, introducing more effective ways of disposing of cigarettes through the adaptation of existing bins or the introduction of more suitable ones, and considering the wider repercussions of decisions such as those removing planting areas on overall environmental quality and the urban smellscape experience.

7.6 Conclusion

The city is a site of constant change, not only in its physical form but also in the activities of the people that inhabit it and the places where they undertake these activities. City authorities play an active role in determining what can occur where, with political imagining of the city and urban life having a direct impact on the sensory lived experiences of cities. Policies introduced in the UK as part of the drive towards the twenty-four-hour city have interacted with the ban on smoking in enclosed public areas, impacting in numerous complex ways on urban smellscape experiences and perceptions. The odours of food and coffee, originally associated with the idealised concept of the European-style café culture in government rhetoric, are experienced far less than those of tobacco smoke, which is now detected frequently in the street. These policies and initiatives also generate the odours of waste in the street, including that produced by cigarette-related paraphernalia, spilt alcohol, urine and vomit. The latter two of these odours are specifically associated with areas that are perceived as dark, run down and unhealthy, such as alleyways and public car park stairwells.

As a result, a range of new and enhanced odour management practices have been introduced, including cleansing, maintenance, and scenting practices with the use of artificial odours as a means of masking more negative odours in the indoor and outdoor environment. The following and final section of this book on odour control, design and placemaking will start by exploring these trends in further detail, considering contemporary treatments of odour in the built environment and examining the ways that city managers seek to organise and influence urban smellscapes.

Part III
SMELLSCAPE CONTROL, DESIGN AND PLACEMAKING

8

Processes of odour control
in the city

Paris used to smell of bakers, pissoirs, pastis and dark tobacco. It was as alluring and decadent a scent as a city could wear. All the smells of old Paris have gone now ... No one drinks pastis, the bakeries are all out-of-town conglomerates, the pissoirs went years ago. And it's not just Paris that smells of bland-city. All over the world, the urban scent has been wiped off the olfactory map. (Gill 2005)

In 1994, geographer Paul Rodaway challenged the dominant view that society sought only to limit the odours of people and the environment. He argued that this perspective was too simplistic, and instead proposed four strategies that he believed were used to control and organise experiences of smells from people and environments. He defined these as follows: *cleansing*, the removal of smells by washing; *deodorisation*, the removal of unwanted smells by the addition of masking odours; *synthesis*, the manufacture of odours either as extractions or as synthetic odours; and *labelling*, the adding of a specific smell with desired properties and culturally-agreed associations to a product or space (Rodaway 1994: 151). However, these same terms are used by others in different ways. Odour masking, for example, is a widely-recognised term used to describe the superimposition of one odour over another with a modifying effect, such as is frequently used in the control of odours emitted from agricultural and industrial sites (Cheremisinoff 1995). Classen *et al.* (1994: 171–172) refer to deodorisation as a strategy of odour reduction through control rather than masking, and highlight the recent development of 'smell suppressing sprays' called antagonists, which block people's ability to perceive certain odours through the release of odourless molecules into the air. Furthermore, when considering Rodaway's strategies of synthesis and labelling within the context of environmental control and management, these two might be argued as two halves of the same process – synthesis being the manufacture of odours, and labelling the application of these within environments.

Without wanting to detract from Rodaway's important contribution to our understanding of the relationships between smell and environments, the identified strategies are clearly problematic when we think about modern

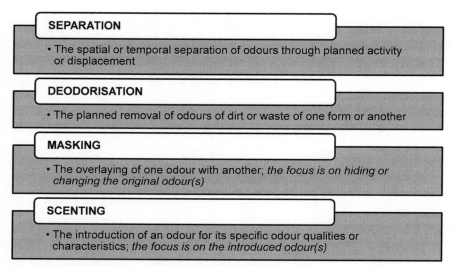

Figure 8.1 Management and control processes: urban smellscapes

terminology regarding the control of environmental odour in cities. I have therefore drawn on Rodaway's original categorisations and redefined them according to the insights gained through the empirical smellwalking studies, and from the specific perspective of the control and management of the urban smellscape (see Figure 8.1).

These revised processes are *separation*, where odours or odour-producing sources are separated from each other or from the source; *deodorisation*, where odours are removed from the environment through waste management, cleansing and maintenance activities; *masking*, where (frequently stronger) odours are intentionally or unintentionally introduced into the environment, mixing with, overlaying and hiding other odours that are present; and *scenting*, where new odours are introduced into areas with the aim of enhancing olfactory experience and/or influencing people's behaviour or mood through the detection of the specific odour (as opposed to its capacity to hide or modify another odour). In this chapter I will discuss each of these strategies in turn, and will both draw from the findings of earlier chapters and introduce additional material relating to deodorisation and scenting in particular.

8.1 Separation

Separation works as a key organising concept in the management, control and design of urban smellscapes. It relates to: the spatial separation of odour-producing activities according to activity type; the separation of odours through displacement; the separation of odours from source through ventilation and other mechanical means; and the temporal separation of odours.

Historically, a range of different industries and trades mixed cheek by jowl in cities, with the consequence that a variety of odours were experienced within close proximity of one another (Classen 2005a). In contrast, many odour-emitting activities, industrial and otherwise, have relocated away from contemporary urban centres either in response to the enforcing of policy and legislation or as a result of rising land values and global forces. The relocation of some activities, namely those perceived by the majority as widely offensive odour emitters such as waste water plants, is considered beneficial to the urban environmental experience by most people. However, not all spatial separation is perceived in such positive terms, with the relocation of some traditional odour-emitting businesses, such as breweries, away from urban centres being perceived by some as detrimental to the urban smellscape experience, with negative implications for place belonging and identity.

Processes of separation also impact on urban smellscapes through the displacement of odours from one place to another. The pedestrianisation of specific streets or areas within urban cores was highlighted in Chapter 5 as separating traffic and its odours into what I will term 'sanctioned' areas. A sanctioned area is a site where society or legislators have deemed it acceptable for specific activities or experiences to take place. Pedestrianisation in Doncaster was widely perceived in positive terms, considered to improve air quality and reduce traffic odours in the heart of the town. However, Doncaster's pedestrianisation scheme has also displaced traffic and its emissions to surrounding areas including Silver Street, an area located on the verge of the town's pedestrian core, where smell experiences were dominated by traffic odours. These odours offered a marked contrast to those within the pedestrianised zone, and they were widely disliked.

The displacement of odour has also occurred as a consequence of smoking regulations preventing the smoking of tobacco in enclosed public places. The identification of areas where smoking can no longer take place effectively shifts this activity and its odours into other areas, including those that are a specified distance away from other premises such as schools, hospitals or premises serving food, as is the case in the US and India, or into private areas only, as in Nigeria. In the UK, the spaces sanctioned for smoking in the city include the yards and outdoor seating areas of licensed premises, office doorways, the street and outdoor public areas, but odours have a habit of leaking from these areas into other areas, and this is disliked by many. One of the most novel examples of the separation of smokers and smoking odours from the rest of the public that I have witnessed was in Stockholm, Sweden, where transparent and ventilated smoking booths are provided in enclosed public areas such as hotel lobbies or the airport (see Figure 8.2). Reminiscent of exotic creatures at the zoo, smokers huddle together in these booths and can be viewed but not smelled by onlookers. Such smoking booths, which provide a smoking area within the confines of a non-smoking space, are also cropping up in other areas of Europe such as Frankfurt Airport, Germany and offices in Helsinki. Recent reports in the Japanese online media have also highlighted the fact that the first pay-for-access smoking booths are being introduced into three sites in Tokyo, Japan; it is claimed that they are used by nine hundred smokers on a daily basis (Daily Yomiuri Online 2012). In these cases, the smoking odours are separated from source with sophisticated ventilation systems which suck the odours out of the smoking booths to prevent them from being released into the immediate external environment, although some of the tobacco odours continue to stick to the clothing, hair and skin of the smokers.

Odours are similarly separated from source at a localised level in city streets through the use of ventilation systems and chimney stacks. Given the relocation of most industrial activities to out-of-town areas, the most common use of these systems in urban areas is in fast food premises, restaurants, pubs and clubs, and individual shop or service units such as nail and hair salons and gyms. Such premises generally fall within the 'nuisance' category of legislation, with the potential to create annoyance and have an impact on quality of life. However, the perception of the odours emitted by these premises varies according to individual, social and cultural experiences and norms, professional perspectives, training and odour identification, expectation and acceptance.

Legislation frequently specifies the types of systems that are required for different uses and the height at which emissions should be released; ultimately most ventilated odours have to be released somewhere, although they may be chemically cleaned of grease or odour molecules as part of the process. In many cities, ventilated emissions are released at the rear of premises and in back alleyways, as was found in Manchester's Chinatown or in Doncaster's Copley Road. As a result, these back-of-house areas frequently become perceived as dirty, smelly and unhealthy places to be. In effect, the separation and redirection of odours into these areas through ventilation systems reinforces existing olfactory differences between the public front and the private backs of houses. Odours such as those from kitchens are separated and displaced from source, and as a result they are no longer as easy to identify or anticipate. Therefore they become inappropriate to the physical space to which they are redirected. Despite these ventilation practices some odours continue to filter out of premises into the street, where food odours are regularly perceived as positive unless they are of a highly greasy nature. Relocating these odours to back of house locations not only has the potential to increase negative perceptions of those areas, but also to increase the likelihood of those odours themselves being considered as negative.

Figure 8.2 Smoking booths, Arlanda Airport, Stockholm, Sweden. ©Finnavia&Finnair

Many extracted odours are released into the air above first floor level in an attempt to reduce detection. In the increasingly common mixed use high-rise urban blocks with restaurant, bar and retail usage at ground level and residential above, even such high-level odour release can be problematic. The development of new residential buildings on plots situated close to odour-producing sources presents similar issues. In such cases, the separation of odours becomes increasingly difficult if not impossible to enforce, with smells leaking between public spaces such as restaurants and bars into private areas of the home. In current UK planning guidelines, consideration is given to the impact on neighbours of proposed developments of new odour-emitting sources, or the change of use of existing premises which might create a source of odour. However, in the development of multi-use urban blocks where a range of uses occur within one development, provided the ventilation systems meet building regulation requirements, the impact on residents above may not be of direct concern to officials. Similarly, when new residential buildings are constructed next to existing odour-emitting sources, the potential for annoyance and complaint can be overlooked. Occasionally, it is only when premises are built and odour complaints are received that conflicts are identified.

The separation of odours can also occur according to times of the day, week and year as well as over longer periods of time, signifying olfactory changes throughout history. The shorter-term temporal changes occur as a result of seasonal activities and the effects of weather on odour experience and expectations throughout the year. Temporality also impacts directly upon odours emitted from planting and green spaces, discussed further in Chapter 9. Warmer weather increases the intensity of many odours:

> ...you do tend to get more of a smell when it's summertime and that's partly because people are outside ... but also the heat from the sun can cause more of a smell. We get much more complaints about smelling rubbish and dog muck and things like that when it is warmer weather. (D44)

Warm weather can reduce the physical separation of outside and inside as premises open their doors, windows and frontages onto the street and more people spill out into pavement cafés. In some hot countries, however, extreme temperatures have the opposite effect as people close their doors and windows and turn up air-conditioning equipment, such as is increasingly the case in Singapore (George 2000). In a study of the effects of microclimatic conditions on public space usage in an urban Mediterranean environment, Nikolopoulou and Lykoudis (2007) found that daytime usage of urban space was three to four hundred per cent higher in the autumn and winter than during the hot summer months.

The idea of the twenty-four-hour city brings the physical and temporal separation of activities, each with varying smell expectations for different times of the day and week. In larger cities the evening and night-time economies run throughout the week, although some evenings are busier than others. In Doncaster, evening activity is concentrated on specific nights, producing varying stereotypical temporal expectations of odour: 'I know what it would smell like on a, probably on a Saturday or Sunday morning ... there would be vomit all over the place' (D10). Similarly, unlike many high street retailers who open every day of the week, Doncaster Market operates on a limited number of days. Olfactory experiences of the market place therefore change considerably, from the varied, strong and widely liked odours of market days to non-market days, where '...it smelt of emptiness ... it reminded me often of Sunday mornings when you sort of get that kind of the morning from the night before kind of smell' (D42).

Experiences of traffic pollution are also influenced by the heat of summer and the cold of winter. The summer increases the perceived pollutant odour strength, mirroring relationships between increased air temperature and actual pollutant levels (DEFRA 2008: 51). In the winter months cold air and fogs can similarly exacerbate pollution levels (Bendix 2000) with the visual nature of emissions in cool air increasing awareness: '...when the traffic's very heavy, particularly when the traffic's stationary, then it does feel quite bad, and on a cold morning you, you get the feeling that it's not very nice' (L17).

Separation therefore influences odour experience and perception in varied and complex ways, and it can be understood both as a consequence of the temporal nature of life and the changing seasons. However, it is also significant of a human desire to exert control over the environment.

8.2 Deodorisation

Deodorisation is a term that I apply broadly across a range of activities that have the general aim of removing or reducing odours of dirt or waste from the environment. It therefore refers to processes such as waste collection and cleansing and maintenance activities, aimed at removing and washing away sources of odour from the surfaces of the city.

The mass generation of waste in a variety of forms, whether from traffic or industrial emissions, sewage, food waste, litter or street urination, is a by-product of the widespread consumption of goods, services and materials in the city. Efforts are made to remove and dispose of waste through: separation according to different *waste types*, such as the separation of organics from non-organics, plastics from metals, toxic from non-toxic; *waste location*, with waste being stored or released as emissions in private areas such as back-of-house alleyways, yards and gardens and kept physically separate from more public areas; or the provision of *waste disposal receptacles* such as litter bins in the street (see Figure 8.3 for a particularly disgusting example) or cigarette disposal units attached to building walls. Once collected in units or sites, public and private waste services transport waste out of the city to venues away from urban cores such as recycling plants, incinerators and landfill sites.

Figure 8.3 Waste disposal bins, Manchester

Processes of waste collection and disposal influence urban smellscape experience and perception in a variety of ways. The frequency of collection services is important in maintaining control: 'I think that maybe there should be minimum requirement in terms of, like refuse collection … if it's a hot morning, it starts to smell pretty quickly' (D26). Although the physical separation of waste to allocated places does produce visual separation, odours regularly leak out. Alleyways are frequently considered smelly areas that need regular servicing, without which they risk polluting public areas through odour leakage: '...we walked past an alleyway and you could smell the rubbish from the bins, and there were plastic bags ... you could smell them from there' (D24). Similarly odours from the drainage system were detected in specific areas, impacting on area perceptions: '...it's very, very, very unpleasant ... on a hot day, it's nasty ... but you would not want it to occur at a time when the town was at its busiest because people would get a bad view of the town' (D11).

However, the infrastructure of waste disposal bins also occasionally fell short of expectations. In the case of cigarette-related litter, the recent introduction of the smoking ban changed disposal requirements; because cigarette butts are no longer disposed of in ash trays provided indoors, an enhanced requirement for outdoor disposal has emerged. Problems occur when waste and its odours are detected in places where contemporary expectations and beliefs suggest that they should not be, such as odours of cigarette ends, cigarette smoke, alcohol spillages, urine or vomit. These odours are heavily associated with dirty, unhealthy and run-down areas, illustrative of places that are uncared for and out of control through their apparent lack of cleaning and maintenance activities: 'I think probably what I would consider a poor area quite often has stale smells about it anyway, you know because it's perhaps not that well looked after, and I think some of the smells come from that' (D28).

In town and city centre cores, city managers frequently take action in an attempt to address the presence of 'out-of-place' waste. These include initiatives such as fines for those dropping litter and cigarette waste in the street, the regulation of street cafés, and requirements on businesses to clean areas immediately outside their premises. The sweeping and washing of outdoor areas has additionally become a common practice in most towns and cities, although individual assessments of cleanliness are highly subjective. These two assessments of the same area in Doncaster were made on the same morning by two different participants:

...it still looks dirty and although it's quite new and not been here that long, even the shop signage looks a bit like they could do with a good wash ... I think the stains of chewing gum on the pavement and cigarette ends ... just general cleanliness really... (D24)

I like Priory Walk ... one of the more clean-looking areas of Doncaster. It's set out really nicely with modern looking buildings, and it's quite pleasant to the eye. (D25)

Assessments are therefore influenced by individual factors, such as occupation, and contextual factors such as an individual's familiarity with, and relationship to, a particular site. Assessments also draw from area preconceptions as well as olfactory and other sensory information gathered while on-site: 'It's just a bit of an unpleasant, a dirty smell, that's the perception that you get and obviously wherever you're walking down here and it's that constantly, it's then perceived as not being a very clean place' (D24). Cleaning and maintenance practices in city centres are now so commonplace that it is frequently only when expectations are not met that comment is made: '…you're gonna get ambience, depending on how good the cleaning up is, of the sweepers in Doncaster, but I have to say it must be good because otherwise I would have noticed if it wasn't' (D15). In these cases clean places are associated with a lack of odour, but this is not always the case. In many areas scented cleansing fluids and detergents are used, themselves contributing directly towards urban smellscape experience. Detergent odours were more widely disliked than scented cleaning fluids, described as strong, heavy smells that were seen as out of context in the outdoor environment:

> …you can kind of ignore background smells but then you get arrested by something and there's a really strong detergent smell … that's sort of actually quite offensive … you might find it bearable in a hospital, but anywhere else it's kind of really unpleasant. (D05)

Odours of scented cleaning fluids were perceived more positively, although descriptions were still in mixed terms:

> Well, I thought it was quite nice at first, but I think … when you smell cleaning products, you think ah, what's that smell, but then you're sort of smelling, and it's like, ah no, it's like disinfectant … as you take it in, it gets a bit heavy. (D12)

Both detergents and scented cleansing products were seen as part of a cleansing process targeted at washing away the negatively perceived odours of waste, including those of stale alcohol, urine and vomit. Indeed, cleaning-related odours were detected most frequently in Doncaster's two areas with active evening economies (Priory Walk and Silver Street), although they were also detected in the market. Odours of detergent and other cleansing fluids were thought to have a masking effect on more negatively perceived odours, although on some occasions, rather than masking these odours, the smells of the cleaning products themselves mixed with the existing odours to create other negatively perceived odours. For example, public toilets were associated with a combined odour of urine and bleach, recalled and observed in very negative terms. However, in close proximity to a block of public toilets in Doncaster Market the odour detected was scented cleansing fluids: '…it's a nice clean smell, like that kind of CIF lemon smell' (D19). This synthetic smell of lemons was associated with cleanliness and was considered appropriate to the place, a fact which is illustrative of human control over the environment. Taken further, the synthetic smell of lemons served the purpose of masking olfactory reminders of the physicality of human existence. Therefore, although both detergents and scented cleaning fluids are used for similar purposes, the scented cleaning products are more positively associated than the smell of detergent, which is more widely associated with other places such as hospitals and toilets.

The deodorisation of urban smellscapes in town and city centres through waste management, cleansing and maintenance cannot therefore be limited to odour removal or sterilisation alone, although these processes play an important role in maintaining the perceived environment quality and in removing unwanted odours. Additionally, they are associated with separation and scenting practices. One underlying theme in deodorisation is a connection between public places and the odours of dirt and other such unsanctioned waste: '...the streets smell ... I suppose it might be an association with kind of public areas and public buses ... grubbiness of that smell ... maybe that is a psychological thing' (D04). This is not to suggest that private places are always perceived to be cleaner than public areas; in the case study analysis of Doncaster's two evening economy areas, it was the privately-owned and managed area that was deemed to be the most poorly cleaned and maintained. Yet despite this fact, the overall smellscape of the private area was preferred, largely as a result of the area being pedestrianised and therefore perceived as unpolluted by the odours of traffic.

8.3 Masking

Cain and Drexler (1974) investigated masking odours and 'counteractant' odours, the latter being a term used to describe the introduction of some odours with the intention of reducing the perceived intensity of another odour. Masking is considered by Cain and Drexler to be an issue of odour quality rather than odour strength. From this perspective, the qualities of an introduced odour combine with an existing odour to change the odour qualities to something new. Someone once described this mixing of odours to me as similar to the visual combination that occurs when one mixes the colours blue and yellow and create green. Although it is created through the combination of two colours, green is neither blue nor yellow but a colour in its own right with its own characteristics. The same is frequently true of masked odours, with one odour mixing with another to create a new odour.

In contrast to masking activities relating to the body, where sprays might be used to overlay and hide other less positively-perceived body odours, the masking of environmental odour in the city is as likely to be an unintended by-product of another action as it is to be a planned effect. The most highly masking activity in contemporary Western cities is the emission of traffic fumes produced as a consequence of the movement of vehicles in and around the city. In this respect, not only does the presence of air pollutants potentially reduce the detection of more subtle environmental odours through their masking qualities, but they can also potentially break down other odours as they travel through the air (McFrederick *et al.* 2008) and reduce human smell performance on a temporary or permanent basis (Hudson *et al.* 2006). Traffic pollution therefore has a significant impact upon odour experience; but this is in no way a result of any odour-related decision making process or strategy.

Odours of cigarette smoke also have a masking effect on experiences of other environmental odours, as was extremely apparent following the introduction of the English smoking ban in enclosed public areas. The full extent of this masking quality was revealed in pubs, clubs and bars once the odours of smoke started to fade, to be replaced by those of body odour and other generally negatively perceived odours. It was only when the activity of smoking was displaced from one site to another that the true masking effect of the odour was realised.

Some planned environmental odour masking practices also occur in the urban environment. The most common of these is the use of detergents and scented cleaning products. Both of these are aimed at washing away negatively perceived sources of odour, but they also overlay remaining odours with their own distinct smell. The reported use of artificial scents specifically in the stairwells of car parks (BBC 2009) mirrors the odour-masking strategies adopted by bar and club licensees following the smoking legislation. Such practices are based on an assumption that the masking of odours through the application of stronger smells will enhance the experience and perceptions of those areas.

8.4 Scenting

An increasing number of multi-national high street stores and restaurants, including non-food stores such as Sony, Nike and Lush (Hirsch 1990, Jenkinson and Sain 2003, Selvaggi-Baumann 2004, Lindstrom 2005a) and food stores KFC and McDonalds (Schlosser 2002, Kentucky Fried Chicken Corporation 2007), use smells that are designed and released as a means of communicating with their customers. Their corporate odours feed into the mix of those detectable on many high streets. In this section we will explore the experiences of scenting activities in urban smellscapes under three broad categories. The first is *non-food odours*, relating to those scents emitted from the retail or service sectors as a consequence of the products they sell. The second category examines more aggressive scenting approaches under the category of *perfumes and synthetic odours*. In Chapter 6 I outlined odour perceptions resulting from the sale of foodstuffs and food preparation. An additional category of food odours not yet discussed forms the third category of scenting activities: *perceptions of commercial scenting practices in food*. In each of these cases the aesthetic qualities of odours are considered by the commercial sector in one form or another, and in exploring them I will highlight some potential ethical implications arising from these activities.

8.4.1 Non food odours – product-related perceptions

A range of non-food odours is released by retail or service businesses into the ambient environment through windows or doorways at the front of premises, or through ventilation systems at the back. Such odours generally create highly localised experiences and provide insights into the nature of the business activities and products available. They additionally contribute towards odour expectation, with people expecting to detect certain types of odours in specific places as they navigate their way around a town or city. People draw from previous experiences of specific or similar shops, for example expecting to detect odours of leather whilst walking past a shoe or handbag shop, or those of sawdust and animal feed outside a pet shop. In some cases less obvious product sources are perceived:

> There are certain smells that resemble certain places … with the [electronic game shop], it always smells sort of new, like it has got lots of new stuff in it … whenever I smell it, it's sort of the new plastic, it always makes me think of games. (D16)

People detect non-food smells from chemists' shops: 'Everything will be correct, the smells of this, of that, you know, when you feel ill, like it smells like you're going to get better right now because you're going to take some tablets and medicine' (D49). These odours have the potential to form part of an individual's emotional attachment to specific stores, and in the case of leather shops, pet shops and book stores, odour perceptions generally ranged from neutral to positive. In Doncaster, when such odours were expected but not detected, participants occasionally passed comment:

> I really tried to smell the pet food place … I didn't pick it up as I went past, I was disappointed … I would have done that automatically as I went past the pet shop, have a smell … it was a missed opportunity to, you know, add something to the environment. (D31)

Odours were also repeatedly detected from clothes shops and market stalls, some being associated with perfuming practices in high-end clothing stores (explored in further detail below). However, several people considered the smells a product of the clothing itself, described as the 'smell of new' and perceived in generally positive terms:

> ...there's been some quite nice smells actually ... quite a strong smell of new clothes as we walked past the clothes stalls ... I do quite like that. (D14)

> There's a certain sort of atmosphere if you go into somewhere like [clothing chain store], which is perhaps almost because you are amongst new fabrics ... almost a smell of things that are new and haven't been soiled or dirtied or worn, and a certain fresh smell that they have about them. (D13)

In fact, positive associations with the 'smell of new' extend much further than those of clothing, mentioned spontaneously by eleven of the Doncaster participants. The 'smell of new' was associated with different aspects of the built environment, feeding into processes of consumption as well as contrasting with perceptions of run-down areas: 'I like the smell of newness, you know, new paint, new fittings, new fixtures, new carpet, you know, newness' (D39). Rather than being understood solely as representative of a naturally 'new' odour in terms of a starting point, newness in this context is also representative of being without the dirt or pollution of other processes, people or things.

Commercial non-food odours from retail and service businesses, such as those emitted by products sold and processes carried out, were experienced differently by different people. All of these stores, whether they were perceived in positive or negative terms, were frequently linked with specific local areas and provided participants with micro-area smellmarks. These odours, and others, therefore have the potential to contribute towards olfactory experience and city legibility as people draw from smell and other sensory information to create a mental map of particular streets, neighbourhoods and other urban areas.

8.4.2 Perfumes and synthetic odours

Perfume and synthetic odours were also detected in the street, from perfumes worn by people, scented products and perfumes sold in stores, and as synthetic odours introduced into stores as part of the store experience and branding. Experiences of these kinds of odours were notable in the extreme judgements participants described when detecting them, and the physical bodily responses and behaviour they exhibited following detection.

Perfume preferences are highly individual, with many participants in the favourite odours survey identifying a specific named perfume as a most preferred smell, and another as a least preferred. Similarly, perceptions of perfumes from people in the street were mixed:

> ...a chap walked past me ... and I went mmm ... I love the smell of Kouros and he had it on when he walked past. (D15)

> ...the only thing I could smell as we were walking up here was the perfume from the woman in front of us, which I found really repulsive, it's actually given me a headache ... I could smell it most of the time actually, her perfume, cheap and nasty. (D10)

Disliked perfumes and synthetic odours, whether from people, products or stores, were described as strong, pungent and invasive: '...the perfume counters at [name of department store], I really can't bear because to me it just stinks, it's overwhelming' (D05). There was one high street store that was identified in three of the case study towns and cities as selling scented products and having a particularly potent odour; this store was Lush, the global cosmetics chain founded in the UK in the 1990s. In a study on experience marketing carried out by the Rotterdam School of Management at the turn of the millennium, the researchers describe the experience of detecting the odours from a Lush store:

> As you walk along the street where there is a Lush shop you start smelling the fragrances from afar; but since the exotic, fragrant scents do not belong to an urban landscape, your senses are alerted. As you pass by the window you realize that this is the source of the pleasant scent diffusing onto the street. And, you are naturally led to enter the shop. (Frank *et al.* 2001)

Of the sixteen Doncaster participants that described their experiences of Lush, six liked its smell and thought that this opinion was representative of the majority: '...if you go to a town where there's a Lush and you see people going, hmm yes, that smells nice... that's an attractive smell and people enjoy that' (D41). However, the strength of the odours emitted by the store provoked equally negative reactions in a similar number of people:

> I hate it, I find that a really offensive smell, awful, it should be banned .... It's so overpowering, it's not smells that I like, they don't hit with my taste at all, and it's just so in your face it's just 'ugghh' awful! (D14)

...it's well too overpowering, a lot of people I know, when they walk past it, they can't stop sneezing ... I think it's the strength of it, I think if it was a lot weaker, it wouldn't be too bad but it's just so strong. (D19)

The intensity of the smells of perfumes and perfumed products was highlighted as a main reason for disliking specific types or brands. As with people's descriptions of their experiences of the Lush stores, the intensity of smells sometimes provoked reactions such as disgust. Many people described physical, bodily reactions to perfumes, explaining these as allergic reactions or related to health conditions such as asthma and hayfever. Symptoms included headaches, catarrh, wheezing, sneezing and tickling noses, with many of those suffering these reactions describing such odour detection as annoying. In such cases, avoidance behaviours similar to those used in avoiding sites with perceived high levels of traffic pollution were adopted. These included exposure limitation – 'I do go in occasionally to buy gifts for people and it's sort of get in and get out because it's so strong' (D36) – and even the avoidance of whole areas – 'I had a girlfriend who hated it and if she smelt it on the street we had to walk around the block to miss it' (D31).

Those who enjoyed specific perfume and synthetic odours provided similar reasons to those who disliked them, mentioning odour qualities, associations and odour strength, although they did not mention health-related effects. Positive associations with and descriptions of odour qualities included reference to these as 'clean', 'fresh', 'girly' or 'sweet', and they were often related to sexual attraction. Participants often inferred such odours had a positive impact upon area image: 'I think it brings a quality to the area' (D38). They also highlighted the 'designed' as opposed to 'artificial' nature of perfumes and scents: 'I suppose it's designed to be liked so I've no problem with smelling ladies' perfumes' (D26). The strong and distinctive odours of some stores were identified as providing smellmarks in the town, assisting with legibility and attracting people to store in some cases. These smells were simultaneously considered 'artificial' by others and resented in some contexts:

I hate air freshener type smells, the sort of canned air, and air conditioned air I guess would come into that ... I feel that something is being imposed on me that I don't have a choice about. I feel the same way about piped-in music ... But with smells I feel that that would be an extra imposition, someone deciding for me what I should be smelling. (M26)

Several people echoed these sentiments explaining they were both aware of, and in principal opposed to, what several of them termed specifically as 'sensory manipulation'. Manipulation is referred to here, and throughout later chapters, as the idea that odour has the ability to influence emotional state and behaviour at a sub-conscious level, without implicit agreement or knowledge of the individual. However, some participants opposed to such 'sensory manipulation' went on to accept and enjoy commercial scenting when it met their expectations:

> I don't like things being contrived; I will react against them in that respect, but ... I can really see it working in high end clothes shops where they really pump in that kind of high quality cologne smell ... I go in [named shop] and it just smells lovely and I can imagine probably some high end nightclubs in some of the big cities, that kind of attractive smell. (D31)

In this case the perfumes are perceived as being in context with the new designer clothes, associated with the imagery of wealth and success in a similar way to the 'new clothes' smell. This experience also highlights processes of separation, since the cologne has no chemical or naturally-occurring association with the products or physical environment within which it is detected. Rather, it is an odour extracted from elsewhere and thus, in literal terms, it is out of place. Yet the odour was introduced with the aim of enhancing experience and ultimately increasing sales (see Kotler 1973). Its use is based on the premise that despite having no natural relationship with the physical products or environment of the store, the odour fits expectations and will be accepted by the store's clientele. The odour association is socially constructed, and is similar to the positive perceptions of the synthetic odours of lemon from scented cleaning fluids; these associations are significant of social relationships, complexity, and indicative of efforts to exert control and order over the environment.

Commercial scenting practices in cities have taken a new turn over the past decade, moving out from the semi-contained internal environments of stores into the street itself. In 2006, scented oils similar to the odours of cookies were introduced into bus stops in San Francisco, US as part of a poster marketing campaign for milk. Within less than twenty-four hours the scents were removed in response to complaints that they induced allergic reactions and were offensive to homeless people who couldn't afford such treats (Gordon 2006). Such scenting campaigns in bus stops have also been introduced into the UK, where my own research as part of a team at the University of Manchester has found these to be experienced very differently by people. One advertising campaign implemented in five UK cities in early 2012 used the smell of baked potatoes, and was predominantly positively perceived by people that used the bus stops. The release of these scents into the bus stop represented a certain novelty value for people, as did the heated, bulbous, potato-shaped protrusion accompanying the scent (see Figure 8.4). The period of time that the bus passengers were exposed to the scent was limited, which was important and perhaps provides a partial explanation of why bus stops were chosen as a site for the smell campaigns, since the smells were experienced very differently after prolonged exposure. I interviewed a local businessman with a market stall sited directly adjacent to one of the bus stops in question, and he reported suffering from headaches, colds and congestion ever since the odours had started to be released, to the point where he had visited his doctor and written a letter of complaint to the council.

These scents also have the potential to mask other odours in the environment, whether they are related to product or place. Although corporate smells provide an opportunity for retailers to reinforce brand through standardising in-store smellscapes or in drawing attention to their advertising campaigns, they might also be argued to present a threat to existing place identity by overlaying more locally occurring and environment-specific odours. Yet, as Massey (1991) argues, rather than being based only on past identity, place identities are continually changing, simultaneously combining local characteristics alongside global factors. From this perspective, such commercial scents might potentially contribute to place smellscapes in the same way that other odours of place would, through regular everyday encounters with these odours in specific areas of the city. What is important to recognise is that the introduction of scents does present the risk of repelling or excluding those that do not like, are sensitive to or have a physical reaction to the odour, as I will explore later.

Figure 8.4 Commercial scenting in bus stops, London, February 2012

8.4.3 Perceptions of synthetic and commercial scenting practices in food

In the case of perfume and odours emitted from non-food sources, participants believed they were intuitively able to differentiate between 'naturally-occurring' and 'synthetic' odours by the nature of the source. 'Synthetic' is defined in the Oxford English Dictionary (2012a) as 'a substance made by chemical synthesis, especially to imitate a natural product' (http://oxforddictionaries.com/definition/english/synthetic). Perfumes, for example, were generally described as synthetic, whereas leather was considered to have its own natural odour. However, the distinction between naturally-occurring odours and those of synthetic origin is not as straightforward as it might seem; the odour of leather, for example, comes about as a result of tanning, which is itself a chemically-dependent process. Also, synthetic odours of leather are frequently used in product manufacturing processes in order to provide an illusion of leather and an association with quality and newness, as is the case when these odours are sprayed into some new cars (Lindstrom 2005a, 2005b). Furthermore, some odours of perfume, including those emitted from the Lush stores, are produced by combinations or extractions of naturally occurring products. The line between natural and unnatural, genuine and synthetic is therefore highly blurred with respect to the perception of smell, with distinctions varying between people.

This differentiation is particularly difficult when examining perceptions of food odours since few clues are provided by the nature of the source. As a result it was very difficult to determine whether participants detected any synthetically-produced food odours or not while undertaking the smellwalks. Instead, I focused upon participants' views of commercial scenting practices in food, with the intention of drawing from these to expand on observations surrounding experiential marketing and smell design practices.

The consideration of smell in food retail environmental design and store layout is not in itself new, given the strict ventilation regulations requiring the food industry to consider odour control as an essential component of their built infrastructure and operations. Many people are aware that smell is utilised by some businesses, with the best-known example being the use of bread odours in supermarkets. In this scenario, some people believe that bread odours are rerouted via ventilation systems from in-store baking areas to store entrances to attract people into the store. In these cases, the odours are considered genuine, with the place of detection, rather than the odour itself, being the designed factor. In other cases, the bread odours in supermarkets are considered synthetic and as having nothing to do with an actual baking process: they are perceived as odours released solely as a means of increasing custom and encouraging sales. In both scenarios, study participants judged these actions negatively, describing them as dishonest, trickery and manipulation:

…with supermarkets I know that they've kind of re-routed their extractor to the door which is almost as good as it having an artificial smell in terms of it kind of being contrived. (D05)

I think the fakery trickery of some shops when they have the bread counter nearest to the entrance to entice you in with the smell of baked bread. Although I love the smell, but again I don't like to be manipulated, I find that a bit annoying. (D42)

One explanation that was offered for the idea of trickery and manipulation in the scenting practices among food businesses was that food items are themselves expected to have particular odours. In introducing other food odours, businesses are thereby judged to infer increased quality, or hide poor quality, with the aim of boosting returns: 'I would think, are they trying to trick me? Does the food actually smell that good? Why are they relying on fake smells to entice you in? Why won't they let the food do the talking?' (D04). Despite these negative judgements about the ethics of the practice, many continued to respond to the odours in the intended manner: 'I don't like the idea, but I fall for it in exactly the same way that everyone else does' (D39). Some participants explained these continued positive responses as a product of the odour qualities: 'There are some smells that you do want to smell and it does enhance the experience. It's like walking in [supermarket] and smelling the fresh bread … I don't know anybody who wouldn't like that' (D47). Similar arguments were also presented by a pub licensee:

…that fresh coffee smell is absolutely beautiful and you just think, oh, I'll have cappuccino, so if you had sort of air freshener and somebody walked past your pub and that fresh coffee smell outside a sort of food pub, 'oh yeah, I think I need to go in for a coffee', it's a win–win. (D35)

Other people commented on the appropriateness of the odour according to context:

…that's a strategy of creating the right ambience for buying which is a cynical marketing device, but then again at least you're smelling food which is what I think you should be smelling when you go into a food retail environment … actually it works quite well 'cos I think what's wrong for me about some retail environments is that they've tried to sanitise food and I don't think you should, I think it should be a complete experience. (D05)

Perceptions of commercial scenting practices as manipulative and dishonest were therefore related to a concern that such strategies were intended to change behaviours and product judgements, rather than being related to the detection of commercial odours themselves. But what is the difference between this and the release of cooking odours into the street?

Half-way through conducting the fieldwork in Doncaster a new open-fronted cooked meat store opened in the main retail area, releasing odours of cooked meats directly out onto the street. One participant observed: '…often that draws people, you know that is a very good business tactic' (D42). Similarly, another described food product odours in the markets area: 'I think that they're attractive, appealing really, they tempt people to buy things' (D32). Such practices were perceived to release 'honest' odours, judged very differently than supermarket bread odours which were considered 'dishonest'.

The point at which olfactory design is judged to switch from being a sound ethical activity, beneficial to society and city life, to being a dishonest and manipulative strategy is complex, varying according to individual beliefs and experiences. Some relate this to the question of whether the food odour is genuine or synthetic: 'Is it being done deliberately to draw us in to those particular shops, and does it matter? I don't think it does matter if it's genuine food smells as opposed to artificially created smells' (D28). Others consider the motivation to be key:

> I think when it's to sell you something, that's the difference, when there's an ulterior motive other than to make you maybe feel happy or maybe improve an environment. I think that's fine because there's no inherent benefit other than you might want to come back and enjoy the space again. (D43)

Commercial scenting practices thus present dilemmas regarding whether these are acceptable and beneficial to society, or manipulative and dishonest. There are no clear-cut answers because perceptions involve a complex interplay of factors such as the genuine or synthetic nature of the odour, the environmental context within which the odour is released and the motivation for release. Other contextual issues are also likely to contribute towards these views, such as positive associations with small independent stores as compared with perceptions of large multinational corporations (Leith 2008). Many of the dilemmas presented in perceptions of scenting practices are equally applicable to wider odour management practices and urban smellscape design. Given that many odours in urban environments are experienced differently by different people, it is important to think about wider ethical complexities when dealing with odour in the environment.

8.5 Scenting the skies?

In the UK's Urban Design Compendium (Davies 2000), a publication that guides local authorities and professionals in designing high quality urban realms, the urban smellscape makes a brief appearance. The Compendium poses the following question: 'What scents can be added?' Its response is that:

> The experience of a place can be heightened by its aromas – whether the scent of flowers, coffee or fresh bread. Even if unpleasant to some, others may consider certain smells to provide the essence of a place – such as the smell of yeast reflecting the presence of a brewery. Birmingham's Brindley Place, for instance, combines the sound of water from fountains and an aromatic coffee shop, which draws people into its centre and creates a lively source of activity. (*ibid.*: 100)

Although this is a brief mention, and is a simplistic response to the question posed, this statement provides evidence that contemporary treatments of odours are perhaps not quite as straightforward as Henri Lefebvre's (2009) argument concerning the complete 'atrophy' of smell might suggest. Indeed, the very way the question is worded speaks volumes regarding some of the issues faced when we think about designing urban smell environments.

When I have interviewed and led architects, urban designers and other built environment professionals on smellwalks, I usually ask them about how they might go about designing and managing smell in the city. In the majority of cases, these individuals express limited knowledge of smell as a design feature: 'In an outdoor space, you couldn't successfully create it, or if there was a smell problem, unless you were able to remove the cause, you wouldn't be able to control it, would you?' (D39). As with the assumption in the Urban Design Compendium, many built environment professionals think of the city as a blank template where a designer can only add odour, rather than thinking of smell as an inherent characteristic of the city that can be influenced through design and management practices. What I find particularly fascinating about this is that although these professionals were unable to identify ways of working with smell in designing and managing areas, they could describe influential factors in urban smellscape experiences whilst undertaking the smellwalks. As sensing bodies themselves, many professionals were able to access knowledge and insights that their training and related decision-making processes did not allow.

In this chapter we have identified city leaders, built environment professionals and commercial businesses as actors who exert an influence on the variety, place and context within which odours can be experienced on an everyday basis. Some odours come about as a consequence of policies unrelated to, but directly impacting on, urban smellscapes. However, processes of environmental odour management and control are being unequally applied in some places and if we examine these in further detail, it is apparent that different types of odours are significant of wide inequalities in society, either by their presence or their absence. An article included in the Washington Times in 2008 criticised the city's elected mayor for describing a range of developments as 'world class', and yet failing to define what he meant by this: 'While the weekend sights, sounds and smells in some neighborhoods showcase the city's ethnic diversity and vibrant retail sector, the sights, sounds and smells in others highlight the short-sightedness posited in City Hall'.

Massey (1991), Atkinson (2003), Herbert (2008) and Minton (2009) highlight cities as becoming increasingly privatised, with different socio-economic groups becoming segregated from one another. Gated communities, business improvement districts and private developments such as Priory Walk in Doncaster are now commonplace, with contracted security patrolling the streets and removing those who are deemed not to belong. As a result, people and communities are perceived as becoming less tolerant of one another. This segregation of people and activities can be sensed as described in the Washington Times article, with the smellscapes of those areas occupied by low socio-economic and ethnic groups being associated with a lack of cleanliness, dirt and poor hygiene, and odours of vomit, urine, smoke and pollutants. The association of specific odours with particular types of places, be they the perfumed odours of the designer clothes store or the smell of greasy food and smoke in run down areas, illustrate that odour is one means by which people come to recognise whether they themselves are in or out of place. Concerns that the synthetic odours of cookies in the scented bus-stop advertising campaign in San Francisco would impact unfairly upon homeless people is a marked and perhaps surprising example of a perceived incongruence between an odour and the people for whom it is intended.

More prosperous commercial areas are zealously controlled in olfactory terms. Such areas have potentially antisocial odour sources separated from them, perhaps through zoning practices or by odour redirection through extraction systems, with the redirected odours being released in areas where they are less likely to be detected. When unsanctioned odour-emitting businesses find their way around the control systems and operate in these areas, the resulting smells become highly unacceptable to those who have responsibility for the street or area, as was the case with an on-street hamburger vendor trading in Doncaster's main retail core. Commercial areas frequently undergo enhanced cleansing and maintenance regimes as public and private resources focus on keeping key public areas clean, with cleanliness occasionally being prioritised above the wider aesthetics of an area.

Masking, on the other hand, occurs in a range of place types, both as an unintended by-product of other actions as well as the result of planned odour-related strategies. Masking occurs as a consequence of the presence of negatively perceived odours such as traffic pollutants, cigarette smoke and bleach combined with urine, since these odours are associated with run down, evening focused and generally 'public' areas. More positively perceived masking odours may include those of scented cleaning fluids, which can overlay highly disliked odours such as those associated with public toilets.

Commercial and synthetic scenting practices are generally associated with core trading areas, with some cities and shopping quarters releasing synthetic odours as part of commercial events. In everyday practice, commercial and synthetic scents are released and detected in commercial districts, usually as a result of the products on sale. However, it can be difficult or impossible to tell the difference between natural and synthetic odours, with considerable variations in people's views of what constitutes a natural or an unnatural odour. In contrast, odours detected in areas such as Doncaster's Copley Road, Manchester's Chinatown or London's Soho area were frequently perceived as providing insights into 'authentic' neighbourhoods and activities, viewed as a window into another world through odour associations. Some people drew from the 'foreign' odours of international foods to explain or express negative perceptions of Doncaster's Copley Road area. These people frequently highlighted a lack of cleanliness in the street, suggesting that this signified a perceived lack of civility and identified the street as an unsafe place to be. Minton (2009) highlights a danger in attempting to create sanitised controlled environments since people quickly adapt their expectations, becoming fearful and over-sensitised to anything alien. By examining experiences of urban smellscapes, it is possible to observe this occurring in urban smellscape experience. The deodorisation of urban environments and the scenting of areas with idealised odours that have no natural association with the place can be understood as part and parcel of the same process that leads people to associate certain food odours with 'the other' in Doncaster's Copley Road. Some of these practices have the potential to reduce place experience and variety: 'I think the more we de-sanitise our lives, smell is part of that de-sanitary thing, it's to the detriment really to the quality of our experience of cities and places' (D05).

Such over-sensitisation through habituation to the point of environmental sterility has been used to explain the rise of environmental sensitivities, particularly in parts of the United States and Canada (see Chapter 3 for a description of odour sensitivity and its causes). Freud (1961) observed: 'Protection against stimuli is an almost more important function for the living organism than reception of stimuli'. Sennett (1994) interpreted this as to mean the following: '…if the body is not open to periodic crisis, eventually the organism sickens for lack of stimulation' (*ibid.*: 372). The phenomenon of environmental sensitivity can be understood from this perspective as the result of over-controlled environments that fail to accommodate sensory stimulation beyond the immediate discomfort of physical existence, with the promotion of bodily comfort a priority as people move through towns and cities. Ironically, although environmental sensitivities might be seen to be influenced by the modernist reductionist approach to urban environmental design and the neo-liberalisation of public space, Fletcher (2005) explains the idealised environment demanded by sufferers as '...a city that is invisible to the nose, a space with no chemical content, a place of olfactory purity'. From this perspective the illness may be considered a vicious circle, which unless broken might lead to the further olfactory reduction of the environmental sensory experience:

> ...the pendulum has swung too far ... I read an article where there's been a huge increase amongst children in allergic conditions, which they attribute to children being too clean these days, they never play with mud or snails in the garden ... the moment they've got a bit of dirt on them we wipe them clean and deodorise them and desensitise them and then when they get into anywhere that's normal they are immediately allergic to things ... we've tried to deodorise our society, we're deodorising people and we've deodorised town centres as well. (D41)

However, environmental sensitivities can also be characterised within the context of research on indoor air quality (e.g. Fanger 1988, Fanger *et al.* 1988, Redlich *et al.* 1997, Wargocki *et al.* 1999). Such studies have found pollutants emitted into the air from a wide variety of sources including office ventilation systems and a variety of furnishings and materials, can combine to create a cocktail that affects the body in different ways. Symptoms include fatigue, allergic-type reactions and respiratory illnesses similar to those described in response to detection of some odours in the ambient urban smellscape. Although many contemporary processes of odour control and management attempt to separate activities and wash selected environments clean, this is not necessarily the healthiest approach in terms of its impact on mental and physical health or societal cohesion. Scenting practices present particular issues since they risk inducing bodily responses such as those found in studies of indoor air quality, are judged to be manipulative by many, and have the ability to repel as well as attract, potentially excluding people through odour associations as well as providing olfactory clues to people that they do not belong in certain places.

8.6 Conclusion

A range of inter-related processes are currently under way in the control and management of urban smellscapes, with some of these being highly organised and sophisticated. Others are an unplanned consequence of different activities such as the masking effect of traffic fumes or the displacement of cigarette odours following the introduction of anti-smoking legislation. In either case, these processes are impacting on everyday experiences and perceptions of odour in the environment in complex ways, and they relate to wider debates about the design of sustainable cities of the future.

Given the various and complex dilemmas raised in an examination of experiences of urban smellscapes, namely issues of social cohesion, environmental sensitivities and perceptions of behaviour manipulation, a clear question emerges regarding whether there are additional approaches and means by which odour might be considered in designing more sustainable towns and cities. Also, given the ability of odours to leak, mix and overlay others, what tools might built environment professionals have at their disposal to assist in shaping olfactory environments, and how might such activities be incorporated into urban management strategies to support the delivery of healthy and inclusive communities? These questions will be explored in further detail in the next chapter on urban smellscape design, including a consideration of restorative aspects of urban environmental experience, the contribution these can make to overall environmental quality with respect to smell, and the way these might improve the quality of life in cities.

9
Designing with smell

Restorative environments and design tools

If you're building to high densities and everything's got to be closer together, you need to think about the whole experience and I think smell would come under that. (D07)

Across the world the number of people living in towns and cities is increasing, with rising urban density levels featuring as a key aspect of strategies aimed at minimising our use of natural resources and delivering more sustainable cities in the future. Closer proximity between people and activities will inevitably impact on lived experiences of the city, with the frequency of odour-related issues and complaints likely to increase and city authorities having to intensify efforts to control urban smellscapes as a consequence. However, there are other approaches to the urban smellscape that built environment professionals might pursue.

In previous chapters we have explored experiences and perceptions of odours according to their sources, and in doing so it has become clear that smell plays an important role in how people make sense of the world around them. For years, environmental odour has been considered by built environment professionals in predominantly negative terms, but if a more proactive approach to odour could be incorporated into existing practice, this would provide opportunities to create more fulfilling, humanistic and ultimately more sustainable urban environments. Here we hit something of a problem, however: designing with smell is not an activity with which we are well versed when undertaking urban design and architectural practice, a fact which became apparent when I asked professionals for their views regarding how they might go about this. Therefore, in this chapter I seek to develop some possible approaches and broaden understanding of the relationship between odour, the environment and design processes. I will do so initially by thinking about the role of the air and the wind in urban smellscape experiences, before examining restorative experiences of smell in the city and potential positive roles for odour. I will go on to draw from the findings of the empirical studies described in earlier chapters to identify environmental design characteristics that influence urban smellscape experience. In doing so, I hope to inform urban design and management practices in a very real and practical sense.

9.1 Air and wind flow

The transmission of odour through the air from source is dependent on the movement of odorous chemicals carried on the wind, and the quality of the air can have a significant impact on urban smellscape experience. Air and wind inevitably play a crucial role in people's odour perceptions, impacting in different ways on olfactory experience and forming a key component of urban smellscape design. Like odour, the air and the wind themselves cannot be seen directly, although unlike odour they have visible effects such as the movement of trees and the circling of leaves in the air. Rather than being seen, air and the wind are sensed through their haptic and thermal qualities on the skin, in the nose, mouth and lungs, heard as the wind moves around and rebounds off the landscape and built environmental form, and detected through the sense of smell. But does the air itself have an odour? If so, how does this relate to urban smellscape design?

Air is a term used to describe the invisible gases forming the earth's atmosphere. It is composed predominantly of nitrogen and oxygen with small percentages of other gases (including those considered to be pollutants) and a variable amount of water vapour. The presence of water vapour is important in smell perception because it influences nasal mucus, which is required to dissolve odours and transfer information about smells to the olfactory receptors. Also a wet atmosphere can lead to smells hanging in the air, as Kate McLean found in her mapping study of the smells of Glasgow, Scotland (STV 2012). Although nitrogen and oxygen are odourless gases, the small percentages of other gases included in the air are not necessarily so. Given that we can detect odours in very small concentrations, the smell of the air itself is highly influenced by the environment in which it is breathed, with a variety of component parts potentially carrying smells. Many participants across the different English cities talked of the smell of 'fresh' air as a favoured odour in and around the city, but when pressed to describe this smell they frequently did so as a product of synaesthetic associations with other characteristics of the air, including its temperature and force of the wind hitting the body. Like the 'smell of new', fresh air is as notable for the absence of some odours as it is for possessing an odour of its own: 'I think as long as it smells clean and there's not loads of traffic fumes, just fresh air and freshness really' (D36). The term 'fresh' is thus frequently used interchangeably with 'clean'.

Fresh air was also associated with odours of vegetation in the city:

> ...something completely in the open in the sense that you know it was purely fresh air ... in a town centre sort of environment I suppose it would be in a park where you've got smells of flowers and things like that, that sort of smell, greenery I suppose. (D44)

Greenspace, trees, planting and water were all thought to improve the quality or 'freshness' of the air, and were widely liked. However, although it is desirable, 'fresh' air was not detected very often in cities. In Manchester, Sheffield and Clerkenwell, London, the air was frequently perceived to be dominated by traffic pollutants. In Doncaster, a different odour backdrop was identified by some participants: 'I suppose this sort of foody smell pervades Doncaster really, a sort of relatively poor food type smells … you can seem to detect it most of the time' (D10). Other studies have identified the Scottish cities of Edinburgh and Glasgow as each having their own distinct olfactory backdrops, of brewing and the smell of damp electric transport respectively (McLean 2013).

This idea of the olfactory backdrop of the city has an important role when we think about the structure and composition of urban smellscapes. In a quest to develop a fuller sensory approach to design, Malnar and Vodvarka (2004) developed a vocabulary reflecting common aspects of sensory response as they relate to time and space. Based on distinctions outlined in Piaget's (1969) investigation into perception, Malnar and Vodvarka (2004: 244–245) considered olfactory stimuli to range between two extremes of 'involuntary' and 'episodic' odours. Episodic odours are described as those that are '…immediately experienced and … recurring through memory', whereas involuntary odours they describe as more general, forming a context or background. When a perfumer creates a new scent they do so by using different top, middle and base note ingredients. In a similar way to Malnar and Vodvarka's distinctions between odours in the environment, these notes are defined by their temporal qualities, or tenacity as it is termed in the perfume industry. Top or high note ingredients are those that are sensed immediately when first smelling a perfume; they exist immediately in the forefront of perception and include smells such as those of citrus fruits and aromatic herbs. Although these top notes are intense because they are formed from volatile smell molecules, they also evaporate quickly as a result. In contrast, base note odours such as those of wood, moss, amber and vanilla are formed from less volatile ingredients, so although they are less intense in the first sniffing of a perfume, they add a depth to the scent and have more staying power, remaining on the skin for hours after the initial application. Middle or heart notes, including odours from ingredients such as flowers, spices and berries, sit somewhere in between the two and add character to the perfume.

The urban smellscape can similarly be thought of as a composition of different odour notes formed from smells emitted by the natural environment, the manmade environment, and people and activities. If we were to step off a plane in a strange country we would be likely to smell the background smell of an area or a city (see Figure 9.1). Unless it was dominated by a specific localised smell such as that of airplane fuel or the after-shave of a fellow passenger, this background odour provides the macro-level base note for the urban smellscape, or the 'involuntary' smells in Malnar and Vodvarka's (2004) terms. As we move through the city we might detect a dominant smell in specific neighbourhoods or areas, such as the smell of a specific factory, or the combined smell of fish and seafood in Doncaster's market area. These mid-level notes blend with the background odour to create an area-based smell. At the micro-level we can detect the high notes of the smellscape, potentially intense, changeable and short-lived odours which are emitted in localised points in space and time. We move through them in the street:

> I could smell … leather goods from the shops … soggy cardboard smell, then the public toilets … as we approached the market I could smell the chip-shop … perfume from the household sprays and store, that was quite strong … candy-floss smell – like a fairground smell of hotdogs and candyfloss and stuff like that. (D04)

The smellscapes of some areas can be fairly uniform, dominated by experiences of the background odours of a city smellscape, whereas some, such as Doncaster's markets area or an alleyway in Manchester Chinatown, are changeable step-by-step. In this respect we can start to think about the different spatial levels at which place-related odours can be considered; this is a point to which I will return later in this chapter.

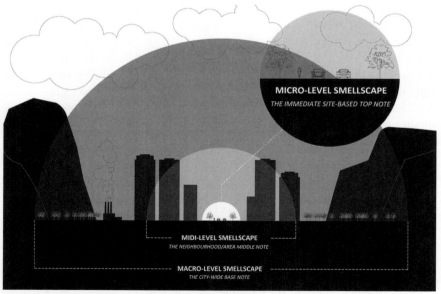

Figure 9.1 The smellscape as a composition of different notes (image drawn by Nabil Awad)

The presence or lack of wind flow can influence urban smellscapes at a variety of spatial levels. Wind is described in the Oxford English Dictionary (2012b) as 'the perceptible natural movement of the air, especially in the form of a current of air blowing from a particular direction', and it is perceived to play contrasting roles in the urban smellscape. In some contexts, people think of wind as a freshener of the air, important in clearing or diluting more negatively-perceived odours such as traffic emissions on a busy stretch of road. The wind is also perceived as a carrier of odour. In some cases this can be of favoured odours, including those associated with freshness:

> ...if you've got trees and flowers etc. coming in, if you've got the greenspaces ... they're adding their scent to the air and it may not be that you get a general feeling but every now and again you get a whiff of them, don't you, if the air current passes you. (D28)

In other cases, however, the opposite is true:

> ...you can never smell freshness, you never smell greenery ... going back to London, the wind would blow in the window, you could smell the park or you could just smell trees. You don't get any of that here, and when the wind blows it's just smog, it's just more fumes, it's like being in the underground all the time. (M18)

The wind is therefore perceived to dilute negative odour intensity with fresh air and odours of vegetation at a micro-level, but in environments where the smellscape is dominated over a wide area by a specific odour or mix of odours, the wind might only 'stir up' environmental odours at a localised or area-based level. I will return later to consider the movement of air and wind in identifying tools for designing urban smellscapes. Before doing so, however, another important issue is raised when we consider fresh air in the city. This relates to the idea of 'restorative' environments: environments that provide people with the opportunity to recharge from the daily stresses and strains of city life.

9.2 Restorative odours

> ...the wind rustling in the trees, the water running out of a pond, the smell of the damp soil, the heat of the sun warming the skin, face, hands and arms, all this is an encouragement to natural relaxation and brings a feeling of physical and mental well-being. (Ousset *et al.* 1998: 372)

Urban environments are generally portrayed as hard, harsh landscapes, areas where streets and spaces are designed primarily for movement, rather than to facilitate any meaningful connection between body, mind and place (Sennett 1994). The idea of restorative environmental experience has emerged in response to a human need for relief from the intensity of modern urban life. Restorative experiences are generally associated with natural areas such as countryside, wilderness and parks, although they have also been considered by Ulrich (1984) and later by Kaplan and Kaplan (1989) in relation to the provision of urban greenspace. Restorative experiences have been examined by environmental psychologists with respect to stress reduction (Ulrich 1983, Ulrich *et al.* 1991) and attention restoration (Kaplan and Kaplan 1989), with the latter including components of recovery and reflection (Morris 2003). Although identifying stress reduction and attention restoration as two distinct aspects of restorative experiences, Kaplan (1995) highlights a relationship between these factors, concluding that this relationship:

> ...points to the significant role that directed attention, a key psychological resource, plays in coping with challenges. In this perspective the role that natural environments play is a powerful one. Experience in natural environments can not only help mitigate stress; it can also prevent it through aiding in the recovery of this essential resource. (*ibid.*: 180)

Kaplan and Kaplan (1989) and Kaplan (1995) progress their theories further, examining the effects that natural environments have upon physical and mental state, and the circumstances in which they do so. They identify four key factors in restorative experiences: *being away* – the feeling that you are away from your usual environment, whether on holiday, in the countryside, or in an urban park; *fascination* – the ability of the environment to hold directed attention; *extent* – the size of the environment and therefore the degree of submersion one can feel within that environment; and *compatibility* – the ability of the environment to match human needs and expectations. Ulrich (1983, 1984) and Ulrich *et al.* (1991) were specifically interested in the restorative benefits to be gained from looking at natural environments, directly or in photographs. Their studies found that these experiences reduced stress and improved well-being, potentially also improving health (Ulrich 1984). Similarly, Moore (1981) found that prison inmates were less likely to require the use of prison health care facilities if they had a view of a natural environment from their cell (Morris 2003). Although some restorative environmental studies have examined whole body experiences of being 'in' nature (e.g. Hartig *et al.* 1991, Chiesura 2004), more often these studies have pursued a tradition of examining restorative experiences through the sense of sight alone (e.g. Moore 1981, Ulrich 1983, 1984, Ulrich *et al.* 1991, Chang *et al.* 2008).

Payne (2008) contributes towards addressing this ocular-centric approach to restorative studies in her examination of the restorative qualities of soundscapes in urban parks in Sheffield. Her survey of four hundred park users explored perceived soundscapes including the sounds heard, their volume and the length of time they were heard for, alongside the participants' perceived restoration. Sound levels within the parks were also monitored to provide contextual information. Payne concluded that soundscape perception has a significant role in restorative experiences of urban parks, and highlights the important role of the individual as an active perceiver of the environment through their relationship with place.

The number of studies examining any potential restorative effects offered by urban smellscapes remains limited, although odour has been examined briefly as part of wider studies investigating overall experiences of natural environments. When considering the key role that smell plays in aromatherapy treatments and relaxation sessions at the spa, its omission from the majority of restorative environmental research illustrates how markedly neglectful our cultural attitude is regarding odour, the roles it can play and the places where it belongs.

The idea of restoration emerged as an important theme in people's experiences in all of the towns and cities included in my empirical studies. Prior to undertaking the Doncaster smellwalks, I asked participants to comment on their general expectations of odour in urban areas. The majority mentioned stereotypical urban odours such as air pollution, waste and food. Few expected to detect odours of planting or greenspace in the town centre. Yet in contrast, when they were asked about their favourite odours many participants highlighted fresh natural smells from woodland, countryside, fresh air, cut grass, trees, flowers or the rain. Despite expectations that experiences of these smells would be limited in Doncaster town centre, they were named across all the studied towns and cities as odours that people wanted to experience more, which they believed would enhance the quality of urban life. However, just as people accepted the presence of air pollution as a trade-off against the more positive benefits of living in the city, they also considered that limited access to greenery was almost inevitable, as this planner explained:

> ...it's a problem for all big cities and all town centres that have got developmental pressures ... councils have to be strong and say 'greenspaces are really important, let's commit to them rather than just let them be built on' ... In Manchester, there's a hell of a lot of urban development gone on and as a result, the pressure on greenspace has increased to such an extent that there isn't that much to go around. Leeds is the same. (D26)

Notably, participants in Sheffield, Manchester and Clerkenwell, London had higher expectations of detecting vegetation odours in the city than participants in Doncaster, although they also believed that these opportunities would be limited.

A range of potential sources of restorative odours in the urban environment featured in comments across the different English cities. These can be grouped into four categories, the first being wind and air flow as highlighted above. The remaining three restorative odour categories are: trees, planting and greenspace; water and waterways; and restorative odours from non-natural sources.

9.2.1 Trees, planting and greenspace

A recurring theme in restorative environmental experiences is the idea that greenspace and planting provide lungs for the city, a concept which is often mentioned with reference to air pollution: 'Smells like fresh air I like best. I mean garden, country, a feeling of, you know, sort of being able to expand the lungs without any, I don't know what it is, fumes perhaps' (S13). Greenspaces and planting were widely perceived to play an important role in air quality:

> ...anything which will absorb pollutants, not necessarily exhausts but in the area where people are, such as trees ... I look at it as carbon absorbed from CO_2. (D50)

> ...it's quite important because ... you know, basically the chemistry as well, it creates more oxygen in the city. (M23)

Some participants observed a lack of vegetation in environments such as Doncaster's traffic-dominated Silver Street, and suggested that the introduction of trees and planting would assist in cleansing the air and improving overall environmental quality. However, as Stewart *et al.* (2002) identify in their work, although trees are effective in absorbing some airborne pollutants, with woodland removing three times more airborne pollutants from the air than grasslands, trees can also release volatile organic compounds (VOCs). It is these that people smell in forests. However, when combined with oxides of nitrogen, VOCs can contribute towards the production of other pollutants that have the potential to damage human health. However, trees and vegetation do have a cooling effect on summer air temperatures in urban environments, as highlighted by Dimoudi and Nikolopoulou (2003) who conclude that greenery can assist in the mitigation of urban heat islands. Furthermore, in a recently published study Pugh *et al.* (2012) examined relationships between urban form and vegetation and found that previous studies had under-estimated the potential impact of planting on air quality in the city. Pugh *et al.* concluded that the contribution of vegetation towards air quality varies according to the movement of air in certain parts of the city, achieving as much as a forty per cent reduction in levels of NO$_2$ and a sixty per cent reduction in PM10s in areas with low air movement.

Trees and planting were believed by participants to serve a purification function both at a site-specific level and with respect to the wider air quality of the city as a whole, irrespective of whether related odours were detected or not. Air quality benefits from tree canopy cover and cooling of the area were also described:

> …they act as filters, physical filters and so if you've got trees, and they offer shade and basically cool the area and pollutants … the cooler they are, the less likely they are to be as vigorous … it's a bit of shade and to sort of absorb pollution. (D50)

Greenspaces were valued for their restorative qualities, providing a contrast to wider urban environments:

> I suppose when you think of a city, you think of the buildings, you think of the roads and the streets … I don't always think of the parks, I think of that almost as a breather from the city, rather than the city itself, it's like a welcome relief. (D26)

As a result, the inhalation of odours of vegetation was perceived to have a cleansing effect on the body and a positive impact on health: 'I mean, there's been a few times when I could smell the fields, it's a good smell to have because you breathe it in and you get bright cheeks type of thing' (D48). These odours were sometimes associated with positive memories, emotional attachments, well-being and feelings of being elsewhere: 'I guess flowers again are what you associate with happiness and contentment and I love my garden… When you've been outside and you can smell all the fresh air around you' (D47). The introduction of more greenery into urban areas was therefore seen as a direct means of improving smell environments: 'We need more green to smell good' (D49).

Odours emitted from plants, trees and other vegetation were generally associated with two types of urban experience. The first was the presence of small-scale planting features, interspaced throughout urban areas and including items such as hanging baskets, individual or lines of trees, and also plants growing wild. The second was urban greenspaces, parks and grassed areas, with these perceived to offer a full-bodied immersive restorative experience. Experiences of the first type of planting tended to be short-lived, sometimes occurring in unlikely places:

> …you know some areas there'll be flowers, like just like across the other side [of the road] there's just sort of a tiny stretch of grassy metres and like bushes

and roses sticking out of the dual carriageway and it just smells lovely, just walking past there, for all of two seconds it's lovely. (S23)

Reynolds (2008: 192) considers such experiences to be especially poignant because of their contrast with less positively perceived stereotypical city odours:

> The lure is stronger when that powerful floral burst ... hits you moments after a gust of the more familiar urban street cocktail of diesel fumes, tobacco smoke and dog shit. The smell of a garden can draw you in before you have even seen the flowers.

Rather than providing immersive restorative effects on the body, these brief olfactory encounters provoke fascination and are associated with positive recollections of environments where more immersive restorative experiences might be gained.

Despite these positive perceptions of vegetation in urban environments, some small-scale planted areas had been removed from Doncaster as they had been filled with litter and smoking-related waste. Similarly, highly-scented plants and flowers were occasionally sited in places where people could see but not smell them:

> ...when Doncaster used to put wallflowers in, they put them down the middle of the dual-carriageway so that the pedestrians never got the benefit, and I think they put them there because they were safe from kids and dogs, so they were just a visual thing, but actually they're quite an aromatic flower and they could put them in the planting boxes in Frenchgate say, but instead they just got some sort of ever-green, ever-lasting stuff. (D09)

The planting in Doncaster's retail primary core includes trees, small-scale planted areas, hanging baskets and floral displays in the summer months (see Figure 9.2). Since concluding the study, more planting has been introduced in the town as part of an initiative to create a new Civic and Cultural Quarter outside the smellwalk route. Some planting features in the town have traditionally been introduced as part of annual floral competitions between towns and cities, such as 'Britain in Bloom' or the European-wide 'Entente Florale'. As the very term 'floral display' suggests, such competitions generally focus on the visual nature of the flower rather than its odour. In the UK these competitions have encouraged the development of a culture where displays are cultivated off-site and transported into urban environments: '...when they go for that ... Doncaster in Bloom thing ... all the flowers pop up from nowhere, don't they!' (D35). Although these displays are enjoyed by many and certainly brighten up the look of the town, the flowers were considered by some to represent a 'disconnect' with the local environment, brought into the town to 'pretty it up' for a few weeks in the early summer.

As well as being on display in baskets and planters, flowers were detected growing in the streets or on waste land in all the studied towns and cities: 'you can walk down by the sort of disused area which is currently a car park and there's some big buddleia bushes which smell rather nice … it would be nice to have more of that' (M21). Occasionally participants went out of their way to smell flowers: '…little low bushes and tiny flowers, a lovely smell … if I'm in the area, I'm going shopping down there and I've got time, I nip in and have a sniff' (L35). Over half of the Doncaster participants described floral odours as contributing positively towards their environmental perceptions: '…the market stalls, the flower stalls there, they make a difference, you know … they probably impact on you subconsciously, there must be a difference to your feeling of pleasure or otherwise' (D41).

Floral odours were also detected while passing shops: '…a very vague scent from the flower-shop, but I don't know whether that was my brain synthesising a previous experience that would have said, well, you're passing a flower shop and that's what you can expect' (D06). As with several other odour sources, flower shops were expected to emit an odour, and when this wasn't detected it was explained as a result of the weather conditions and temperature: 'I think they

Figure 9.2 Small-scale planting in Doncaster's primary retail core

kind of smell more when they warm up, I think that's part of their nature, it's like the grass, isn't it? Warming up, it smells, so that would kind of change as a seasonal thing' (D27).

Unlike other aspects of the natural environment, flowers were also perceived in negative terms by some participants. Occasionally this was allergy-related: 'I do like the smell of flowers, that sort of smell, but only because it triggers me, I tend to stay away from it' (D48). Others expressed a view that flowers were incongruent in urban environments specifically: '…it has a certain value in the countryside, I'm not too keen on it in cities' (D10). For a small number of others, this perceived incongruence was linked to the idea that flowers were forced products with idealised odour associations:

> I'm never really one for flowers … I don't think they smell nice … people associate flowers with the natural environment. Most flowers are nothing to do with the natural environment; it's an industrial process, the same as making cars or anything else. (D26)

The negative perception of the floral odours is, in these scenarios, linked with a perceived 'unnatural' quality of the flower. In one case it is the urban environmental context that leads to this judgement, while in the other it is the associations with the plant origin. The flower was not perceived as truly natural, or naturally occurring, and therefore its odours were not enjoyed. This is reminiscent of Radford's (1978) work on 'Fakes'. Radford investigated the impact of origin upon people's perceptions of the aesthetic qualities of paintings following their discovery these were not painted by specific named artists. Elliot (2003) develops these ideas with respect to natural and unnatural environments and explains: 'The castle by the Scottish loch is a very different kind of object, value-wise, from the exact replica in the appropriately shaped environment of some Disneyland of the future' (*ibid.*: 384–385). Flowers are perceived in negative terms as a result of the value judgements placed on them, with these perceptions intertwined with commercial associations and the idealisation of floral odours. This also relates to perceptions of bread odours in supermarkets, as outlined in the previous chapter. Like the odour of the bread, the perceived unnatural nature of the flower, whether caused by context or odour source, becomes associated with the idea of an odour experience having been planned or designed by someone else, and therefore being contrived. The point at which people interpret odours of flowers as contrived, and indeed whether they interpret the odour in this way at all, is individually, socially, culturally and contextually situated. However, although odours of urban flowers are judged to be unnatural by some, the vast majority of people consider these experiences to be part of the naturally occurring environment.

Doncaster also has trees in its town centre core, introduced over the past two decades as part of urban realm improvements including the development of new public spaces in the town. The majority of these new trees are small in size, with limited canopies. They were selected due to a lack of space in the town and local policing requests regarding the need to monitor the streets through CCTV cameras unobstructed by foliage. However, the town centre is generally considered to lack greenspace: '…it is very, I don't know, sort of hard and cold in a way, isn't it? There is no natural great space at all' (D35). In the absence of greenspace, the new public spaces offer some restorative functions. One such area is Frenchgate, the last stopping point in the Doncaster smellwalks (see Figure 9.3). When vegetation odours were detected in these areas they were thought to positively contribute towards the immediate experience of the area: '…it does introduce some greenery in the summer into the place, which helps to baffle the noise and smells from the traffic from beyond' (D13). Although no prior studies have been identified studying the effects of planting barriers in reducing odours of traffic, there have been relevant studies by Malone and van Wicklen (2001) and Colletti *et al.* (2006) examining the effects of planting barriers on odours released from livestock sites. However, the results of these studies have, to date, been inconclusive.

Conversely, experiences of larger urban greenspaces and parks in the cities of Sheffield, Manchester and Clerkenwell, London sometimes failed to meet odour expectations:

Figure 9.3 Frenchgate, Doncaster

...it's difficult in the summer to smell the local greenspaces even though they're there, and they're well maintained, because of other things that are, that are going on, be it the traffic and building and all sorts of other things like that. (M28)

In such cases, non-detection was influenced by other factors, including the effects of air pollution on overall urban smellscape experience.

In summary, odours of trees, planted areas and greenspaces were some of the most widely favoured odours in the smell preference survey and in the studied towns and cities, with these positive perceptions related to the benefits planting is thought to afford. These include perceived improvements in air quality, health and well-being, odour qualities and associations, and a related restorative function where such odours offer both brief and more immersive opportunities for respite from the city.

9.2.2 Water and waterways

Across all its variety of forms, water was described in widely positive terms in all the studied English cities. It was perceived to have a restorative effect similar to that of greenspaces: 'I like to go there 'cause I think it's, in the absence of a park, it's nice to just be near something natural ... it's good to use the canals' (M18). Another commented: '...the Peace Gardens, there are fountains like in the main square, I went there just a few days ago 'cause it's really nice just to relax' (S15). Akin to vegetation, water was thought to have a cleansing and freshening effect on the air. Sometimes this related to characteristics of the water: '...you get anywhere near the river, that has that sort of, I don't know if it's ozone, or what it is, but it has a kind of fresher smell' (D10). Rain was also thought to cleanse pollutants from the air and assist in the release of other positively perceived odours through evaporation following rainfall in the summer (a frequently-mentioned favoured odour). Others described the freshening effect associated generally with water:

> ...flowing water ... if not physically improving the pollution, it will aesthetically improve people's perception, because if there's clean running water people think it's a clean environment ... If you go to Sheffield and see the water trickling down, as soon as you come out it always feels refreshing. I've been to Barcelona and seen all the fountains and things like that and it just gives you an air of freshness. (D50)

Water also emits its own odours: 'I like the smell of water ... if we go down one of the canals, sometimes it smells bad, you know it smells, smells stagnant and it is, but I love the smell of the water' (M18).

Water was therefore identified as a means by which a perceived air of freshness might be introduced to urban spaces through small-scale interventions such as water features (see Figure 9.4). Larger bodies of water such as rivers and canals afford more substantial and immersive olfactory environments similar to those of parks or greenspaces providing a restorative function (see Figure 9.5).

9.2.3 Non-natural restorative odours

As we have identified, previous research on restorative environments has focused on natural environments, with Karmanov and Hamel (2008: 115–116) outlining a general belief from policy makers, urban planners, architects and the public that urban environments lack the same restorative potential. However, other environmental types and forms, such as museums, churches or favourite places, have been shown to also serve restorative functions (Kaplan *et al.* 1993, Korpela and Hartig 1996, Herzog *et al.* 2010). The study by Karmanov and Hamel (2008: 122) found that urban environments have stress-reducing and mood-enhancing potential equal to that of natural environments. In undertaking smellwalks in cities, it becomes clear that restorative experiences can occur in a variety of non-natural environments. A London resident commented of an old building they regularly visited: 'I just relax and just breathe in the history of this place. And it's just great, I just love this place, I just love my couple of nights here, it's just fantastic' (L36).

Figure 9.4 Water-feature in public space, Manchester city centre

Figure 9.5 Immersive restorative experience, Manchester's urban canals

In Doncaster town centre, the markets area was the most liked area visited on the smellwalks, and it also scored highest in smellscape ratings. Its varied odours of fish, fruit, vegetables, cardboard, clothing and food, not to mention those emitted from the public toilets, were very different from the odours of natural environments. However they contributed towards overall place experience and were associated with restoration: '...that's what you associate with the market isn't it? It's part of it, it's nice, I like it, it's not off-putting, it's nice and there's people around eating and just relaxing enjoying themselves' (D37). Doncaster's mixed-use Priory Walk similarly served a restorative function in the form of its café culture: 'I think it's quite a nice area, a nice area to walk through, a nice area to sit down and relax' (D44). However, due to the design and management of the area, opportunities to sit down and enjoy the environment were limited to paying customers located in and outside the street's cafés and public houses. Although urban, these areas have the potential to offer a restorative experience similar to those associated with more natural environments such as green spaces and waterways.

More notably, when thinking about urban smellscape experience and design, odours can be identified as playing a role in restorative experiences within a range of environments, both natural and non-natural, whether experienced as a brief olfactory encounter or as part of a more immersive restorative experience.

9.2.4 Restorative odours in smellscape management and design

As cities become increasingly dense and the demand for space becomes ever more competitive, access to natural environments is likely to be threatened and existing greenspaces will be more heavily used. At the same time growing density is likely to increase the intensity of city life, with more frequent potential for conflicts between people and closely proximate odour producers. As a result, the need for restorative environments increases, and those cities better able to meet this demand will have healthier and possibly also happier inhabitants as a result. The provision of greenspaces and planting in the city is also of importance in remediating against urban heat island effects and improving air quality, thereby protecting the longer-term interests of the city's inhabitants.

Smell is an important part of the overall experience of green areas: '…if you're gonna have greenspace, the sensory perception of smell should be treated as highly as any' (D26). Even small-scale urban planting schemes provide relief in the city, seen as freshening the air and introducing widely positively perceived odours into the city. However, the provision of greenspace, planting and trees throughout the city, as well as the management of public space, does present challenges for those with responsibility for overseeing the development and maintenance of the city. City managers and professionals are tasked to consider issues such as land values, commercial and economic development, maintenance and vandalism, and they are under pressure to balance budgets while delivering high standards of environmental quality, community cohesion, access to public space and quality of life. As a result, smaller-scale environmental features are sometimes removed because of maintenance and vandalism concerns, thereby reducing opportunities for potentially restorative odours to be experienced. Even the selection of trees with minimal foliage to facilitate monitoring of the public via CCTV cameras is an indicator of an approach where opportunities for fascination and delight become limited, with the mechanics of running and maintaining the city taking priority over the everyday embodied experiences of the people who inhabit it.

The identification of a role for odour in restorative experiences within the city therefore provides an important conceptual foundation, from which built environment professionals might start to consider odour in a different way in their everyday practice. This positive role for odour in the environment provides an opportunity for such actors to adapt their current practices, stepping towards a more ecological approach to urban smellscape design.

9.3 Smell design tools

In earlier chapters I highlighted urban smellscape experience as being influenced by a range of factors that come together to influence perceptions of odour and place. Despite pre-conceptions that urban environments are filled with generally negatively perceived odours, in fact a variety of odours can be detected in cities, perceived differently according to individual, social and cultural experiences and norms. I have argued that the congruence between odour and place impacts on perceptions of both. In analysing people's varied perceptions of odour it is also possible to identify physical and spatial characteristics of the city that influence urban smellscapes; these characteristics can be adapted into everyday practices by built environment professionals when designing with smell in mind. They are grouped as follows: air movement and micro-climates; activity density; materials; and topography.

9.3.1 Air movement and microclimates

> Smells in town, the same as anywhere else, it depends on how calm it is or how windy it is. If it's calm, you'll get a lot more, and they'll be a lot stronger smells, and if it's windy you're likely to miss a lot of smells. (D08)

Built environmental form has a known impact on pedestrian experiences of wind-flow (Penwarden and Wise 1975, Cochran 2004, Pugh *et al.* 2012) and thermal comfort (Nikolopoulou *et al.* 2001; Nikolopoulou & Lykoudis 2007; Nikolopoulou 2003, 2004; Tahbaz 2010; Tseliou *et al.* 2010). Given the importance of air movement in influencing smell experiences in the city (see Figure 9.6), built environmental form can impact directly on odour concentration, dilution and movement. Bentley *et al.* (1985: 75) draw from a study carried out by Penwarden and Wise (1975) highlighting the effect of wind speeds on the body, and conclude that designers should aim to use the built form to limit wind speeds to a gentle breeze of less than five metres per second. However, as the smellwalking studies have illustrated, perceptions of appropriate wind-speed levels vary from place to place and depend on factors such as area usage and type. They are also closely interlinked with judgements of urban smellscape and overall environmental quality. In areas where traffic emissions were detected, the wind was regularly considered to have a positive freshening effect on the air.

In Doncaster's Silver Street, an area with a busy road and bus route running through it, participants described a strong wind blowing along the length of the street, encouraged by the built form of the long relatively straight road enclosed by buildings on both sides. This strong wind was thought to assist in

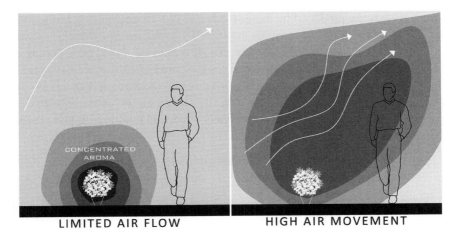

LIMITED AIR FLOW   HIGH AIR MOVEMENT

Figure 9.6 Air flow and odour concentration (image drawn by Nabil Awad)

dissipating negatively perceived odours of traffic emissions and remnants of odours from 'the night before'. On less windy days participants described the area differently: '…because it's a main bus route so you can smell the buses … it's not blowing away, it's there in your face, it can get overpowering' (D38). Similarly, scenting practices were thought to be more appropriate in areas where odours could disperse quickly: '…I think that's fair enough in an area which is open to the elements, but in an enclosed mall I think that can lead to problems' (D28).

Wind was mentioned too in Doncaster's enclosed Priory Walk: '…it's enclosed, you imagine that a smell in here might get trapped … it's not going to easily dissipate unless there's movement of air in some direction' (D10). This enclosure was described in generally positive terms and was linked with bodily restoration. However, in smell terms the enclosure was occasionally considered to exert a negative influence:

> I like the fact that it's quite enclave, and you have to sort of like physically find it … But I know that I've been here sort of like night time and it's been just like a big ray of smoke … that kind of puts me off. (D42)

Therefore, enclosure has the potential to both channel the wind and direct air flow, *and* to limit it. However, it is important to remember that although a strong wind might be perceived in positive terms by improving air quality or clearing odour, it might simultaneously be considered in negative terms through its cooling effect on the body. Care must therefore be taken to incorporate considerations of odour within a wider full-bodied sensory approach to design.

In fact, the use of the environmental form as a tool for shaping sensory experience is by no means alien to designers. The use of earth-banks in remediating noise produced by major roads and the use of planting to improve the visual aesthetics of an area are both well established practices. Similarly, trees and planting are also thought to provide a physical shield from odours in the same way as buildings: 'I think if you screen, either visually as well as actually physically, with trees and maybe a few barriers before the roads, it does ameliorate that [air pollution and odour] quite a lot really' (D17). However, these beliefs are more likely to be related to association than to an actual shielding of such odours.

9.3.2 Activity density

…when I'm advising people on markets … then I would say that the more dense they are the better, and that the more you can contain the smells and that you can contain the atmosphere and the activity, it actually creates even more excitement … I think it's that intensity of space which creates a drama. (D05)

Recent efforts to redevelop Doncaster's markets area have presented particular issues to those involved, who seek to achieve a balance between delivering a modern retail offering without reducing the haphazard sensory nature of the markets. As one participant explained:

…there's clearly places where it's [sensory design] easier to do, I mean around the market … it could kill it, you'd lose that critical mass and intensity of the buzz and the feel and the excitement of the markets … it would be easy to create smell as a really important factor in the regeneration of the markets. (D31)

The enclosed and concentrated nature of markets is a critical aspect of their success, both within market buildings and in the wider ambient environment, with odour experiences playing an important role in place perception and enjoyment. With many other activity types, such as the concentration of the evening economy in one area or nationally associated food businesses in international districts, such spatial concentration or activity zoning contrasts with the mixed-use approaches to development that have been advocated in urban design theory and have filtered into city regeneration mantra in recent years. In Doncaster, those with responsibility for cleaning, maintaining and policing the street were generally positive about a concentrated evening zone because it enabled resources to be allocated to specific areas during and after core evening trading hours. Effectively, such activity zoning both concentrates problems, including those relating to smell (odours of vomit, urine, spilt alcohol, food and cigarette related waste), *and* focuses corresponding odour control and management practices into one area.

9.3.3 Materials

...different sorts of buildings defined the different smells in each area that we've been to ... you can smell the buildings, like the stone and the brickwork, you can sort of get a sense of that. (D12)

In any one given place in the city, there can be a huge variety of materials that together form the streetscape. Ranging from the materials included in the buildings and walls through to those of the flooring, street furniture and public art, combinations vary dramatically between places and cities and are highly influenced by local stone types, period of build, building styles and norms. Some participants were sceptical about the potential for streetscape materials to impact on urban smellscape experiences, although others detected odours from materials or talked about the influence these had on their experience.

Natural materials such as wood were rarely detected during smellwalks, but when they were these odours were positively perceived: '...they were working on refurbishing one of the restaurants, you could smell the wood that they were sawing ... I love that smell' (D21). Although stone was considered a subtler odour, it also featured in experiences:

I like the smell of wood, I do like the smell of stone ... I think when you're sat maybe twenty meters away from a stone building it wouldn't make a difference, but I think when you're say in a church, if the church was built in concrete, it wouldn't have that same smell to it. (D26)

In these examples, the materials were thought to possess odours in their own right. However, more often it was the effect of materials on other odour sources that was considered to be of greater influence. Absorption or non-absorption qualities in particular were highlighted:

I think that the surface textures of the brick are kind of reflective and if you had a York Stone or a Portland it would absorb that rather than that kind of engineered clay brick ... it just feels like that smells are just reflecting back off them. (D31)

In other cases, difficulties faced when cleaning flooring materials were mentioned:

...if you were designing a market square, you'd probably not use the bricks that they've used here because I think they just collect dirt and I think possibly by using other materials, that would wash away a bit easier. (D05)

Different materials, and the odours they brought with them, were also associated with particular types of areas:

> ...this kind of mono block type paving tends to be in areas where there's quite a lot of smell ... and then to more traditional sort of tarmaced areas, because they're older they can hold certain smells, it's not really the pavement, it's more the juxtaposition with the buildings or alleyways and things like that. (D07)

Odours of materials were thought to be at their strongest when construction and maintenance activities were under way. Just as the sawing of the wood in construction works released odours into the air, the cutting and drilling of stone and other materials also had an olfactory impact: '...they have a big drill sometimes and a digger, and there's billows, there's like billows of smoke and stuff coming out. And I mean I didn't like inhale it but the smell of it' (S15). Similarly, road works emitted odours: '...we crossed the road, you know, where the people were digging up, I could smell tarmac like building work' (D42). Perceptions of these odours were mixed, but they were generally accepted as temporary phenomena to be put up with, although the odour source played a role in determining whether the odours were enjoyed (wood sawing) or not (stone drilling).

9.3.4 Topography

The topographies of the towns and cities where I have led smellwalks have varied significantly – from the glorious hills of Montreal, Canada to the flats of downtown New York. Doncaster town centre has a level topography while both Sheffield and London are hillier in areas, allowing me to investigate different aspects and impacts of topography on odour experiences in the city. Topography influences smell in a number of ways:

> [Doncaster] suffers from this drainage system because it's flat ... that's been problematic for many years ... there's no natural flow, so everything has to be pumped ... as soon as it rains it'll flush the stuff through ... there's underground sumps which sit there and fill up ... if it sits there any length of time with no rainfall, as soon as it moves it's stagnant already. They have tried injecting oxygen at the points to help them; it suffers from a low natural flow. (D50)

Negatively perceived odours of drainage can be detected on a daily basis in Doncaster town centre, and are stronger at particular times of the year and in different weathers. They are concentrated in specific places, most significantly at the edge of the medieval town with its older drainage infrastructure. Certain areas in the town have developed notoriety with local people, with the drains providing distinct smellmarks in the town centre: '…as you come around that corner … it absolutely stinks of sewers and that is every day, that's a regular occurrence' (D24). Realistically, the steps that can be taken to resolve issues with drainage are tied up with investment in drainage infrastructure; not all flat towns suffer from drainage odours. The smells are therefore indicative of a drainage system that falls short of modern requirements and expectations.

Hillier topographies were also problematic at times, with traffic odours being particularly strong in areas where vehicles and specifically buses were required to stop and start on inclines.

This highlights a more direct approach that designers and city managers might adopt in attempting to reduce the strength and frequency of negatively perceived experiences. Through modelling varying emission levels and likelihood of pedestrian/emission encounters with relation to gradient, professionals can better inform decision-making regarding bus routing and the positioning of bus stops and traffic lights. Equally, such modelling might also consider the positioning of bus stops in relation to residential blocks, attempting to reduce experiences of emissions in the home.

Topography therefore impacts on olfactory experiences in very real ways, and in both highlighted scenarios these impacts had negative impacts on olfactory perception. However, topography also plays a significant role in the movement of air in and around the city, important in promoting more positive experiences.

9.3.5 Smell design tools – summary

In examining people's experiences and perceptions of odour in the streetscape, it has been possible to identify a range of tools by which odour might be better considered as part of the design and management of the urban environment. Air movement and microclimates, activity density and concentration, materials and topography are all factors that are currently considered, in one way or another, as part of existing design, development or management practice. A wider, more holistic sensory approach to design could therefore easily be incorporated into existing practices. Clearly these findings present only a glimpse into the impact of these factors on everyday experiences of urban smellscapes, and it is likely that with further research studies in this field, and the wider implementation of sensory design practice, other factors of influence would also emerge. However, for our purpose in identifying practical means for designing with odour, it is helpful to recognise that issues relating to built environmental form and content can, and do, influence odour experiences. In light of this realisation, such tools can be incorporated into a new urban design approach that better meets the sensory requirements of city inhabitants.

9.4 A new approach to odour in urban design

In this chapter I have drawn from the experiences of people *in situ* to identify useful factors in urban smellscape design and specifically in thinking about the role of smell in restorative environments. However, I do not suggest that odour itself leads to restoration, although I have identified examples where the mere presence of an odour is able to provide significant feelings of delight and fascination. Rather, I argue that smell should be pro-actively considered, rather than overlooked, in the delivery of areas where people can escape from the stresses of modern urban life. I have also provided examples of restoration gained from non-natural environments. Such environments include public spaces in the city or other areas of particular meaning for the individual. Restorative experiences, like wider odour experiences, are likely to vary according to the past experiences and memories of the individual.

Moreover, the identification of a positive role for odour in the urban environment is significant because it provides an opportunity for designers, architects and city managers to think about urban smellscapes in a different light. If odour has the potential to assist in providing bodily restoration *and* a number of practical odour design tools have been identified, then steps can be taken towards developing and practising a more sympathetic and responsive approach to the sensory needs of urban dwellers. Indeed, odour may provide a way by which built environment professionals can start to think about restoration as a factor that can easily be incorporated into the urban environment in the form of small-scale interventions. Odour might also be more proactively considered in attempts to improve the experiences of immersive restorative environments such as urban parks or waterways.

Furthermore, restorative odours have the potential to interface with certain olfactory tools in creating odour-designed effects similar to those pursued within existing urban design practices. City legibility, for example, serves as a means by which Kevin Lynch (1960) suggested that people form an internal image and map of the city, for use in recollection, navigation and city image. Odour was highlighted in Chapter 7 as playing a role in legibility, a possible consequence of frequent experiences of odours from site-specific sources such as flowers growing on wasteland, speciality stores such as pet shops and leather shops, as well as on a larger scale in areas such as Doncaster's Copley Road and Manchester Chinatown. Such odours can be interpreted as smellmarks, a concept which is equally applicable to negatively-perceived odours (such as those emitted from Doncaster's drains) as to more positive examples.

In the previous chapter I categorised and described existing processes of managing and controlling the olfactory environment as falling within the four broad areas of separation, deodorisation, masking and scenting. Restorative odours and identified olfactory design tools can similarly be situated within these four approaches. Restorative odours such as those of fresh air have a deodorising effect which dilutes odour concentration, with built environmental forms encouraging or preventing this freshening effect. Trees and planting also play a deodorising role through their ability to absorb pollutants, a masking effect through a perceived ability to screen off other odours, and a scenting effect through contributing positively perceived odours into the olfactory environment.

9.5 Conclusion

In this chapter I have argued that it should be possible for built environment professionals to think about odour in more positive ways, without this necessarily having to incorporate scenting practices since these are seen as controversial by some. A potential role for smell in enhancing restorative experiences from urban environments, whether derived from natural or non-natural sources, has previously been overlooked in research on restorative environments. However, the examples I highlight in this chapter might complement the findings of other studies, such as that undertaken by Payne (2008) on the role of sound in restorative experience, in developing a multi-sensory approach to restorative environmental knowledge and design.

A broad range of odours can be detected in English towns and cities, as I outlined in Chapter 4. Some of these are perceived differently by different people, such as the nationally associated food odours in Copley Road or the odours emitted from stores selling highly scented products. Other odours are perceived very similarly by most people, such as the odours of traffic fumes, perceived in widely negative terms, or those of vegetation which are widely liked. In examining experiences of these odours, including those from 'natural' sources within the built environment, I have outlined tools for use by architects and designers to actively shape odour experiences of places, rather than such experiences coming about as an accident or oversight or a by-product of urban policy, outlined in Chapter 7. Designing with odour is therefore within the grasps of practitioners, and this knowledge can be used to complement design guidance and tools emerging in other fields such as urban soundscapes and thermal comfort.

In Chapter 10, I will build on this knowledge by further developing the study's findings on perceptions of odour and their relationship with place perception, and I will consider the active role of odour in placemaking.

10

Odour, placemaking and urban smellscape design

A few years ago I visited Grasse in the south of France, famous for its reputation as the world centre of the perfume industry. The town featured in Patrick Süskind's novel 'Perfume: The Story of a Murderer', and although it was one of the wealthiest areas in France in the mid-twentieth century, it is now host to both extremely wealthy and extremely poor communities. As I drove into the valley of Grasse on a hot sunny day with the car windows open I could smell flowers long before I arrived in the town. Once there, I stood among tourists on a beautiful stone patio and wondered over the intensely floral smell surrounding me, only to realise that I was standing directly next to a perfumed fountain (see Figure 10.1). In Grasse there are many odour-themed features throughout its streets, and the boundaries of what is appropriate and acceptable are rather different than in most other cities. Odour themes include visual representations of scent and flowers in the public art features sited in public parks, and murals painted on empty shop units or situated outside school buildings. A huge mock bottle of Chanel No. 5 sits on the mini-traffic island outside the town hall (see Figure 10.2). In one of the cafés, I marvelled at the taste of my crème brûlée flavoured with lavender grown in the local fields.

Scenting features dominate the urban smellscape experience, with aromatic vegetation (primarily jasmine), trees and flowers planted throughout the town's streets. These can be found in pots alongside busy trafficked streets, growing next to water fountains on shaded squares, or as large manicured bushes next to grand old stone houses. Town leaders, in collaboration with the perfume industry, promote the area's smellscape and relationship with scent to the world's tourism, business and conference markets, and organise an annual Festival of Jasmine in early August as well as an annual exhibition of roses.

However, scenting practices are not all that is responsible for the urban smellscape in Grasse, as can be witnessed by taking a five minute walk away from the tourism centre into the city's poorer streets where much of the city's northern African immigrant community is concentrated. Here the smells of scented flowers are absent; instead one detects dampness, stone and cooking smells in the dark, dense urban streets. In the spaces between buildings where the hot sun penetrates, young men play basketball among graffiti, dust and broken stonework, and washing hangs from high windows. The ambience is

Figure 10.1 Perfume fountain, Grasse, south of France

Figure 10.2 Chanel No.5 traffic island feature, Grasse, south of France

markedly different to that of the tourist areas only a few streets away, and may be threatening to those who do not belong.

Venturing back into the main tourist area of the town, there is clear evidence of other processes of odour management and control. With the exception of smells emitted from the traffic, sitting nose-to-tail through the town's winding roads at busy times of the year, the only other obvious potential negative odour source is the town's population of dogs, who walk with their owners in the greenspaces and manicured lawns. Dog faeces, along with other forms of waste, is dealt with via a zealous deodorisation campaign with waste bins provided every few metres, street cleaning, public toilets provided and large signs outlining a wide range of regulations – including the rule that under no circumstances should anyone pick the flowers.

Given its unique association with the perfume industry, it would be easy to reject Grasse as a one-off case of limited relevance in examining everyday efforts to manage, control and design the smellscapes of most towns and cities. Indeed, cities are far more likely to be 'infamous' for odour associations than celebrated for their positive smell environments, and such features as perfumed fountains would be considered wholly inappropriate in the streets of many cities. However, those odour management and control processes observed in English towns and cities, namely separation, deodorisation, masking and scenting, can also be observed in Grasse. Smell clearly plays an important role in the place identity, design and control of Grasse. However, given the variety of interactions occurring on a daily basis between odours, people and environments, what kind of contribution might smell provide to wider understandings of place and placemaking activities, and how do we respond to perceptions of smell design as a potentially manipulative and dishonest practice?

10.1 The contribution of odour to placemaking

Barbara and Perliss (2006) consider current debates on smell and place and categorise them according to two positions – a search for the authentic smell of place and the capture of a memorable and extraordinary experience – but each of these positions is problematic. The term authentic is used in everyday language to characterise things, objects and environments as genuine, truthful or conforming to 'reality'. In describing experiences of urban smellscapes, very different views are expressed regarding the meaning of place authenticity. Massey (1991) talks of complex social flows and inter-connections across the globe, and describes how many theorists interpret this as unsettling for individuals. She argues that these theorists adopt a 'reactionary approach', concluding that a strong sense of place provides

'…a kind of refuge from the hubbub'. Massey observes that this is problematic in a number of ways: 'One is the idea that places have single, essential, identities. Another is the idea that place – the sense of place – is constructed out of an introverted, inward-looking history'.

In Doncaster's Copley Road, some participants described the neighbourhood's authentic place identity as associated with local residential and business communities including the town's minority black ethnic population, many of whom are recent immigrants. These participants enjoyed the international food odours of Copley Road and described them as authentic and cosmopolitan (see Chapter 5). Other participants rejected the presence of local minority residents and businesses, perceiving related odours as foreign and unrepresentative of the true character of the neighbourhood and town. These participants referred back to, and described in idealised terms, the historical smellscapes in the area, and although they expected non-indigenous food odours in the area today, they did not accept them.

For Relph (1976: 49), authenticity relates to a distinction between insideness and outsideness in experiences of place: 'To be inside a place is to belong to it and identify with it'. For those emphasising the foreign nature of the odours of Copley Road the odours were incongruent with their associations with that place, a sign of their outsideness as individuals. Place authenticity is thus conflicted, with odour perception acting as one means of formulating and expressing opinions regarding wider social and environmental factors at play. Individuals might accept or reject an odour, perceiving it in positive or negative terms according to its congruence with their personal perception of any one particular place.

The idea of an authentic sense of place further relates to concerns about urban smellscape design as a potentially manipulative process. Just as synthetic food odours are suspected to hide the true quality of food, smell design activities are perceived to potentially trick people into developing false area impressions that hide the authentic character of a place. However, as noted above, the authenticity of any one place is itself fluid in its definition, differing according to individual, social and cultural perspectives and beliefs. In many cases authenticity is associated with the historical aspects of a certain place – the authentic street pattern, local stone or the traditional use of the street. As observed in Copley Road, authenticity also relates to people and communities – some well established, others new to an area. Similarly, many transient or temporal activities might be considered authentic by some, intrusive or annoying by others. The on-street burger van and hot dog vendors located on Doncaster's primary shopping street were thought by the majority to add to the street theatre with their smells, sounds, tastes and sights. Those with responsibility for managing the street, however, perceived these odours very differently, signifying a lack of control and an incongruity with their perceptions of the place, both in terms of how it exists currently and how they imagine it might evolve in the future.

The point here is not to suggest that authenticity does not matter; rather, that it is made up of a complex range of factors and there will be a multitude of perspectives on what makes up the authenticity of any one place. Engagement with a wide range of stakeholders is therefore critical in assessments of urban smellscapes so as to ensure that one particular view does not dominate, take priority over, and potentially exclude others.

Smell is well known for its special link with memory, with associations being retained for much longer periods over time than visual images (Engen 1977, referenced in Engen 1982) and familiar odours generally being more positively perceived than unfamiliar odours (Porteous 1990). However, as a result of habituation and adaptation, people are more likely to unconsciously process known odours, with only unfamiliar or particularly strong odours being brought to our conscious attention as a potential threat or a source of pleasure. As a result, it might often be a town's visitors who observe the overall background smell of an area, or its 'base notes', the broader background and relatively unchanging odours of a place, neighbourhood or whole city described in Chapter 8.

In their comments on urban environments, Barbara and Perliss (2006: 125) suggest: '…cities have odours, and not in the sense of metropolitan-type smells or pollution, but in the proper sense of an olfactory essence, of an identity that at times, only a few are able to recognise'. Here, Barbara and Perliss might be thought to refer to the background smell of a place, but if an area has traffic fumes or poor air quality as part of its smellscape, then the 'olfactory essence' becomes only an idea or memory, an odour place identity possibly existing in the past but no longer existing in the present. The olfactory essence might also be formulated through imagery and other associations, many potentially disputed – hence Barbara and Perliss's cautionary note that these subtle sensory experiences might only be recognised by a few.

The service and hospitality sectors have increasingly responded to the idea of using odour to create environments offering memorable and extraordinary experiences, with extraordinary being interpreted here as unusual, exceptional or outside the normal order. These sectors draw their odour references from other times, places and experiences with the intention of creating copies or idealised versions of originals, and also use smell in creating experiences of places that have previously only existed in fiction. Thorpe Park, a high adrenaline theme park in England, uses smell as a key component in its new attractions. In 2010, the park ran a competition to find the country's smelliest urine, with the aim of incorporating this into the design of a new horror-film themed attraction (Merlin Entertainments Group 2010). In doing so, the park's team drew from associations between urine odours and dark, undesirable places with the specific intention of enhancing the fears of those experiencing it. The park's entertainments manager explained:

> We want [the attraction] to be as authentic and terrifying as possible to make visitors feel as if they are living in a real-life horror film. To do this we need to really push the boundaries of what our guests experience from a sensory point of view with the use of smells, special lighting and effects such as electrocution and vibrating floors that will create a full-on attack of the senses. We've begun creating some of the stenches of [the attraction] but need the help of the public to create the most realistic and unsavoury urine odour. (*ibid.*)

In contrast to the highly controlled environment of the theme park and other such commercial settings, towns and cities operate as living, changing organisms. As Relph (1976: 140), Massey (1991) and Smith (2007: 101) observe, towns and cities combine global and local elements co-existing within the urban fabric. In English cities local and global odours co-exist: the strong smell of Doncaster's fish market, the odours of cigarette smoke, perfumes and scented products, wafts from a basement kitchen, and those from a branded coffee chain store can all be detected literally within a few metres of one another. As Massey (1991) argues, places must change and move forward out of necessity, and cannot just look inwardly to their heritage in gaining a sense of place. Instead they must merge both local and wider elements to create a uniqueness of place specific to that one area.

Tuan (1977: 183–184) observes:

> Abstract knowledge about a place can be acquired in short order if one is diligent. The visual quality of the environment is quickly tallied if one has the artist's eye. But the 'feel' of a place takes longer to acquire. It is made up of experiences, mostly fleeting and undramatic, repeated day after day and over the span of years. It is a unique blend of sights, sounds and smells, a unique harmony of natural and artificial rhythms.

Within this context smellmarks, even things as low-key as ventilation emissions released from one of Doncaster's basement restaurants, can be argued to contribute towards a sense of place. They do so by forming a part of people's everyday memories and associations with the street in which they are experienced, regardless of whether those same people would like or dislike the same odours if they were sniffing them from a test-tube. These odours instead become biographical, forming part of people's individual and social memories and their sense of 'insideness' or belonging.

Dann and Jacobsen (2003) suggest that to increase their success as contemporary tourism destinations, towns and cities should retain or recreate as authentically as possible their historical infrastructure, while attempting to remove negatively perceived odours and introduce more pleasant varieties. In the context of the insights offered by Relph (1976), Tuan (1977) and Massey (1991), this approach is clearly too simplistic, failing to acknowledge the progressive and evolving nature of urban smellscapes. Furthermore, it prioritises the experience of the tourist above those of other stakeholders, failing to recognise the important role that odours can play in local place identity and experience. Thus, the smell of the fish in Doncaster's market area, the ventilation emissions from the basement restaurant and the smell of fumes in London's Soho were not only frequently enjoyed or fondly recalled by people, both meeting expectations and enhancing legibility in the same way that a landmark might be used (e.g. May *et al.* 2003), but they also assisted in developing a sense of familiarity and belonging.

Dann and Jacobson's suggested strategy therefore raises many important questions about the stakeholders for whom the city and its constituent parts are being designed, and whose perceptions will be considered as part of the process of doing so.

10.2 Urban smellscape design: a practice of value or question?

We know the world through our senses, and despite our many protests to the contrary, through our senses we imbue our world with value. (Postrel 2003: 191)

In a detailed chronicle and discussion of aesthetic value in the twenty-first century, Virginia Postrel (2003) recognises the sensory qualities of design to be deeply contested, influenced by a line of thinking where aesthetics are seen as an unnecessary luxury; indeed, she quotes Bell (1996) in suggesting that aesthetics are based upon 'a world of make believe'. This world of make believe, she argues, is built on a fear that aesthetic design has the power to override rational thought by seducing the senses, and she reflects on '…the widespread fear that surface and substance cannot coexist, that artifice inevitably detracts from truth' (Postrel 2003: 70).

Smell, perhaps more than any of the other senses, is thought to have the potential to influence emotional state and behaviour at an unconscious level, without the implicit agreement or knowledge of the individual. As a consequence, urban smellscape design is labelled by some as a manipulative and dishonest practice, which in the context of city design and debates on authenticity has the potential to disguise the 'true' characteristics of place. Within this context, it is useful to clarify the limitations of the effects of odours on emotions and behaviours.

There are documented effects that many smells or emissions can have upon body and mind following inhalation, as outlined by the World Health Organisation (2008). Some odours of air pollutants have potentially harmful, even life-threatening effects on the body (*ibid.*), worsening existing respiratory illnesses (Jensen and Fenger 1994) and impacting negatively on the sense of smell on a temporary or permanent basis (Hudson *et al.* 2006). The odours of some flowers and plants and synthetic smells such as perfumes are also associated with allergic reactions (Fletcher 2005, 2006). At a concentrated level or following long periods of repeated exposure, all odours, even those that are usually enjoyed, can cause annoyance and nuisance, increasing stress levels and indirectly harming health (Evans and Cohen 1987, Miedema and Ham 1988, Cavalini *et al.* 1991).

There is some evidence that odours in general can affect psychological state. Heili *et al.* (1998) suggest that the odour of amniotic fluid has a calming effect on newborn mammals including humans, and a wide range of retail and marketing studies have argued in favour of a link between emotion and odour (e.g. Aggleton and Waskett 1999, Hirsch 2006). Given the particular functions of the sense of smell, including the role of the trigeminal nerve (Doty 2001), the important link that smell has with memory and associations (Engen 1991, Hirsch 2006) and a tendency towards favouring known odours (Porteous 1990: 24), it would seem that it is predominantly thinking or cognitive processes – the triggering of memories, emotional attachments and associations with odour – that make odours smell good, bad or mediocre, and perhaps also imbue them with a restorative function.

It is thinking and association that results in people holding their breath when they walk through a group of smokers on their way into a bar or restaurant, or prompts them to take a specific walking route to detect the smell of a particular plant. However, people's views and responses to these odours vary depending upon the point in space and time where the odours are detected. Following an overarching review of the marketing and retailing literature, Fitzgerald Bone and Scholder-Ellen (1999) suggest that the belief that odours can directly affect emotion and influence behaviours regardless of context is a myth. They argue that more useful and meaningful insights into odour-influenced judgements and behaviours may be gained from theories indicating that information gained from the environment, or accessed from memory, has the greatest effect (*ibid.*: 253). In my work in English cities and further afield I have found the combination of smell information with insights gained from other sensory modes, and prior experiences of specific or similar places, related associations and resulting expectations, to be critical in creating an ambience of place and perception and producing resulting behaviours.

The idea that odours might affect emotion regardless of context is complex and deep-rooted, situated within historical thought (Classen 1993, Classen *et al.* 1994), reflected and reinforced in art and fiction such as Süskind's novel *Perfume* (1987), and used in sophisticated scent marketing campaigns associating sexual attractiveness with odour (Drobnick 2000). These perceptions are further encouraged by our everyday passive perception of odours, with the vast majority being processed at an unconscious level; these subconscious effects are associated by people with a perceived vulnerability or lack of control. It is this perception that stimulates people into interpreting the act of designing with smell as manipulative. As one participant commented with regard to planting with the aim of masking odours of traffic:

> I mean, it's a bit dishonest, but on the other hand if it's a means of making people happy and they don't mind being manipulated like that, or even if they don't know they're being manipulated ... trying to make a place seem nicer, which is all well and good, I guess. (D06)

This perception of the purposeful design of urban smellscapes as a manipulative practice contrasts significantly with perceptions of wider built environmental design practices which change the visual aesthetics of an area. Indeed, decisions are made regarding the look of urban environments on an everyday basis by city leaders, planners, urban designers and architects, driven by an intention to attract certain groups of people to particular areas or buildings, portray specific images of place, or provide areas in which people can feel relaxed. In this context such factors are not accused of being manipulative; instead these factors are considered to be the essence of design: 'Design is what links creativity and innovation. It shapes ideas to become practical and attractive propositions for users or customers. Design may be described as creativity deployed to a specific end' (Cox 2005: 2). In contrast, design involving odour is generally considered and practised today as an artistic endeavour in the home or on the body, manifested in the form of perfuming or scenting, although there is increasing use of experiential design including scenting at commercial venues and events.

The wider consideration of odour in urban design practice and placemaking activities thus presents valuable opportunities for practitioners to enhance and protect city experiences and character, enhance place perceptions, and potentially improve the physiological and psychological state of city inhabitants. Equally, without careful consideration and meaningful engagement with a wide range of local stakeholders, designing with odour by removing existing odours and overwriting them with others has the potential to influence perceptions of areas with little regard for local context, familiarity or meaning.

Faced with such complexities, city leaders and built environment professionals would be forgiven for wondering how they might most effectively go about incorporating this sense into their urban management and design activities, given such conflicted perceptions and without risking the exclusion of some or allergic reactions in others. Some years ago I asked myself this same question as I considered how to progress my research from a theoretical position to one of practical use and application in urban and architectural design. To make this transition I drew from the philosophy of pragmatism, which recognises and embraces contextual pluralism and focuses on experience and practice on a case-by-case basis when dealing with issues of environmental ethics and morality such as those presented when designing urban smellscapes. Farmer and Guy (2010: 371) describe pragmatism as '...a philosophy of environments (not the environment) where value is understood to emerge in the ongoing transactions between humans and those environments'. Drawing from Light (2009), Farmer and Guy argue that pragmatism in sustainable design presents a philosophical position where abstract theorising has the most value in practical application: '...its proper aim is to clarify, coordinate and inform practice. Theory without practice becomes an intellectual game only weakly connected to the challenges it is supposed to understand and explain' (Farmer and Guy 2010: 371).

In adopting a pragmatic approach to urban smellscape design, I acknowledge that even with detailed consultation with local stakeholders and the subsequent proactive consideration of odour within the smellscape design decision-making process, it is unlikely that the resulting smellscape will be liked by everyone. Postrel (2003) notes that people are inevitably different, with differing tastes, values and perspectives, and identifies: 'To avoid design tyranny we need to find the right boundaries – to discover rules that preserve aesthetic discovery and diversity, accommodating plural identities and tastes while still allowing the pleasures of consistency and coherence' (*ibid.*: 123). The design of urban smellscapes must therefore acknowledge and allow for difference, both in recognising that odours will be perceived differently by different people, and in thinking about the variety of odours that may be detected in a city or neighbourhood.

I do not advocate a strict standard to be used across a multitude of places and environments, such as the ISO International Standard 7730 (ISO 1994) which recommends that designers of environmental thermal comfort should seek to satisfy ninety per cent of the population. Such a pre-set target is, I believe, too prescriptive to apply across the totality of urban smellscape design, because the risk in attempting to please such a large majority in all areas is that resulting environments become homogenised blandscapes. Equally, not all sites or neighbourhoods are suitable places for strong or challenging odours to be detected on a regular basis; consider, for example, the different responses people had in San Francisco in comparison with London and other English cities when they detected scented advertisements at bus-stops. In San Francisco there was public outcry, whereas in London the advertisements were liked as long as exposure was kept to a minimum.

I therefore suggest that built environment professionals should aim towards a scenario where the range, type and strength of odours detected in an area or development should be experienced by the majority of its users as appropriate and acceptable, given the context of the environment. In some areas an exciting, stimulating and challenging smellscape would work better than in others; likewise, in other areas, such as alongside busy urban roads, fresh, clean air supported by a good airflow might provide the most desirable option.

The urban smellscape should therefore be designed and managed with overriding attention to the local context, the purpose of the development and its users, and site-related issues. When designing public areas and city streets designers should seek to create inclusive urban smellscapes which work with other sensory modes to provide elements of fascination and delight.

10.3 The strategic context for designing urban smellscapes

...for so long, the way that places are made has been dominated by people who fill things and [smell] is not something you can do, it's not something you can make and form and fabricate yourself, it's a different way of designing or thinking about design, it's not about bricks and mortar... (D43)

In designing urban smellscapes, city leaders and built environment professionals will have very different intentions and perspectives, not only limited to personal, social and professional paradigms but also in terms of the constraints presented by the site itself. The term urban smellscapes, as we have identified, refers to different spatial levels – from the micro level, such as momentary encounters with the smell of flowers, perfumes or food from a café in the street, through to macro level contributors such as the smell of the sea, nearby mountains or countryside, or the smell of traffic emissions in highly polluted towns and cities (see Figure 9.1). Many of these macro-scale characteristics cannot be dealt with on a scheme-by-scheme basis. Instead they provide the context within which an ambient smell design project must operate. Take for example the city of Rotorua on New Zealand's North Island, famous for its geothermal activity and the odours emitted from its many geysers. To outsiders the smell of Rotorua, nicknamed 'Sulphur City' might be considered offensive and disagreeable, but this certainly does not deter the many thousands of visitors to the city every year. The odours of the hot springs are referred to fondly by many of the local people, contributing towards their feeling of home, just as the smell of manure may have similar associations for those who have lived or worked on farms.

As I write this section of the book I am in the city of Grenoble in the Rhône-Alpes region of France. The air is filled with the cold peaty smell of the mountains, one of my favourite smells. A colleague of mine described how, when she moved into the area, she tried for months to remove the odour from her apartment, since it combined with the old stone of the building in which she lives to create an odour she found fusty and disagreeable. However, as we have seen, such pervasive smells provide the base note of a city's smellscape and are characteristic of both city and site; they cannot be ignored. Although we become habituated and adapt to them over time, they still remain and we continue to detect them on a day-by-day basis as we emerge into the street from our apartments, or when we return to a city after some time away. Instead, such macro-level smellscapes, the backdrops to cities, should be acknowledged and worked with, whether they are considered in generally positive, negative or mixed terms.

The same is true with sound environments. A few years ago I visited Stockholm, the capital city of Sweden and while I was there I was taken to Mariatorget, a small public park situated in a square in the heart of the city, including manicured lawns, a fountain, carts serving food and drink and benches for people to sit and relax (see Figure 10.3). On three sides of the square were buildings, and on the remaining side a busy road. City designers were aware that the space served as an important location for workers from nearby office buildings to eat their lunch and relax for a while away from their desks, but the noise from the road was significant and certainly above the level that most people would find conducive to an al fresco picnic. In their long-term strategic plans, city designers might consider re-routing the road, encouraging people onto public transport and requiring vehicles to be regularly checked and emissions limited, and indeed all of these options have been explored in visions, master-planning and strategic plans in the city. However, what actions might be taken *now* to improve people's experiences of the square, given these limitations and challenges of the site?

Faced with these issues, the city's designers followed a pragmatic and experimental approach, commissioning Björn Hellström, an Associate Professor of Architecture and a practising sound artist, to design and introduce a sound installation for the site. The resulting scheme adopted a masking approach, introducing small sound speakers and piping more favourable sounds into the square. These included sounds such as water (emphasising the sounds of the fountain) and recordings of birds, each introduced with the aim of drowning out the sounds of the road. Similar schemes have been introduced into other cities, including a number of sonic gardens across Italian cities including Milan, Rome, Florence and Venice (see Licitra *et al.* 2011). However, these schemes go further by combining sound and visual elements, with the speakers also playing an ornamental role (see Figure 10.4).

Figure 10.3 Mariatorget, Stockholm, Sweden. Image by Holgar Ellgaard

Figure 10.4 Sound speakers in a sonic garden, Venice, Italy. ©architetturasonora

The design of urban smellscapes similarly requires attention to broader long-term strategic issues within a city in addition to those experienced at a neighbourhood or site-based level. Therefore, the model I have developed to assist built environment professionals in the process of designing urban smellscapes operates and is situated within a strategic, political and legislative framework (see Figure 10.5).

Air quality and odours of pollution, specifically those originating from traffic, operate in a similar manner to high levels of noise within the city; they are large-scale strategic issues which individuals feel powerless to resolve themselves, and therefore they assign responsibility to city leaders. International policies and environmental legislation provide guidance and targets aimed at reducing pollution and limiting harmful effects on human and environmental health in many countries. However, traffic levels continue to rise, key pollutant levels remain high and air pollution impacts in very real ways on everyday experiences of contemporary urban smellscapes. Traffic fumes are widely disliked, considered both unhealthy and of poor odour quality. Furthermore, such pollutants have the ability to impact on human olfactory function on both a temporary and permanent basis. However, all of these risks are accepted by people as one of the downsides of living in a city, to be traded off against more positive aspects of city life.

To improve the smellscapes of urban areas, air quality is therefore a key factor for consideration. In addition to policy initiatives aimed at reducing overall emission levels, built environment professionals can influence the frequency, location and potential concentration of exposure in the city. The sense of smell plays a key role in people's assessment of air quality within their locality (Bickerstaff and Walker 2001) and consequently, in exploring experiences of urban smellscapes in English cities it is possible to identify a number of ways to potentially remediate or limit the effects of emissions:

- *Manipulating wind and air flow:* Just as the built environmental form plays a role in influencing thermal and acoustic experiences of the city, it can also reduce odour concentrations, and have a freshening effect on the air surrounding busy roads.
- *Pedestrianisation:* These schemes reduce the detection of traffic pollutants in city centre cores, although traffic odours concentrate in those areas immediately surrounding pedestrianised zones as a result, impacting on perceptions of those areas.
- *Trees and planting:* These are considered to cleanse and freshen the air, a finding supported by a recent study from Pugh *et al.* (2012), although should be considered carefully as the effects of planting vary in different types of urban spaces. Trees and planting might also be perceived to mask traffic odours through the creation of a physical barrier, although

evidence from related studies of this 'barrier' influence has been inconclusive.

- *Parks and greenspaces:* These are also thought to cleanse the air, providing lungs for the city and an opportunity to escape into an immersive environment. However, opinions vary from city to city and according to pollution levels.
- *Water and waterways:* With the exception of waste water, water in all of its spatial forms – from large immersive canal environments through to small-scale water features and fountains – is perceived to freshen the air.
- *Vehicular stopping points, strategic location of traffic lights/bus stops/taxi ranks:* Any area in the city where vehicles wait with their engines running is potentially problematic. The strategic location of traffic lights, bus stops and taxi ranks can assist in reducing the frequency, strength and period of exposure of such encounters.

The processes of decision-making within any given city also have a huge influence on urban smellscapes, and provide a context within which any one scheme has to operate. Across developed nations this context exists primarily in the form of environmental legislation and guidance, as well as planning regulations which limit the amount, type and location of developments. For effective and locally appropriate odour-related decisions to be made, these two strands of legislation and guidance must work together. On the one hand, environmental guidance determines the categories and levels of potentially harmful emissions which can be released into an environment, while on the other hand, planning guidance separates odours from potentially sensitive receptors (i.e. people) through strategic land allocations, and devolves power to planners to decide what kinds of businesses are allowed to operate in different areas of the city. The focus of both of these legislative types is to exert control over potentially negative odour emissions for the benefit of the wider population, but in focusing on the negative odours they usually fail to take into account many locally significant and enjoyed odours. Here, city authorities would benefit from more positive strategic odour initiatives such as that initiated by the Japanese Ministry of the Environment, which consulted its communities in identifying 'One Hundred Sites of Good Fragrance' and incorporated these into its environmental policies (see Chapter 2).

Planning bodies guide and control the 'quality' of future development through area assessments, aesthetic decisions and urban design and master-planning work. City authorities can add to associated guidance which sets design styles relating to the look, size and location of different types of buildings and the locations of public spaces, to supplement the regulation of potential nuisance with a more positive approach to odour: '...if the council had a fragrance policy ... they could actually say we're doing this on purpose' (D09).

Such an approach might single out smell within a design guide for a city and clearly state the city's policy on olfactory matters. This might include a position on the city's macro-smellscape, recognising important contextual odours such as geographical features or meteorological conditions, as well as important and significant smells in and about the town. The determination of these odours would require city officials to consult with local communities and other key stakeholders, just as they would be advised to do so at a site-specific assessment and design stage. Guidelines should outline the city's position regarding neighbourhood disputes and odour complaints: does the city believe new or existing residents living close to a long-existing odour producer have a valid basis on which to complain about the odours it produces, and what limits might be set? How would the city assess the odours of existing or proposed odour-producing sources in the city? Does the city take into account benefits provided to the wider community by odour-producing sources, such as jobs, products, a local place to buy food or beverages, transport facilities or in design terms, local legibility, place identity or the simple enjoyment of the odour for its own sake?

Equally, a city might choose to incorporate such considerations throughout its wider strategic documents regarding all aesthetic guidance. After all, the sense of smell is merely one of the sensory modes through which we receive information, with all forms of sensory information working together to form an overall place perception, experience and identity. Should this approach be adopted, it remains important for city authorities to be clear to themselves, and to their stakeholders, what their positions are on all the factors outlined above, since without them opportunities are missed to protect significant features within the existing smellscape, and to explore possibilities to improve the urban smellscapes of the future.

In Grasse, the town leaders clearly have a plan, and unlike most towns or cities the plan includes the positive promotion of odour as an important aspect of everyday experiences of urban life. In some areas of the town, detailed attention is paid to the design and management of the smellscape, whereas in others, smell is less important in comparison with other aspects of environmental quality. In the following section I outline a process of urban smellscape design, and introduce tools to assist city leaders and built environment professionals in its implementation.

10.4 Urban smellscape design process and tools

As we have seen, designing urban smellscapes can be a complex business. It is also a relatively rare activity, given the primacy of vision in contemporary built environmental practice. As such, the introduction of a model highlighting different processes for undertaking urban smellscape design, and the identification of different tools for doing so, is helpful to guide these activities. The process I will outline includes four stages in urban smellscape design, as illustrated in Figure 10.5. These adhere to Tippett *et al.*'s (2007: 19) re-conceptualisation of different stages in the environmental and spatial planning process as part of an approach to sustainable development. Each of the four stages is discussed in further detail below, but the stages are inter-dependent, frequently requiring reference back to previous stages – for example, in seeking stakeholder input in the process of design development. Rather than acting as a standalone scheme, this process of urban smellscape design is intended to act as a cycle, informing the design and delivery of future schemes.

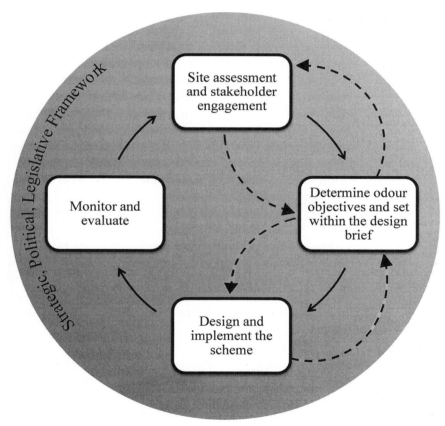

Figure 10.5 Processes of urban smellscape design

10.4.1 Site assessment and stakeholder engagement

Most urban site assessments, if carried out well with the inclusion of stakeholder engagement, will provide knowledge about which smells exist within any one place and over different points in time. Given the highly individual, social and cultural nature of odour perception and its relationship with place context, it is critical that urban smellscape design should be based on a sound understanding of locally significant odours and the varying perceptions that people hold in relation to them. A thorough smellscape assessment can be carried out as an activity separate from other sensory evaluations of site, for example as part of a scheme specifically aimed at improving the smellscape of a particular site. More frequently, it will be implemented in conjunction with other assessments of site as part of a multi-sensory evaluation, since it is only through such consideration that a truly synergistic sensory approach to urban design can be adopted.

Whether it is a standalone evaluation, or applied in conjunction with assessments of other sensory information, an olfactory evaluation of a site should realistically aim to achieve three key goals: provide an evaluation of the existing environment and related perceptions and experiences; examine the wider context of the area and historical odour references; and explore future smellscapes for the site through imagining exercises and linking into overall city master-planning and strategy work. Detailed desk research on the identified site will assist in providing contextual information via the review of official records and strategic documentation, such as air quality figures for the site, and a review of the popular media, including local and regional print and electronic media and blog-sites where different perceptions of the site might be highlighted. What is the history of the site? Does the site have any documented relationship with odour – is there a known odour-producing source in the area, or has there been one in the past? Where does the site fit and what role does it play within overall city strategic plans – is it a mixed use area, a primary retail site, a recreation space? What are the neighbouring sites and what role have they played, both historically in relation to the existing site and in the future imagineering of the city?

Early in this stage, built environment professionals will visit the site and undertake their own evaluations of the area and context. Out of the burgeoning field of sensory studies and design, some tools have already emerged to aid the recording of the smell characteristics of a site, in combination with perceptions through other sensory modes. Malnar and Vodvarka (2004), for example, feature smell as one aspect of their 'sensory slider' and suggest that odour has immediate, ambient or episodic qualities. The sensory slider provides an individual assessor with a tool for recording the strength of smells in an area as they perceive them, to identify whether these are characteristic of the space and to evaluate whether the odour is consistent or temporary. Lucas (2009, Lucas *et al.* 2009, Lucas & Romice 2010) introduced a Sensory Notation Tool (see Figure 10.6), which similarly considers the temporal characteristics of odour. This tool also facilitates an assessment of the priority placed on the different forms of sensory information detected within a site at the time of assessment. For example, if the sensory information gained through one specific sense is dominant, this would be recorded as a high existing priority, whereas a less dominant sense would be recorded as a low existing priority. This model follows traditions introduced by Gibson (1966) in combining smell and taste stimuli into the category of 'chemical stimuli'.

Each of these tools requires notation at one or more specific points of the site. While on sensory walks, I have therefore experimented with mobile methods of evaluating stimuli perceived through different sensory modes as one moves through spaces. Figure 10.7 illustrates one such evaluation I undertook in Doncaster in 2010, following a section of the route of the

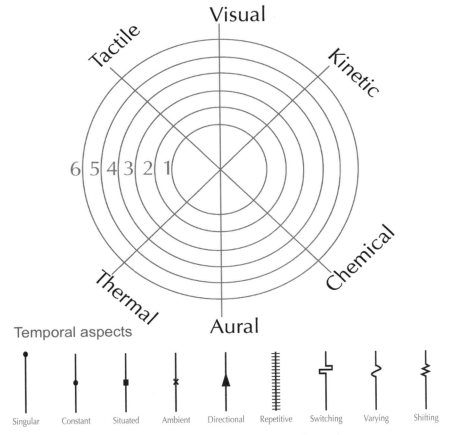

Figure 10.6 Sensory notation tool: radar diagram (Lucas *et al.* 2009)

qualitative sensory walks. This method, although useful in evaluating sensescapes at specific points in time and from the perception of one person or the consensus of a group of individuals, is too simplistic a tool to be used in isolation in assessing smell and sensory environments for wider design purposes. It fails to capture the complexity of olfactory perception and difference, presenting an impression of uniformity and lacking contextual and historical factors of influence. Nevertheless, this method does provide insights into relationships between different senses and has the potential to provide a simple and user-friendly tool by which built environment professionals might start to make steps towards site assessments of sensory experiences, including smell.

Because of the variations that exist between people's individual perceptions of urban smellscapes and the different smells within them, it is important to involve a broad range of stakeholders and potential users in on-site assessments. If the site is public urban space and is therefore serving a broad range of populations, the site assessment should ideally include people from different age groups, genders, classes and ethnicities, as well as those with different smoking habits. The people responsible for organising stakeholder engagement might also target special interest groups such as people with respiratory illnesses, or complainants regarding odours within a particular area. Smellwalking provides one method which can be used by professionals when evaluating olfactory components of different areas or neighbourhoods within a city. Additionally, this technique might be used on a site-by-site basis, acting in a similar manner to other established site evaluation techniques such as Enquiry by Design and Planning for Real. Each of these techniques bring different stakeholders together, using maps, models and signs in different ways to encourage people to identify their specific perceptions, concerns or aspirations for particular areas. Different techniques for involving stakeholders in planning and design processes are outlined and critiqued in detail by Tippett *et al.* (2007).

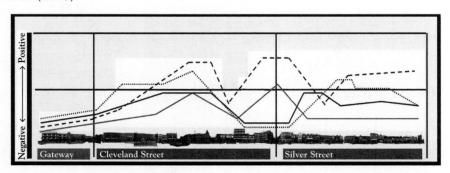

····· Sound aesthetics — Olfactory aesthetics − − Visual aesthetics —Textures/materials

Figure 10.7 Sensory experience ratings across site, Doncaster

People's pre-conceptions of the smells of any one particular site can be limited if they are drawing from memory rather than being stimulated by on-site assessments, an effect that was highlighted in pre-walk perceptions of urban environments. Although such pre-conceptions are revealing in their own way because they illustrate people's expectations of different sites, recollections of urban smellscapes should not be considered reliable or comprehensive. In-situ assessments more accurately reflect on-site experiences, providing the opportunity for detection and immediate perceptions to inform assessments. Stakeholders should be encouraged to visit the site, either as individuals or on a group basis, and asked to record the smells they detect and what they think about them. Following the site visit, stakeholders should gather together and mark the smells they detected on a plan. They could identify the potential source of odours on the plan using either words or images, and highlight whether they enjoyed the odours or not using words or numbers in a rating system, such as the place liking system I used while smellwalking (see Chapter 4). Stakeholders might be encouraged to talk about their experiences and negotiate with other stakeholders regarding priorities for future development on the site. An interesting example of site-based assessments involving the senses includes the method developed by Thwaites and Simkins (2007, 2010) in their work on experiential landscapes. According to this method, stakeholders are asked to evaluate sites as they stand currently, and to highlight aspirations for the future by identifying what is 'theirs', 'ours' and 'mine'.

New technologies also offer increasing opportunities for gathering site-related information and facilitating debate between different sectors of the community. In encouraging the participation of stakeholders in assessments of sites, built environment professionals are better placed to develop meaningful odour objectives situated within the context of specific sites or places.

10.4.2 Determine the odour objectives and set within the design brief

The development of meaningful odour objectives and their incorporation into a design brief is highly dependent on insights gained from site evaluation and stakeholder engagement activities. Perceptual and contextual information gained through inclusive site assessments should identify which odours are particularly meaningful, appropriate and acceptable to local communities and area users within any given place. They should assist in protecting or enhancing place identity through future urban smellscape design and management activities, guide decision-making regarding local sensitivities to odour, and go some way in alleviating concerns about olfactory manipulation.

Consequently, built environment professionals can work in continued collaboration with local stakeholders to develop objectives which complement and support the delivery of wider aims for a scheme or environmental initiative, without destroying the local sense of place. For example, this might include the enhancement of a restorative environment within which people might relax, the acknowledgement of smell as a signpost for activities in a multi-cultural neighbourhood where independent businesses operate, or sympathetic measures aimed at protecting existing historic area characteristics and components. The identification of odour-related design objectives thus provides additional means for communicating and agreeing aspirations and facilitating planning and design work.

10.4.3 Design and implement the scheme

Following the incorporation of meaningful odour objectives into an overall design brief, built environment professionals are faced with the challenge of planning and turning designs into reality. This challenge should not be underestimated because it represents a change in thinking from more traditional approaches on behalf of the designer. When we think about the issues presented by the adaptation and habituation characteristics of the sense of smell, we can begin to appreciate the rationale behind plug-in air fresheners which switch between three different scents every fifteen to twenty minutes so the odours can be detected by customers in their homes. The same challenges are presented when designing in the urban environment, and should inform decisions made by a design team throughout the design's development and implementation.

In her work in France exploring experiences of indoor smellscapes, Suzel Balez offers useful tools to start thinking about smell design from a fresh new perspective. Balez (2001) carried out smellwalks similar to those I have undertaken, but within the enclosed environment of a shopping mall. From people's perceptions of odour, she identified a range of thirty-two odour 'effects' associated with smellscape experience and design; see Balez (2002) for a summary of all of her identified odour effects. Effects ranged from those focused on the characteristics of the sense of smell and quality of the air, through to the behaviours and judgements made by people following odour perception. Of particular interest are Balez's odour effects relating to environmental characteristics and air movement, which I have drawn from below, and in some cases adapted.

The history and nature of a site will feed into people's expectations of the smellscape of that area. This also translates into design terms, creating an *Anticipation effect* prior to arrival on site. Designers might consider using other sensory means of enhancing this effect prior to arrival, through the use of creative signage, related sounds or a trail of textures or patterns on the floor. An *Entrance effect* can be considered as people arrive in a space; in olfactory terms this might relate to specific types of odour in particular entrances and exits to a space. The point of arrival in some sites might be clearly defined if the space serves a specific purpose. However, more often than not, there will be a multitude of arrival points in a space with these same points also serving as exit points, thus providing a simultaneous *Departure effect*. Different priorities or characteristics might be placed at different arrival points to determine the approach to odour in those areas. Additionally, a *Transition effect* occurs as people move both into a specific area and through it. This effect focuses on the perspective of the person detecting the odours, rather than the sources emitting them in the form of body odour or perfumes etc. If a person has moved from a very different type of area into the site being designed, then their smell receptors are likely to be more alert and open to new odour types. However, if the smells are very similar within the designed site as in the surrounding areas, then the smellscape might easily pass unnoticed, which itself might be an odour objective in some schemes.

Within the site area, the movement of people, air and objects throughout the space impacts significantly on the resulting smellscape. Not only will each of these factors carry their own odours, such as perfumes, cigarette smoke or odours from other areas, but they can also stir up the odours present, creating a *Wake effect* behind them which can be detected by others. If the air is still it might have a *Static effect* on an odour, but air movement could provide a *Neutralising effect* whereby odours are diluted to a concentration below human detection thresholds. Air movements might also create a *Diffusion effect*, reducing concentrations over time and potentially moving from a fixed to a wider location. Odours can have a *Flooding effect*, dominating an area smellscape either in part or as a whole, and an *Impregnation effect*, where they attach to other items or materials either in or moving through the space, such as might be the case when walking through cigarette smoke in an enclosed area. As odours are emitted they might create a *Burst effect*, where they release in short sharp emissions, or they might gradually build or fade in *Crescendo* or *Decrescendo effects*. Smells might also be specifically identifiable as belonging to a particular place, whether as an individual odour or as a mix, recognisable by odour quality or strength and thus creating a smellmark. This might be termed an *Iconic effect*.

These effects can be used by designers as techniques for planning the spatial implications of different olfactory components of urban smellscapes. The analysis also offers a range of terms by which designers can express their intentions, and these can be applied and adapted across design schemes according to the odour objectives and the nature of odour source(s). In fact, here it is important to return to odour source, since the odour effects provide us with techniques and related language for structuring and planning our ideas, but the smellscape of any given place is determined by the smell ingredients themselves as they combine with other environmental factors, and are then perceived by people.

Designers can draw from the knowledge gained through site assessment and stakeholder engagement, and should also pay attention to local area odour sensitivity levels and area type in selecting and implementing their design effects. In doing so, they might consider issues and techniques relating to the spatial and temporal *Separation* of odours, reviewing the separation or combination of odours according to source as a means of delivering desired odour effects. Existing and future *Deodorisation* processes on the site can be reviewed, with decisions made as to whether these should be enhanced, reduced, retained or targeted at specific areas within a site footprint, such as the regular cleaning of alleyways or stairwells. Designers can interrogate any *Masking* effects in operation on the site, such as the detection of traffic emissions, and consider actions to remediate the effects. Finally, designers can review the use of existing *Scenting* on the site, or consider the possible introduction of new smells into a site depending on the scheme objectives. If a scenting approach is found to be appropriate, then designers will need to specify the nature of those odours. They may consider introducing vegetation as scenting into a scheme, or work towards attracting particular businesses to an area such as introducing street vendors selling food, beverages or products.

As with wider sustainable design practices, the design of urban smellscapes requires designers to think about the ongoing maintenance of sites in addition to the delivery of a physical scheme on day one. If the smell components grow, do they require pruning and watering? What are the ongoing implications of cleaning regimes in particular areas? Has provision been made for the replacement of cigarette disposal units on walls if these are regularly vandalised? In cases where synthetic scents are utilised, how will these be emitted on site? Will related equipment require maintenance? Will scents need replacing or changing?

It is worth noting that smell design, whether related to outdoor urban environments, indoor spaces or large-scale leisure attractions, remains in its infancy when compared with other forms of design such as visual design and urban soundscape design. Technologies are starting to emerge, such as those facilitating the scenting of bus-stops in some towns and cities, but these do not yet operate to the same degree of sophistication as for the other senses. However, we are in the midst of change, and I predict that it will not be long before technologies are available to support designers of urban smellscapes in creating experimental smell environments. Careful attention will need to be paid in a number of areas, particularly the balance between odour ingredients with existing relationships to place, such as vegetation, materials, foods and geographical features, the fluid and changing nature of these places, such as culturally specific odours associated with new immigrants to an area, and the risk of local smellscapes being overlaid with synthetic odours extracted from elsewhere.

10.4.4 Monitor and evaluate

Expanded supply creates expanded demand, which in turn feeds even more supply. Over time, people learn. They discover more about what's aesthetically possible and more about what they like. Exposure changes tastes. (Postrel 2003: 55)

In her review of the relationship between contemporary aesthetic design, society and the marketplace, Virginia Postrel highlights a 'ratchet' effect that occurs when individuals are exposed to new products, people, places and ideas. This phenomenon relates to urban smellscape design in many ways, not least regarding the acceptability of the idea that smell might be worthy of incorporation into the everyday practices of built environment professionals. Examples of the direct consideration of smell as a potential positive contributor towards urban environmental experience remain few and far between. Even though the perfumed fountains of Grasse would not be to everyone's taste, they at least provide an example from which people might begin to think more proactively about smell in their cities. The implementation, monitoring and promotion of additional schemes will assist in normalising urban smellscape design as an important component of wider urban design practices.

However, the ratchet effect also presents a potential danger in that just as people become used to more and more technologies surrounding them, they might also demand more and more detailed urban smellscape design and control. This could go one of two contrasting ways: on the one hand, it might result in an increase in the introduction of synthetic scents into an environment, risking the exclusion of some people such as those with respiratory illnesses, other health issues or sensitivities. On the other hand, however, in placing a spotlight on olfactory control practices it might encourage the further deodorisation of environments such as is currently demanded in parts of Canada and the US where environmental sensitivities are common. In short, the rise in environmental sensitivities acts as evidence of the ratchet effect at work, with a demand for increasingly hygienic environments leading to more people demanding scent-free environments. On a more positive note, an increasing demand for urban smellscape design will also drive the development of new technologies and knowledge to assist scheme implementation, providing wider options for delivering and managing smell in the future.

The practical delivery of projects which consider, and on occasion experiment with, odour are therefore important in furthering knowledge and understanding regarding the design and implementation of urban smellscapes, and also in monitoring their wider effects on the physiological and psychological well-being of city inhabitants. Where feasible, this should include the collection of data in qualitative and quantitative forms. Evaluations will be most useful if data can be collected or is available before schemes are delivered, to facilitate rigorous investigation into the wider effects and implications of a scheme. Lessons learnt should be shared at a city-wide level and beyond. For example, a potential role for odour in restorative environmental experiences was highlighted in Chapter 8, and it is only through further work, including post-scheme monitoring and broader evaluation, that a deeper understanding will be gained of the role of odour in bodily restoration.

It is also important that post-scheme evaluation should be carried out for the practical purposes of exploring whether olfactory objectives have been delivered, producing environments that better meet the needs and requirements of the local stakeholders and users of the area, as anticipated at the design stage.

10.5 Conclusion

We already know that smells play an important role in urban place perception, influencing how people perceive areas, and interacting with place-based expectations. In investigating the relationship and contribution of smell towards place, as well as thinking about what it means to design with smell, we reveal compelling ideas regarding place and odour authenticity and identify some misapprehensions about smell design as manipulative, underpinned by fears that odours might override rational thought and decision making. In exploring the evidence regarding the ability of odours to influence our emotional state, it becomes apparent that the sense of smell cannot ambush and bypass our rational thought to make us do something we would not want to do; rather, it can enhance our experiences of places in complex ways.

However, smell perception is conflicted, and for this reason urban smellscape design must include the views of other people beyond those of the immediate design team. Ideally, the design process should include a range of smell perceptions of site gained from a wide variety of stakeholders, particularly if the area being designed is public space. The process of urban smellscape design described above provides a way of structuring such design activities, and identifies a range of different techniques and tools from which designers might draw, adapting them into their existing practices. In doing so, they will be better equipped to avoid the unintentional removal, replacement or overlaying of local odours with others of little local significance, meaning or potential to provide enjoyment and delight.

11

Conclusion

...you go to London and you've got the bustle, which is visual, spatial ... then you've got the smell of the people with the food ... the noise and there's the music blurting out ... and the traffic as well ... the smell is part of that buzz, that activity, without smell it's not quite as strong. (D09)

The sense of smell is playing an ever more important role in the design of products, services and commercial environments, and odours are destined to spill out into city streets in the form of commercial scenting activities at an increasing rate over the years to come. During the past twelve months alone a minimum of three UK-wide outdoor scented bus-stop campaigns have been reported in the British media, and the trend looks set to continue here and across geographical and public/private boundaries. Harold Vogt, President of the US-based Scent Marketing Institute, reported that commercial scenting practices were already worth $100 million in 2008, and he predicted that the industry would increase to a value of $1 billion within a decade (in Herz 2008).

However, existing urban smellscapes are not blank canvasses on which scenting campaigns may be applied. Towns and cities and the areas within them in some circumstances conform to urban stereotypes, containing odours of pollution, waste and greasy fast-food, but they simultaneously play host to other more positively perceived odours such as those of vegetation, food, beverages and markets. Cities certainly are not sterile and static environments from which odour has been removed as a combined effect of olfactory control processes and design, but rather places where a variety of odours can be found. Most of these odours are not unique to specific places, neighbourhoods or cities, but can be detected in cities around the world. However, they frequently combine in unique ways and strengths to create odours which can become associated with specific locales. I would also go a step further here and extend this idea of a unique combination to include stimuli gained through other sensory modes. Odours of place might be conceptualised as similar to the ingredients included in a perfume. Imagine a perfume with twenty different ingredients. Others might attempt to duplicate that perfume using exactly the same ingredients, but they would fail to do so if they included incorrect amounts of each. The same is true of urban smellscapes. Different odours combine and are detected by our smell receptors in a unique pattern, which is recognised by our brain and associated with a specific place. Sometimes we might visualise different colours or sights which accompany memories of a specific place, person or object; sometimes we can almost feel the warmth of the sun on our bodies or the cold of the winter air, taste a particular foodstuff, or hear a song, depending upon our wider sensory recollections of that place. However, it is the smell which is stubbornly retained in our memories over long periods of time, allowing us to access and revisit the memory at a later date or to mourn the passing of the smell if it is wiped away for one reason or another. As Ascherson (2007) recalls nostalgically:

> [East Germany] vanished from the atlas in 1990 … yet it did have its own authentic scent, a spicy reek brewed out of People's Cleaning Fluid, two-stroke petrol, brown-coal briquettes and cheap police tobacco … how can I accept that I will never again breathe that whiff which said: You are entering 'Stasiland', and nowhere else on earth? Can a republic of seventeen million people, three hundred thousand secret policemen or informers and five million personal files melt away without leaving even a tang in the air?

Such olfactory memories are autobiographical, significant of who we are, the places we have lived, loved and visited, and the people we have met along the way. If we are habituated to the odour of a particular place we encounter in our everyday lives we might not even notice it, unless we return to that place to find its odour changed. Although the sense of smell therefore presents challenges, requiring city leaders and built environment professionals to adapt their approach and practice to managing and designing urban smellscapes, it also generates fresh opportunities to protect meaningful odour sources, acknowledge and work with existing smellscapes, and, where appropriate, to challenge or delight the people who occupy them.

In *Urban Smellscapes* we have examined experiences and perceptions of smell in English cities and beyond, and have encountered olfactory elements of the built environment from the ridiculous to the sublime, ranging from paid-for smoking cubicles and stinky bins to smell-emitting bus-stops, from scented car-parks and perfumed fountains to pop-up urinals. If people believe smell to be completely disregarded in existing urban management and design practices, they are mistaken. Urban smellscapes are not static or in decline; rather, they are constantly shifting.

A wide variety of factors shape urban smellscapes, many of which do not come about as directly targeted and planned odour management or design activities, but as olfactory hangovers, temporal, spatial and cultural, from other activities. Urban and health policies – for instance, changes in licensing laws, the promotion of the evening economy, the closure of public toilets and the criminalisation of smoking in enclosed public places – all have an impact on urban smellscapes, changing the location and concentration of existing odours such as cigarette smoke, litter, spilt alcohol, vomit and urine. In response, odour control regimes are frequently applied in the form of separation, deodorisation, masking and scenting activities. These processes are used in attempts to remove, limit and hide some odours and introduce others in their place. However, given the observed differences between people's perceptions of which odours are 'fragrant' and which ones 'stink', these practices can at times be based on dubious assumptions regarding the odours that should be removed or added. Even disliked odours have the potential to contribute towards some positive aspects of urban design such as city legibility, and if positive smells are detected in incongruent areas they can impact negatively upon place experience. As a result, any efforts made by designers to simply remove negatively perceived smells and replace them with more positive ones raise important questions about whose perception is considered as part of the process. Furthermore, such an approach is also likely to reduce the variety and unique quality of many urban smellscapes, potentially reducing place experience and perception as well.

When I started out on my olfactory journey of discovery in cities around the world, I was concerned that in singling out experiences of smellscapes, I was creating an unnatural separation between odour and other aspects of sensory experience, in much the same way that many design disciplines are accused of prioritising visual aspects of cities above those gained through other sensory modes. I sought counsel from some of my esteemed colleagues, who quite rightly pointed out that in order to gain a full and detailed knowledge of bodily experiences of cities, it is necessary to both understand the unique qualities and challenges of perception gained through each of the senses, and to understand how these relate to one another. Brown (2011:13) similarly wrestles with these issues in his work on urban soundscapes. He explains: 'While experts tend to dissect environments into their component parts, the reality is that people's experience is of the whole of their environment.'

A good deal of work has been undertaken on visual characteristics of cities, although new and interesting research continues to emerge relating to the use of lighting and colour in the city. Indeed, some years ago, Charles Landry's work on colour inspired me to find out more about sensory environments (see Landry 2006, 2008). The study of acoustics has provided an established disciplinary platform from which an increasingly sophisticated body of research on urban soundscape experience and design has been carried out, with many fascinating experimental schemes now implemented in cities around the world (see Axelsson 2011). Linking into the discipline of acoustics, experiences of vibration in the environment have also come under scrutiny with a primary focus on environmental annoyance. Although the majority of these studies have adopted a quantitative approach by measuring vibration and attempting to establish correspondence with annoyance ratings, other detailed qualitative studies on vibration are now materialising, such as the work by Condie and Brown (2009). Research and projects with a focus upon thermal experiences or 'comfort' in indoor and outdoor space have been placed under the spotlight as a result of concerns regarding energy consumption and conservation, alongside issues of global climate change and urban heat islands in outdoor environments; for example, see Nikolopoulou (2003, 2004), Nikolopoulou *et al.* (2001) and Nikolopoulou and Lykoudis (2007).

However, as I noted at the beginning of this book, knowledge of urban smellscape experience and design has been limited to a small number of studies, with more published in French than English. Although I have drawn from studies referencing smell from other perspectives, such as assessments of air quality like those of Bickerstaff and Walker (2001, 2003) or smell as one aspect of twenty-four-hour city experiences (Adams *et al.* 2009), there is clearly a dearth of literature aimed at supporting the transition from theory to practice. It is this deficit that I have sought to tackle in *Urban Smellscapes*, informing and guiding built environment professionals around the problems and opportunities presented by smell design in the city. In doing so, it has been necessary to draw from research across a number of disciplines and well established bodies of work, such as those of restorative environments or stakeholder engagement in environmental design. I have explored experiences of urban smellscapes to identify processes of olfactory control and outline tools of use in structuring the development, design and delivery of urban smellscape schemes. Until further projects are delivered in strategies on the ground that specifically include or target smell within their objectives, it is difficult to provide more detailed guidance. Therefore, at this final stage I must acknowledge that a number of unanswered questions remain such as what different sensory profiles might we expect to encounter in different types of urban space, and how might these vary according to the various cities and nations in which they are detected?

However, of some things I am certain. First, smell does have a role to play in urban environmental experience, perceptions and place identity, and it should be considered in wider urban design and city management practices. Second, odours are perceived very differently by different people, and those with responsibility for delivering smellscapes in the city should seek to understand relationships between odour and site where feasible and certainly prior to the implementation of new schemes and projects in an area. Finally, the urban smellscape is but one sensory aspect of place experience, and therefore design schemes need to pay attention to smell and its interactions with other forms of sensory information, such as the sounds, textures, sights, temperature and tastes of an area, in designing more humanistic places for the future.

Glossary

Adaptation	The reduced ability of smell receptors to detect an odour following initial exposure
Anosmia	A temporary or permanent lack of a sense of smell
Anosmic	A person lacking a sense of smell
AQMA	Air Quality Monitoring Area
BME	Black Minority Ethnic
Built environment professionals	City managers, planners, architects, urban designers, engineers and environmental health officers
Chemical senses	A term used to describe the senses of taste and smell, and occasionally also touch
DEFRA	Department for the Environment, Food and Rural Affairs (England)
DMBC	Doncaster Metropolitan Borough Council
EPSRC	Engineering and Physical Sciences Research Council
Habituation	An adjustment to a familiar odour based on an unconscious judgement that it is of no significance and can be ignored
Haptic	Relates to the sense of touch, and therefore includes those aspects of the environment that can be sensed through touch (including vibration and temperature)
Olfactory	The physical odour perception system, and smell-related aspects or characteristics of objects or people
ONS	Office of National Statistics (UK)
PM_{10}	Particulate Matter (with the number used to describe particles of 10 micrometres or less)
Sensitivity	The individual response (physical, emotional and behavioural) following odour perception with respect to both positive and negative effects
Smell receptors	Receptors linking to the olfactory nerve, providing the primary route for odour detection
Smell perception	Includes both the detection and mental processing of odours
Smellmark	The olfactory equivalent of a landmark or soundmark. An odour that has distinctive meaning within a specific environmental context
Smellscape	The total smell landscape, including individual odours, odours that have mixed, and the overall background odour

Trigeminal   The sensation nerve in the face. Olfactory nerve
                                    endings on the trigeminal nerve can detect even low
                                    concentrations of some odours, producing bodily
                                    sensations
VOCs   Volatile Organic Compounds

References

Adams, M., Moore, G., Cox, T.J., Croxford, B., Refaee, M., and Sharples, S. (2007) 'The 24-Hour City: Residents' Sensorial Experiences', *The Senses and Society*, 02 (2): 201–215.

Adams, M.D. and Askins, K. (2009) *Sensewalking: Sensory Walking Methods for Social Scientists*, available at: http://www.iaps-association.org/blog/2008/12/19/sensewalking-sensory-walking-methods-for-social-scientists/ (accessed 11 May 2013).

Adams, M.D., Cox, T.J., Croxford, B., Moore, G., Sharples, S., and Rafaee, M. (2009) 'The Sensory City', in R. Cooper, G.W. Evans and C. Boyko (eds), *Designing Sustainable Cities*, Chichester: Wiley-Blackwell.

Aggleton, J.P. and Waskett, L. (1999) 'The Ability of Odours to Serve as State-Dependent Cues for Real-World Memories: Can Viking Smells Aid the Recall of Viking Experiences?', *British Journal of Psychology*, 90 (1): 1–7.

Ascherson, N. (2007) 'Beware, the Walls have Ears', London: *The Observer*.

ASEAN (2008) *The ASEAN Charter*, The ASEAN Secretariat, Jakarta, Indonesia (First published December 2007).

Atkinson, R. (2003) 'Domestication by Cappuccino or a Revenge on Urban Space? Control and Empowerment in the Management of Public Spaces', *Urban Studies*, 40 (9): 1829–1843.

Axelsson, Ö. (ed.). (2011) *Designing Soundscape for Sustainable Urban Development*, Stockholm, Sweden, available online: http://www.decorumcommunications.se/pdf/designing-soundscape-for-sustainable-urban-development.pdf

Barbara, A. and Perliss, A. (2006) *Invisible Architecture – Experiencing Places through the Sense of Smell*, Milan: Skira.

Balez, S. (2001) *Characterisation of an Existing Building according to Olfactory Parameters*, PhD Thesis, The Graduate School of Architecture, Grenoble, France.

Balez, S. (2002) *Characterisation of an Existing Building According to Olfactory Parameters*, The Graduate School of Architecture, Grenoble, France.

Baron, R.A. (1983) 'The Sweet Smell of Success? The Impact of Pleasant Artificial Scents on Evaluation of Job Applicants', *Journal of Applied Psychology*, 68: 709–713.

Baron, R.A. (1997) 'The Sweet Smell of Helping: Effects of Pleasant Ambient Fragrance on Prosocial Behavior in Shopping Malls', *Personality and Social Psychology Bulletin*, 23: 498–503.

Baumbach, G., Vogt, U., Hein, K.R.G., Oluwole, A.F., Ogunsola, O.J., Olaniyi, H.B. and Akeredolu, F.A. (1995) 'Air Pollution in a Large Tropical City with a High Traffic Density: Results of Measurements in Lagos, Nigeria', *Science of the Total Environment*, 169 (1–3): 25–31.

BBC (2002) 'Smoking Ban on Tokyo's Streets', available at: http://news.bbc.co.uk/1/hi/world/asia-pacific/2292007.stm (accessed 28 March 2011).

BBC (2004) 'History of Manchester's Chinatown', Manchester, available at: http://www. bbc.co.uk/manchester/chinatown/2004/01/history.shtml (accessed 3 August 2010).

BBC (2007a) 'Chinese Sniffers to Hunt Fumes', BBC News World (20 June).

BBC (2007b) 'New Yorkers Puzzled by Smell', available at: http://news.bbc.co.uk/1/hi/ world/americas/6243165.stm (accessed 29 April 2008).

BBC (2008a) 'What Does the Stink Smell Of?' News Broadcast, UK, available at: http:// news.bbc.co.uk/1/hi/uk/7355574.stm (accessed 23 April 2008).

BBC (2008b) 'Unintended Consequences of the Smoking Ban', BBC News, available at: http://news.bbc.co.uk/1/hi/magazine/7483057.stm (accessed 3 July 2008).

BBC (2009) 'NCPs to come up Smelling of Roses', available at: http://news.bbc.co.uk/1/hi/ uk/7967251.stm (accessed 21 April 2009).

BBC (2011a) 'Are Public Toilets Going Down the Pan?' London (9 March).

BBC (2011b) 'Tetley's Closes Leeds Brewery Landmark', available at: http://www.bbc.co. uk/news/uk-england-leeds-13768975 (accessed 13 July 2011).

BBC Radio 4 (2009) 'Who Knows What The Dog's Nose Knows?' London, available at: http://www.bbc.co.uk/pressoffice/proginfo/radio/2009/wk5/tue.shtml (accessed 3 February 2009).

Bell, D. (1996) *The Cultural Contradictions of Gratification*, 2nd edn, New York: Basic Books.

Bell, D. (2008) 'Two Views of Outside in British City Centres', *Urban Design* 108: 24–27.

Bendix, J. (2000) 'A Fog Monitoring Scheme Based on MSG Data', presented at *The First MSG RAO Workshop*, CNR, Bologna, Italy: European Space Agency.

Bentley, I., Alcock, A., Murrain, P., McGlynn, S. and Smith, G. (eds) (1985) *Responsive Environments*, Oxford: Architectural Press.

Berrigan, C. (2006) '*The Smelling Committee*', New York, available at: http://membrana.us/ smellingcommittee.html# (accessed 12 July 2008).

Bhaumik, S. (2007) 'Oxygen Supplies for India Police', *BBC World News*, available at: http://news.bbc.co.uk/1/hi/world/south_asia/6665803.stm (accessed 12 August 2012).

Bichard, J.A. and Hanson, J. (2009) 'Inclusive Design of 'Away from Home' Toilets', in R. Cooper, G.W. Evans and C. Boyko (eds), *Designing Sustainable Environments*, Chichester: Wiley-Blackwell.

Bickerstaff, K. (2004) 'Risk Perception Research: Socio-Cultural Perspectives on the Public Experience of Air Pollution', *Environment International*, 30 (6): 827–840.

Bickerstaff, K. and Walker, G. (2001) 'Public Understandings of Air Pollution: The Localisation of Environmental Risk', *Global Environmental Change*, 11 (2): 133–145.

Bickerstaff, K. and Walker, G. (2003) 'The Place(s) of Matter: Matter Out of Place – Public Understandings of Air Pollution', *Progress in Human Geography*, 27 (1): 45–67.

Blackett, M. (2007) 'The Smells of Toronto', in *Spacing Toronto – Understanding the Urban Landscape*, Toronto, available at: http://spacing.ca/wire/2007/11/29/the-smells-of-toronto/ (accessed 6 June 2008).

Bokowa, A.H. (2010) 'Review of Odour Legislation', *Chemical Engineering Transactions*, 23: 31–36.

Bonnes, M., Uzzell, D., Carrus, G. and Kelay, T. (2007) 'Inhabitants' and Experts' Assessments of Environmental Quality for Urban Sustainability', *Journal of Social Issues*, 63 (1): 59–78.

Booth, R. and Carrell, S. (2010) 'Iceland Volcano: First Came the Floods, then the Smell of Rotten Eggs', London: *The Guardian*.

Boring, E.G. (1942) *Sensation and Perception in the History of Experimental Psychology*, New York: Appleton-Century.

Bouchard, N. (2013) *Le Théâtre de la Mémoire Olfactive: le Pouvoir des Odeurs à Modeler notre Perception Spatio-temporelle de l'Environnement*, unpublished thesis, Université de Montréal, Canada.

Bristow, M. (2012) 'Beijing Sets 'Two Flies Only' Public Toilet Guidelines', BBC News (23 May).

Brody, S.D., Peck, B.M. and Highfield, W.E. (2004) 'Examining Localized Patterns of Air Quality Perception in Texas: A Spatial and Statistical Analysis', *Risk Analysis*, 24 (6): 1561–1574.

Brown, L. (2011) 'Acoustic Design of Outdoor Space', in Ö. Axelsson (ed.), *Designing Soundscape for Sustainable Urban Development*, Stockholm, Sweden: 13–16, available at: http://www.decorumcommunications.se/pdf/designing-soundscape-for-sustainable-urban-development.pdf

Buck, L. and Axel, R. (1991) 'A Novel Multigene Family may Encode Odorant Receptors: A Molecular Basis for Odor Recognition', *Cell*, 65: 175–187.

Burr, D. and Alais, D. (2006) 'Combining Visual and Auditory Information', in S. Martinez-Conde, L.M. Martinez, P.U. Tse, S. Macknik and J.M. Alonso, (eds), *Visual Perception Part 2: Fundamentals of Awareness, Multi-Sensory Integration and High-Order Perception*, Oxford: Elsevier Science & Technology.

Burrows, E., Wallace, M. and Wallace, M.L. (1999) *Gotham: A History of New York City to 1898*, Oxford: Oxford University Press.

Cain, W.S. (1982) 'Odor Identification by Males and Females: Predictions vs. Performance', *Chemical Senses*, 7: 129–142.

Cain, W.S. and Drexler, M. (1974) 'Scope and Evaluation of Odor Counteraction and Masking', *Annals of the New York Academy of Sciences*, 237 (1): 427–439.

California Healthy Nail Salon Collaborative (2010) *Framing a Proactive Research Agenda to Advance Worker Health and Safety in the Nail Salon and Cosmetology Communities – Research Convening Report*, available at: http://saloncollaborative.files.wordpress.com/2009/03/collab_researchrpt_final.pdf (accessed 16 January 2013).

Carmona, M., Heath, T., Oc, T. and Tiesdell, S. (2003) *Public Places – Urban Spaces: The Dimensions of Urban Design*, Oxford: Architectural Press.

Carolan, M.S. (2008) 'When Good Smells Go Bad: A Sociohistorical Understanding of Agricultural Odor Pollution', *Environment and Planning A*, 40: 1235–1249.

Cavalini, P.M., Koeter-Kemmerling, L.G. and Pulles, M.P.J. (1991) 'Coping with Odour Annoyance and Odour Concentrations: Three field studies', *Journal of Environmental Psychology*, 11 (2): 123–142.

Chan, S. (2007) 'A Rotten Smell Raises Alarms and Questions', New York: *New York Times*, available at: http://www.nytimes.com/2007/01/09/nyregion/09smell.html?scp=4&sq=Good%20Smell%20Vanishes&st=cse (accessed 12 July 2008).

Chang, C.Y., Hammitt, W.E., Chen, P.K., Machnik, L. and Su, W.C. (2008) 'Psychophysiological Responses and Restorative Values of Natural Environments in Taiwan', *Landscape and Urban Planning*, 85 (2): 79–84.

Cheremisinoff, P. (1995) 'Work Area Hazards', in *Encyclopedia of Environmental Control Technology*, Oxford: Butterworth-Heinemann.

Chiesura, A. (2004) 'The Role of Urban Parks for the Sustainable City', *Landscape and Urban Planning*, 68 (1): 129–138.

Chiquetto, S. and Mackett, R. (1995) 'Modelling the Effects of Transport Policies on Air Pollution', *Science of the Total Environment*, 169 (1–3): 265–271.

Christiansen, F. (2003) *Chinatown, Europe: An Exploration of Overseas Chinese Identity in the 1990s*, London: Routledge.

Chudler, E.H. (2010) *Amazing Animal Senses*, available at: http://faculty.washington.edu/chudler/amaze.html (accessed 16 January 2013).

City of Montreal (1978) By-law No. 44: Air Purification.

Classen, C. (1993) *Worlds of Sense: Exploring the Senses in History and Across Cultures*, London: Routledge.

Classen, C. (1999) 'Other Ways to Wisdom: Learning through the Senses across Cultures', *International Review of Education*, 45 (3/4): 269–280.

Classen, C. (2001) 'The Senses', in P. Stearns (ed.), *Encyclopedia of European Social History*, New York: Charles Scribner's Sons.

Classen, C. (2005a) 'The Sensuous City: Urban Sensations from the Middle Ages to Modernity', in *Sensing the City: Sensuous Explorations of the Urban Landscape*. Montréal: Canadian Centre for Architecture.

Classen, C. (2005b) 'The Witch's Senses – Sensory Ideologies and Transgressive Femininities from the Renaissance to Modernity', in D. Howes (ed.), *Empire of the Senses – The Sensual Culture Reader*, Oxford: Berg.

Classen, C., Howes, D. and Synnott, A. (1994) *Aroma – The Cultural History of Smell*, New York: Routledge.

Cochran, L.S. (2004) 'Design Features to Change and/or Ameliorate Pedestrian Wind Conditions', in *ASCE Structures Congress*, Nashville, Tennessee.

Cockayne, E. (2007) *Hubbub: Filth, Noise and Stench in England, 1600–1770*, London: Yale University Press.

Cohen, Eric. (2006) 'The Broken Cycle - Smell in a Bangkok Lane', in J. Drobnick (ed.), *The Smell Culture Reader*, Oxford: Berg.

Colletti, J., Hoff, S., Thompson, J. and Tyndall, J. (2006) 'Vegetative Environmental Buffers to Mitigate Odor and Aerosol Pollutants Emitted from Poultry Production Sites', in V.P. Aneja, J. Blunden, P.A. Roelle, W.H. Schlesinger, R. Knighton, Dev Niyogi, W. Gilliam, G. Jennings, C.S. Duke (eds), Workshop on Agricultural Air Quality: State of the Science, Potomac, Maryland.

Condie, J and Brown, P. (2009) 'Using a Qualitative Approach to Explore the Human Response to Vibration in Residential Environments in the United Kingdom', *The Built & Human Environment Review*, 2(1).

Cooper, R., Evans, G.W. and Boyko, C. (eds) (2009) *Designing Sustainable Cities*, Chichester: Wiley-Blackwell.

Cornell University (2009) 'Improved Air Quality During Beijing Olympics Could Inform Pollution-curbing Policies', *Science Daily* (5 August).

Corwin, J., Loury, M. and Gilbert, A.N. (1995) 'Workplace, Age, and Sex as Mediators of Olfactory Function: Data from the National Geographic Smell Survey', *The Journals of Gerontology*, 50B (4): 179–186.

Cox, G. (2005) *The Cox Review of Creativity in Business*. London: HM Treasury, HMSO.

Cullen, G. (1961) *The Concise Townscape*, Oxford: Architectural Press.

Curren, J., Synder, C., Abrahams, S. and Seffet, I.H. (2013) 'Development of Odor Wheels for the Urban Air Environment', in *The International Water Association Specialized Conference on Odors & Air Emissions*, San Francisco, USA (4–7 March).

Daily Yomiuri Online (2012) 'Smokers Face Increased Restrictions in Tokyo', *The Daily Yomiuri*, http://www.yomiuri.co.jp/dy/national/T120725004117.htm (26 July).

Damhuis, C. (2006) 'There is More than Meets the Nose: Multidimensionality of Odor Preferences', in *A Sense of Smell Institute White Paper*: Sense of Smell Institute.

Damian, P. and Damian, K. (2006) 'Environmental Fragrancing', in J. Drobnick (ed.), *The Smell Culture Reader*, Oxford: Berg.

Dann, G. and Jacobsen J.K.S. (2002) 'Leading the Tourist by the Nose', in G. Dann (ed.), *The Tourist As a Metaphor of the Social World*, CAB International, Wallingford, UK: 209–236.

Dann, G. and Jacobsen, J.K.S. (2003) 'Tourism Smellscapes', *Tourism Geographies*, 5 (1): 3.

Davies, L. (2000) *Urban Design Compendium*, English Partnerships (ed.).

Davies, W., Adams, M.D., Bruce, N.S., Cain, R., Carlyle, A., Cusack, P., Hume, K.I., Jennings, P. and Plack, C.J. (2007) 'The Positive Soundscape Project', in *19th International Congress on Acoustics*, Madrid.

Davis, F. (1979) *Yearning for Yesterday: A Sociology of Nostalgia*, New York: The Free Press.

Day, R. (2007) 'Place and the Experience of Air Quality', *Health & Place*, 13 (1): 249–260.

DCLG (2008) *The Provision of Public Toilets – Twelfth Report of Session 2007–08*, London: HMSO.

DeBolt, D. (2007) 'Neighbors dislike smell of KFC', in *Mountain View Voice*, available at: http://www.mv-voice.com/morguepdf/2007/2007_09_14.mvv.section1.pdf (accessed 16 January 2013).

DEFRA (2002) *Air Pollution: What it Means for Your Health'*, available at: http://archive.defra.gov.uk/environment/quality/air/airquality/publications/airpoll/documents/airpollution_leaflet.pdf (accessed 16 January 2013).

DEFRA (2007a) *The Air Quality Strategy for England, Scotland, Wales and Northern Ireland*, London: HMSO.

DEFRA (2007b) *Human Response to Vibration in Residential Environments*, London: HMSO.

DEFRA (2008) *Air Pollution in the UK 2007*, DEFRA (ed.), available at: http://www.airquality.co.uk/annualreport/annualreport2007.php (accessed 16 January 2013).

DEFRA (2010) *Odour Guidance for Local Authorities*, London: HMSO, available at: www.defra.gov.uk/.../files/pb13554-local-auth-guidance-100326.pdf (accessed 16 January 2013).

Degen, M. (2008) *Sensing Cities: Regenerating Public Life in Barcelona and Manchester*. London and New York: Routledge, Taylor & Francis Group.

DePalma, A. (2005) 'Good Smell Vanishes, But It Leaves Air of Mystery', New York: *New York Times*, available online: http://www.nytimes.com/2005/10/29/nyregion/29smell.html?_r=1&scp=1&sq=Good%20Smell%20Vanishes&st=cse&oref=slogin (accessed 16 January 2013).

Desor, J.A. and Beauchamp, G.K. (1974) 'The Human Capacity to Transmit Olfactory Information', *Perception and Psychophysics*, 16: 551–556.

DETR (2000) *Our Towns and Cities: The Future – Delivering an Urban Renaissance*, London: DETR.

Devlieger, P.J. (2011) 'Blindness/City: The Local Making of Multisensorial Public Spaces', in M. Diaconu, E. Heuberger, R. Mateus-Berr and L.M. Vosicky (eds), *Senses and the City: An Interdisciplinary Approach to Urban Sensescapes*, London, Transaction Publishers: 87–98.

Diaconu, M. (2011) 'Mapping Urban Smellscapes', in M. Diaconu, E. Heuberger, R. Mateus-Berr and L.M. Vosicky (eds), *Senses and the City: An Interdisciplinary Approach to Urban Sensescapes*. London: Transaction Publishers.

Diaconu, M., Heuberger, E., Mateus-Berr, R. and Vosicky, L.M. (eds) (2011) *Senses and the City: An Interdisciplinary Approach to Urban Sensescapes*. London: Transaction Publishers.

Diamond, J., Dalton, P., Doolittle, N. and Breslin, P.A.S. (2005) 'Gender-Specific Olfactory Sensitization: Hormonal and Cognitive Influences', *Chemical Senses* 30 (1): 224–225.

Dickens, C. (1837–39) *Oliver Twist*, London: Bentley's Miscellany.

Dimoudi, A. and Nikolopoulou, M. (2003) 'Vegetation in the Urban Environment: Microclimatic Analysis and Benefits', *Energy and Buildings* 35: 69–76.

DMBC (2005) *Doncaster M.B.C. Air Quality Action Plan*, available online: http://www.doncaster.gov.uk/sections/environment/pollution/air/Air_Quality_Reports_available_to_the_public.aspx (accessed 16 January 2013).

DMBC (2008) '*Estimating and Profiling Population and Deprivation in Doncaster*', in Mayhew, L. and Harper, G. (eds), Doncaster, UK.

Dodd, G. (1856) *The Food of London: A Sketch of the Chief Varieties, Sources of Supply, Probable Quantities, Modes of Arrival, Processes of Manufacture, Suspected Adulteration, and Machinery of Distribution, of the Food for a Community of Two Millions and a Half*, London: Longman, Brown, Green and Longmans.

Doty, R.L. (2001) 'Olfaction', *Annual Review of Psychology*, 52 (1): 423.

Doty, R.L., Brugger, W.E., Jurs, P.C., Orndorff, M.A., Snyder, P.J. and Lowry, L.D. (1978) 'Intranasal Trigeminal Stimulation from Odorous Volatiles: Psychometric Responses from Anosmic and Normal Humans', *Physiology & Behaviour*, 20 (2): 175–185.

Doty, R.L., Applebaum, S., Zusho, H. and Settle R.G (1985) 'Sex Differences in Odor Identification Ability: A Cross Cultural Analysis', *Neuropsychologica*, 23: 667–672.

Douglas, M. (1966) *Purity and Danger*, London: Routledge & Kegan Paul.

Dove, R. (2008) *The Essence of Perfume*, London: Black Dog Publishing.

Doyle, K. (2008) 'Smoking Ban Increases Litter', BBC1 (09 February 2008).

Drobnick, J. (2000) 'Inhaling Passions, Art, Sex and Scent', *Sexuality & Culture* 4 (3): 37–56.

Drobnick, J. (2002) 'Toposmia: Art, Scent and Interrogations of Spatiality', *Angelaki* 7 (1): 31–46.

Drobnick, J. (ed.) (2006) *The Smell Culture Reader*, Oxford: Berg.

Elliot, R. (2003) 'Faking Nature', in A. Light and H. Rolston (eds), *Environmental Ethics*, Oxford: Blackwell Publishing.

Engen, T. (1982) *The Perception of Odors*, London: Academic Press Inc.

Engen, T. (1991) *Odor Sensation and Memory*, New York: Praeger.

English Heritage (2010) '*Understanding Place Historic Area Assessments: Principles and Practice*', available at: http://www.english-heritage.org.uk/publications/understanding-place-principles-practice/.

EUKN (2002) 'NOZONE – An Intelligent Responsive Pollution and Odour Abatement Technology for Cooking Emission Extraction Systems', available at: http://www.eukn.org/susta/themes/Urban_Policy/Urban_environment/Environmental_sustainability/Air_quality/NOZONE_1069.html (accessed 14 July 2008).

European Parliament (2009) 'Decision No 406/2009/EC on the Effort of Member States to reduce their Greenhouse Gas emissions to meet the Community's Greenhouse Gas Emission reduction commitments up to 2020', in *Official Journal of the European Union*, European Parliament and the Council of the European Union (ed.), L 140/136. Strasbourg, France.

Evans, G. (2003) 'Hard-Branding the Cultural City – From Prado to Prada', *International Journal of Urban and Regional Research*, 27 (2): 417–440.

Evans, G.W. and Cohen, S. (1987) 'Environmental Stress', in D. Stokols and I. Altman *Handbook of Environmental Psychology*, New York: Wiley.

Fanger, P.O. (1988) 'Introduction of the Olf and the Decipol Units to Quantify Air Pollution Perceived by Humans Indoors and Outdoors', *Energy and Buildings*, 12 (1): 1–6.

Fanger, P.O., Lauridsen, J., Bluyssen, P. and Clausen, G. (1988) 'Air Pollution Sources in Offices and Assembly Halls, Quantified by the Olf Unit', *Energy and Buildings*, 12 (1): 7–19.

Farmer, G. and Guy, S. (2010) 'Making Morality: Sustainable Architecture and the Pragmatic Imagination', *Building, Research and Information*, 38: 368–378.

Fitzgerald Bone, P. and Scholder-Ellen, P. (1999) 'Scents in the Marketplace: Explaining a Fraction of Olfaction', *Journal of Retailing*, 75 (2): 243–262.

Fleming, R.L. (2007) *The Art of Placemaking – Interpreting Community Through Public Art and Urban Design*, London: Merrell Publishers Ltd.

Fletcher, C. (2005) 'Dystoposthesia – Emplacing Environmental Sensitivities' in D. Howes (ed.), *Empire of the Senses – The Sensual Culture Reader*, Oxford: Berg.

Fletcher, C.M. (2006) 'Environmental Sensitivity: Equivocal Illness in the Context of Place', *Transcultural Psychiatry*, 43 (1): 86–105.

Fox Claims (2008) 'Fox Claims', available at: http://www.foxclaims.co.uk/Claims.htm (accessed 3 July 2008).

Fox, K. (2006) *The Smell Report*, Social Issues Research Centre, available at: http://www.sirc.org/publik/smell.pdf (accessed 24 April 2010).

Frank, A., Hill, B., Lalloo, V., Possa, P., Ren, H., Tjoa, J., and Brod, D.V. (2001) *Experience Marketing: Lush Gets a Makeover*, Rotterdam School of Management, Erasmus Graduate School of Business.

Fraser, S. (2002) 'Odours – What a Nuisance – Regulation and Quantification of Environmental Odour', in *The Chartered Institute of Water and Environmental Management – National Odour Conference*, Hatfield.

Freud, S. (1961) *Beyond the Pleasure Principle*, New York: W.W. Norton.

Furniss, J. (2008) 'Purity and Pollution between Researcher and Researched: Barriers to Ethnography among a Community of Egyptian Garbage Collectors', *Oxford Researching Africa Day 2008*, Oxford: Oxford University.

George, C. (2000) *Singapore: The Air-Conditioned Nation: Essays on the Politics of Comfort and Control, 1990–2000*, Singapore: Landmark Books.

Gibson, J.J. (1966) *The Senses Considered as Perceptual Systems*, Westport: Greenwood.

Gilbert, A.N. and Wysocki, C.J. (1987) 'The Smell Results: Survey', *National Geographic*, 172 (4): 1.

Gill, A.A. (2005) 'A Sense of Loss', *Australian Gourmet Traveller*, 5 (11): 61–62.

Gordon, R. (2006) 'Aromatic ads pulled from city bus shelters', *San Francisco Chronicle*, available at: http://www.sfgate.com/bayarea/article/SAN-FRANCISCO-Aromatic-ads-pulled-from-city-bus-2483659.php (accessed 31 March 2013).

GOYH (2009) *Yorkshire and the Humber Regional Sustainable Development Indicators Factsheet*, available at: http://www.defra.gov.uk/SUSTAINABLE/GOVERNMENT/PROGRESS/regional/documents/yorkshire_and_humber_factsheet.pdf (accessed 31 March 2009).

Grant, A. (2006) 'Smoking ban has unexpected spin-offs', BBC, available at: http://news.bbc.co.uk/1/hi/magazine/7483057.stm (accessed 31 March 2013).

Greed, C. (2003) *Inclusive Urban Design: Public Toilets*, Oxford: Architectural Press.

Grésillon, L. (2010) *Sentir Paris: Bien-être et Matérialité des Lieux*, Paris: Collection Indisciplines, QUAE: 192.

Grimwood, C.J., Skinner, C.J. and Raw, G.J. (2002) 'The UK National Noise Attitude Survey 1999/2000', in *Noise Forum Conference*, 20 May.

Guski, R. and Felscher-Suhr, U. (1999) 'The Concept of Noise Annoyance: How International Experts See It', *Journal of Sound and Vibration*, 223 (4): 513–527.

Hamanzu, T. (1969) 'Odour Perception Measurement by the Use of an Odourless Room', *Sangyo Kogai*, 5: 718–723.

Harrison, R.M. (2000) 'Studies of the Source Apportionment of Airborne Particulate Matter in the United Kingdom', *Journal of Aerosol Science*, 31 (1): 106–107.

Hartig, T., Mang, M. and Evans, G.W. (1991) 'Restorative Effects of Natural Environment Experiences', *Environment and Behavior*, 23 (1):3–26.

Heath, T. (1997) 'The Twenty-Four Hour City Concept – A Review of Initiatives in British Cities', London: Routledge.

Heili, V., Christensson, K. Porter, R.H and Winberg, J. (1998) 'Soothing Effect of Amniotic Fluid Smell in Newborn Infants', *Early Human Development*, 51 (1): 47–55.

Henshaw, V., Adams, M.D. and Cox, T.J. (2009) 'Route Planning a Sensory Walk: Sniffing Out the Issues', paper presentation at *The Royal Geographical Society Annual Conference*, University of Manchester (26–28 August).

Herbert, S. (2008) 'Contemporary Geographies of Exclusion I: Traversing Skid Road', *Progress in Human Geography*, 32 (5): 659–666.

Herz, R.S. (2006) 'I Know What I Like – Understanding Odor Preferences', in J. Drobnick (ed.), *The Smell Culture Reader*, Oxford: Berg.

Herz, R. (2008) 'Art & Commerce: Buying by the Nose', *Adweek*, available at: http://www.adweek.com/aw/magazine/article_display.jsp?vnu_content_id=1003695821 (21 January).

Herzog, T.R., Ouellette, P., Rolens, J.R. and Koenigs, A.M. (2010) 'Houses of Worship as Restorative Environments', *Environment and Behavior*, 42: 395–419.

Hillier, B. and Sahbaz, O. (2009) 'Crime and Urban Design: An Evidence Based Approach', in R. Cooper, G.W. Evans and C. Boyko (eds), *Designing Sustainable Cities*, Chichester: Wiley-Blackwell.

Hinton, D.E, Pich, V., Chhean, D. and Pollack, MH. (2006) 'Olfactory-Triggered Panic Attacks Among Khmer Refugees', in J. Drobnick (ed.), *The Smell Culture Reader*, Oxford: Berg, 68–81.

Hirsch, A.R. (1990) *Preliminary Results of Olfaction Nike Study*, The Smell and Taste Treatment and Research Foundation Ltd., Chicago, IL.

Hirsch, A.R. (1995) 'Effects of Ambient Odors on Slot-Machine Usage in a Las Vegas Casino', *Psychology and Marketing*, 12 (7): 585–594.

Hirsch, A.R. (2006) 'Nostalgia, the Odors of Childhood and Society', in J. Drobnick (ed.), *The Smell Culture Reader*, Oxford: Berg.

Howes, D. (1991) 'Olfaction and Transition', in D. Howes (ed.) *Varieties of Sensory Experience*, Toronto: University of Toronto Press.

Howes, D. (2005) 'Architecture of the Senses', in M. Zardini (ed.), *Sense of the City – An Alternative Approach to Urbanism*, Montreal: Lars Muller Publishers.

Hudson, R., Arriola, A., Martinez-Gomez, M. and Distel, H. (2006) 'Effect of Air Pollution on Olfactory Function in Residents of Mexico City', *Chemical Senses*, 31: 79–95.

Illich, I. (1986) H_2O *and the Waters of Forgetfulness*, London: Marion Boyars Publishers Ltd.

Invest in Doncaster (2009) *Prosper de Mulder to Invest £12m in Cutting Edge Recycling Plant*, Doncaster: DMBC.

ISO (1994) *ISO 7730:1994 – Moderate Thermal Environments – Determination of the PMV and PPD Indices and Specification of the Conditions for Thermal Comfort*, Geneva, 1994, International Organisation for Standardisation.

Jacobs, J. (1961) *The Death and Life of Great American Cities*, New York: Random House.

Japanese Ministry for the Environment (date unknown) Measures for Problems Relating to Local Living Environment, http://www.env.go.jp/policy/hakusyo_e/honbun.php3?kid=221&bflg=1&serial=67 (accessed 6 January 2013).

Jenkinson, A. and Sain, B. (2003) *Lush, the scent of success*, Luton: Centre for Integrated Marketing.

Jensen, F. P. and Fenger, J. (1994) 'The Air Quality in Danish Urban Areas', *Environmental Health Perspectives*, 102 (4): 55–60.

Kang, J. and Yang, W. (2003) 'Sound Preferences in Urban Open Public Spaces', *Journal of the Acoustical Society of America*, 114: 2352.

Kaplan, R. and Kaplan, S. (1989) *The Experience of Nature: A Psychological Perspective*, New York: Cambridge University Press.

Kaplan, S., Bardwell, L.V. and Slakter, D.B. (1993) 'The Museum as a Restorative Environment', *Environment and Behavior*, 25: 725–742.

Kaplan, S. (1995) 'The Restorative Benefits of Nature: Toward An Integrative Framework', *Journal of Environmental Psychology*, 15 (3): 169-182.

Karmanov, D. and Hamel, R. (2008) 'Assessing the Restorative Potential of Contemporary Urban Environment(s): Beyond the Nature versus Urban Dichotomy', *Landscape and Urban Planning*, 86 (2): 115–125.

Keep Britain Tidy (2003) *Fast Food Study 2003*, available at: http://www.keepbritaintidy.org/ImgLibrary/fastfood_study_641.pdf (accessed 16 January 2013).

Keep Britain Tidy (2009) *Call for more action on Cig Litter*, available at: http://www.keepbritaintidy.org/News/Default.aspx?newsID=869 (accessed 16 January 2013).

Keep Britain Tidy (2010) *Smoking Related Litter*, available at: http://www.keepbritaintidy.org/AboutUs/Policy/WhatWeThink/SmokingRelatedLitter/Default.aspx (accessed 16 January 2013).

Keller, A., Hempstead, M., Gomez, I.A., Gilbert, A.N. and Vosshall, L.B. (2012) 'An Olfactory Demography of a Diverse Metropolitan Population', *BMC Neuroscience*, 13:122.

Kentucky Fried Chicken Corporation (2007) *Special Delivery: Scent of Freshly Prepared Kentucky Fried Chicken to Tempt Tastebuds of American Office Workers*, press release, available at: http://www.kfc.com/about/pressreleases/082807.asp (accessed 6 June 2008).

King, P. (2008) 'Memory and Exile: Time and Place in Tarkovsky's Mirror', *Housing, Theory & Society*, 25 (1): 66–78.

Kivity, S., Ortega-Hernandez, O.D. and Shoenfeld, Y. (2009) 'Olfaction – A Window to the Mind', *IMAJ*, 11.

Knasko, S.C. (1995) 'Pleasant Odors and Congruency: Effects on Approach Behavior', *Chemical Senses*, 20: 479-487.

Knopper, M. (2003) 'Cities that Smell: Some Urban Centres use Common Scents', *Expanded Academic ASAP*, 22 (3).

Korpela, K. and Hartig, T. (1996) 'Restorative Qualities of Favorite Places', *Journal of Environmental Psychology*, 16 (3): 221–233.

Kostner, E.P. (2002) 'The Specific Characteristics of the Sense of Smell', in C. Rowby (ed.), *Olfaction, Taste and Cognition*, Cambridge: Cambridge University Press.

Kotler, P. (1973) 'Atmospherics as a Marketing Tool', *Journal of Retailing*, 49(4): 48–64.

Kreutzer, R., Neutra, R.R. and Lashuay, N. (1999) 'Prevalence of People Reporting Sensitivities to Chemicals in a Population-Based Survey', *American Journal of Epidemiology*, 150: 1–12.

Lagas, P. (2010) 'Odour Policy in the Netherlands and Consequences for Spatial Planning', *Chemical Engineering Transactions*, 23: 7–12.

Laing, D. G., Legha, P.K., Jinks, A.L. and Hutchinson, I. (2003) 'Relationship between Molecular Structure, Concentration and Odor Qualities of Oxygenated Aliphatic Molecules', *Perception*, 28: 57–69.

Landry, C. (2006) *The Art of City Making*, London: Earthscan.

Landry, C. (2008) *The Creative City: A Toolkit for Urban Innovators*, London: Routledge.

Larssona, M., Finkeld, D. and Pedersenc. N.L. (2000) 'Odor Identification: Influences of Age, Gender, Cognition, and Personality', *The Journals of Gerontology*: Series B 55 (5): 304-310.

Le Guerer, A. (1993) *Scent: The mysterious and essential powers of smell*, London: Chatto & Windus.

Lefebvre, H. (2009) *The Production of Space*, Oxford: Blackwell.

Leino, T. (1999) *Working Conditions and Health in Hairdressing Salons*, London: Taylor & Francis.

Leith, S. (2008) 'Supermarkets are evil: What a shame we love Tesco and Waitrose so', London: *The Telegraph*.

Li, W., Howard, J.D. Parrish, T.B. and Gottfried, J.A. (2008) 'Aversive Learning Enhances Perceptual and Cortical Discrimination of Indiscriminable Odor Cues', *Science* 319 (5871): 1842–1845.

Licitra, G., Brusci, L. and Cobianchi, M. (2011) 'Italian Sonic Gardens: An Artificial Soundscape Approach for New Action Plans', in Ö. Axelsson (ed.), *Designing Soundscape for Sustainable Urban Development*, Stockholm, Sweden, available online: http://www.

decorumcommunications.se/pdf/designing-soundscape-for-sustainable-urban-development.pdf: 21–24.

Light, A. (2009) 'Contemporary Environmental Ethics', in C.B.M. Reynolds, S. Smith and J. Mark (eds), *The Environmental Responsibility Reader*, London, Zed: 94–102.

Lindstrom, M. (2005a) *BRANDSense*. London: Kogan Page Ltd.

Lindstrom, M. (2005b) 'Broad Sensory Branding', *Journal of Product & Brand Management* 14 (2): 84–87.

Linklater, A. (2007) 'The Woman who was Afraid of Water', London: *The Guardian* (10 February).

Low, K.E.Y. (2006) 'Presenting the Self, the Social Body, and the Olfactory: Managing Smells in Everyday Life Experiences', *Sociological Perspectives*, 49 (4): 607–631.

Low, K.E.Y. (2009) *Scents and Scent-sibilities: Smell and Everyday Life Experiences*, Newcastle: Cambridge Scholars Publishing.

Lucas, R. (2009) 'Designing a Notation for the Senses', *Architectural Theory Review*, 14 (2): 173.

Lucas, R. and Romice, O. (2008) 'Representing Sensory Experience in Urban Design', *Design Principles and Practices: An International Journal*, 2 (4): 83–94.

Lucas, R. and Romice, O. (2010) 'Assessing the Multi-Sensory Qualities of Urban Space', in *Psyecology*, 1 (2): 263–276.

Lucas, R., Romice, O. and Mair, G. (2009) 'Making Sense of the City: Representing the Multi-modality of Urban Space', in T. Inns (ed.), *Designing for the 21st Century: Interdisciplinary Methods & Findings*, Burlington: Ashgate.

Lynch, K. (1960) *The Image of the City*, Cambridge, MA: MIT Press.

Macdonald, L., Cummins, S. and Macintyre, S. (2007) 'Neighbourhood Fast Food Environment and Area Deprivation-Substitution or Concentration?', *Appetite* 49 (1): 251–254.

Macintyre, S., McKay, L., Cummins, S. and Burns, C. (2005) 'Out-of-Home Food Outlets and Area Deprivation: Case Study in Glasgow, UK', *International Journal of Behavioral Nutrition and Physical Activity*, 2.

Malnar, J.M. and Vodvarka, F. (2004) *Sensory Design*, Minneapolis: University of Minnesota Press.

Malone, G. and Wicklen, G. Van (2001) 'Trees as a Vegetative Filter', *Poultry Digest Online* 3 (1).

Manalansan, M.F. (2006) 'Immigration Lives and the Politics of Olfaction in the Global City', in J. Drobnick (ed.), *The Smell Culture Reader*, Oxford: Berg.

Mason, K. (2009) 'Residents Don't Want Bad Smells on their Doorstep', *Doncaster Free Press*, Doncaster, available online: http://www.doncasterfreepress.co.uk/free/Residents-don39t-want-bad-smells.4922881.jp.

Massey, D. (1991) 'A Global Sense of Place', *Marxism Today*, 38.

Mavor, C. (2006) 'Odor di Femina', in J. Drobnick (ed.) *The Smell Culture Reader*, Oxford: Berg.

May, A.J., Ross, T. and Bayer, S.H. (2003) 'Drivers' Information Requirements when Navigating in an Urban Environment', *Journal of Navigation*, 56 (1): 89–100.

McFrederick, Q.S., Kathilankal, J.C. and Fuentes, J.D. (2008) 'Air Pollution Modifies Floral Scent Trails', *Atmospheric Environment*, 42 (10): 2336–2348.

McGinley, C. M., Mahin, T.D. and Pope, R.J. (2000) 'Elements of Successful Odor/Odour Laws', *WEF Odor/VOC 2000 Specialty Conference*, Cincinnati, Ohio.

McLean, K. (2012) 'Emotion, Location and the Senses: A Virtual Dérive Smell Map of Paris', in J. Brasset, J. McDonnell and M. Malpass (eds), *Proceedings of the 8th International Design and Emotion Conference*, London.

McLean, K. (2013) 'Sensory Maps (Cities)', available at http://www.sensorymaps.com/maps_cities/glasgow_smell.html (accessed 31 March 2013).

Mean, M. and Tims, T. (2005) *People Make Places: Growing the Public Life of Cities*, London: DEMOS.

Mehrabian, A. and Russell, J.A. (1974) *An Approach to Environmental Psychology*, Cambridge, MA: MIT Press.

Merlin Entertainments Group (2010) 'Ur-ine the money with new THORPE PARK attraction, SAW Alive!', press release, available at: http://www.thorpepark.com/press/releases/2010/24-02-10.doc (accessed 16 January 2013).

Miedema, H.M.E. and Ham. J.M. (1988) 'Odour Annoyance in Residential Areas', *Atmospheric Environment (1967)*, 22 (11): 2501–2507.

Miedema, H.M.E., Walpot, J.I., Vos, H. and Steunenberg, C.F. (2000) 'Exposure-Annoyance Relationships for Odour from Industrial Sources', *Atmospheric Environment*, 34: 2927–36.

Milligan, (2005) *Wake Up and Smell the Coffee!*, press release, available at: http://www.milliganrri.co.uk/News-Press/Triangle/Wake-up-and-smell-the-coffee.aspx (accessed 10 June 2008).

Minton, A. (2009) *Ground Control – Fear and Happiness in the Twenty-First-Century City*, London: Penguin.

Moore, E.O. (1981) 'A Prison Environment's Effect on Health Care Service Demands', *Journal of Environmental Systems*, 11: 17–34.

Morris, N. (2003) *Health, Well-Being and Open Space – Literature Review*, Edinburgh: OPENspace.

Moss, M. and Oliver, L. (2012) 'Plasma 1,8-Cineole Correlates with Cognitive Performance Following Exposure to Rosemary Essential Oil Aroma', *Therapeutic Advances in Psychopharmacology*, 1–11.

Mukherjee, B.N. (1993) 'Public Response to Air Pollution in Calcutta Proper', *Journal of Environmental Psychology*, 13 (3): 207–230.

Muiswinkel, W.J. Van, Kromhout, H. Onos, T. and Kersemaekers, W. (1997) 'Monitoring and Modelling of Exposure to Ethanol in Hairdressing Salons', *Annals of Occupational Hygiene*, 41 (2): 235–247.

Netcen (2005) *Guidance on the Control of Odour and Noise from Commercial Kitchen Exhaust Systems*, (ed.), London: DEFRA.

New Economics Foundation (2005) 'Clone Town Britain', in A. Simms (ed.), *The Survey Results on the Bland State of the Nation*, available online: http://www.neweconomics.org/sites/neweconomics.org/files/Clone_Town_Britain_1.pdf (accessed 10 May 2010).

Nikolopoulou, M. (2003) 'Thermal Comfort and Psychological Adaptation as a Guide for Designing Urban Spaces', *Energy and Buildings*, 35: 95–101.

Nikolopoulou, M. (ed.) (2004) *Designing Open Spaces in the Urban Environment*, Athens: Centre for Renewable Energy Sources.

Nikolopoulou, M. and Lykoudis, S. (2007) 'Use of Outdoor Spaces and Microclimates in a Mediterranean Urban Area', *Building and Environment*, 42: 3691–3707.

Nikolopoulou, M., Baker, N. and Steemers, K. (2001) 'Thermal Comfort in Outdoor Urban Spaces: Understanding the Human Parameter', *Solar Energy*, 70 (3): 227–235.

Nordin, S., Bende, M. and Millqvist. E. (2004) 'Normative Data for the Chemical Sensitivity Scale', *Journal of Environmental Psychology*, 24 (3): 399–403.

Nordin, S. and Lidén, E. (2006) 'Environmental Odor Annoyance from Air Pollution from Steel Industry and Bio-Fuel Processing', *Journal of Environmental Psychology*, 26 (2): 141–145.

ONS (2012) '2011 Census: Ethnic Group, Local Authorities in England and Wales', available at: http://www.ons.gov.uk/ons/publications/re-reference-tables.html?edition= tcm%3A77-286262.

Ousset, P.J., Nourhashemi, F., Albarede, J.L. and Vellas, P.M. (1998) 'Therapeutic Gardens', *Archives of Geronotolgy and Geriatrics*, 6: 369–372.

Oxford English Dictionary (2012a) *Definition: Synthetic*, available at: http:// oxforddictionaries.com/definition/english/synthetic (accessed 27 December 2012).

Oxford English Dictionary (2012b) *Definition: Windflow*, available at: http:// oxforddictionaries.com/definition/english/wind?q=wind (accessed 5 October 2012).

Pallasmaa, J. (2005) *The Eyes of the Skin*, Sussex: John Wiley and Sons Ltd.

Payne, S.R. (2008) 'Are Perceived Soundscapes within Urban Parks Restorative?', *Journal of the Acoustical Society of America*, 123: 3809.

Penwarden, A.D. and Wise, A.F.E. (1975) 'Wind Environment around Buildings', in *Building Research Establishment Report*, London.

Piaget, J. (1969) *The Mechanisms of Perception*, New York: Basic Books.

Pocock, I. (2006) 'California Town Bans Public Smoking', BBC.

Porteous, J.D. (1990) *Landscapes of the Mind - Worlds of Sense and Metaphor*, Toronto: University of Toronto Press.

Postrel, V. (2003) *The Substance of Style: How the Rise of Aesthetic Value is Remaking Commerce, Culture and Consciousness*, New York: Harper Collins.

Pottier, J. (2005) 'Food', in A. Barnard and J. Spencer (eds), *Encyclopaedia of Social and Cultural Anthropology*, London and New York: Routledge.

Proust, M. (2006) *Remembrance of Things Past*, Hertfordshire: Wordsworth Editions Ltd.

Pugh, T.A.M., MacKenzie, A.R., Whyatt, J.D. and Hewitt, C.N. (2012) 'The Effectiveness of Green Infrastructure for Improvement of Air Quality in Urban Street Canyons', *Environmental Science & Technology*, 46 (14): 7692–7699.

Quality of Urban Air Review Group (1996) *Airbourne Particulate Matter in the United Kingdom*. Available online: http://uk-air.defra.gov.uk/reports/empire/quarg/q3intro. html (accessed 17 January 2013).

Radford, C. (1978) 'Fakes', *Mind, New Series*, 87 (345): 66–67.

Rasmussen, S.E. (1959) *Experiencing Architecture*, Cambridge, MA: MIT Press.

Redlich, C.A., Sparer, J. and Cullen, M.R. (1997) 'Sick-Building Syndrome', *The Lancet*, 349 (9057): 1013–1016.

Reinarz, J. (2013) *Past Scents: Historical Perspectives on Smell*. DeKalb, IL: University of Illinois Press.

Relph, E. (1976) *Place and Placelessness*, London: Pion.

Reynolds, R. (2008) *On Guerrilla Gardening*, London: Bloomsbury.

Riessman, C.K. (2004) 'Narrative Analysis', in M.S. Lewis-Beck, A. Bryman and T.F. Liao (eds), *The Sage Encyclopedia of Social Science Research Methods* (1–3), California: Sage.

Rivera, L. (2006) 'Where the Air Leaves Them Breathless', New York Times, New York, available at: http://www.nytimes.com.2006/11/05/nyregion/thecity/05asth.html?_r=0 (accessed 31 March 2013).

Rodaway, P. (1994) *Sensuous Geographies*, London: Routledge.

Rouse, J. (2003) Factories in Wheatley, http://archiver.rootsweb.ancestry.com/th/read/ENG-YKS-DONCASTER/2003-07/1059426556 (accessed 16 January 2013).

Sacks, O. (2005) 'The Mind's Eye – What the Blind See', in D. Howes (ed.), *Empire of the Senses – The Sensual Culture Reader*, Oxford, Berg: 25–42.

Sardar, Z. (2000) 'Our Fetish for Fake Smells', *New Statesman*, available at: http://www.newstatesman.com/200009110018 (accessed 24 September 2009).

Schafer, R.M. (1994) *Our Sonic Environment and the Soundscape – The Tuning of the World*, Rochester, VT: Destiny Books.

Schemper, T., Voss, S. and Cain, W.S. (1981) 'Odor Identification in Young and Elderly Persons: Sensory and Cognitive Limitations', *The Journal of Gerontology*, 36: 446–452.

Schenker, S. (2001) 'Gruesome Gourmets', *Nutrition Bulletin*, 26 (1):2.

Schiffman, S.S., Graham, B.G. Sattely-Miller, E.A., Zervakis, J. and Welsh-Bohmer, K. (2002) 'Taste, Smell and Neuropsychological Performance of Individuals at Familial Risk for Alzheimer's Disease', *Neurobiology of Aging*, 23 (3): 397–404.

Schleidt, M., Neumann, P. and Morishita, H. (1988) 'Pleasure and Disgust: Memories and Associations of Pleasant and Unpleasant Odours in Germany and Japan', *Chemical Senses*, 13 (2): 279–293.

Schlosser, E. (2002) *Fast Food Nation*, London: Penguin Books Ltd.

Selvaggi-Baumann, C. (2004) 'New Sony Store to Woo Women with Style', *Orlando Business Journal*. Available at: http://www.bizjournals.com/orlando/stories/2004/10/04/story6.html?page=2 (accessed 2 January 2013).

Sen, U., Sankaranarayanan, R., Mandal, S., Ramanakumar, A.V., Maxwell-Parkin, D. and Siddiqi, M. (2002) 'Cancer Patterns in Eastern India: The First Report of The Kolkata Cancer Registry', *International Journal of Cancer*, 100: 86–91.

Sennett, R. (1994) *Flesh & Stone – The Body and the City in Western Civilization*, London: W.W. Norton & Company.

Shaw, S., Bagwell, S. and Karmowska, J. (2004) 'Ethnoscapes as Spectacle: Reimaging Multicultural Districts as New Destinations for Leisure and Tourism Consumption', *Urban Studies*, 41 (10): 1983–2000.

Sibun, J. (2008) 'Carlsberg to close Tetley brewery in Leeds after 186 years', London: *The Telegraph*, available at: http://www.telegraph.co.uk/finance/newsbysector/retailandconsumer/3385146/Carlsberg-to-close-Tetley-brewery-in-Leeds-after-186-years.html (accessed 28 December 2012).

Smith, M. (2007) 'Space, Place and Placelessness in the Culturally Regenerated City', in G. Richards (ed.), *Cultural Tourism*, Binghamton, NY: Haworth Press Inc.

Smith, R.S., Doty, R.L.. Burlingame, G.K. and McKeown, D.A. (1993) 'Smell and Taste Function in the Visually Impaired', *Perception & Psychophysics*, 54 (5): 649–655.

Southworth, M. (1969) 'The Sonic Environment of Cities', *Environment and Behavior*, 1 (1): 49–70.

Spangenberg, E.A., Crowley, A.E. and Henderson, P.W. (1996) 'Improving the Store Environment: Do Olfactory Cues Affect Evaluations and Behaviors?', *Journal of Marketing* 60 (2): 67–80.

Stallen, P. (1999) 'A Theoretical Framework for Environmental Noise Annoyance', *Noise and Health*, 1: 69–80.

Starr, C. (1969) 'Social Benefits versus Technological Risks', *Science*, 165 (3899): 1232–1238.

Steel, C. (2008) *Hungry City – How Food Shapes our Lives*, London: Vintage Books.

Stein, M., Ottenberg, M.D. and Roulet, N. (1958) 'A Study of the Development of Olfactory Preferences', *Archives of Neurological Psychiatry*, 80: 264–266.

Steinheider, B., Both, R. and Winneke, G. (1998) 'Field Studies on Environmental Odours Inducing Annoyance as well as Gastric and General Health Related Symptoms', *Journal of Psychophysiology Supplement*, 64–79.

Stewart, H., Owen, S., Donovan, R., MacKenzie, R., Hewitt, N., Skiba, U. and Fowler, D. (2002) *Trees and Sustainable Urban Air Quality – Using Trees to Improve Urban Air Quality in Cities*, Lancaster: Lancaster University.

Strous, R.D. and Shoenfeld, Y. (2006) 'To Smell the Immune System: Olfaction, Autoimmunity and Brain Involvement', *Autoimmunity Reviews*, 6 (1): 54–60.

STV (2012) 'Glasgow Smells of 'Square Sausage and the Subway' According to Map Project', available at: http://local.stv.tv/glasgow/187583-glasgow-smells-of-hot-bovril-and-the-subway-according-to-map-project/ (26 August).

Suffet, I. H. and P. Rosenfeld (2007) 'The Anatomy of Odour Wheels for Odours of Drinking Water, Wastewater, Compost and the Urban Environment', *Water Science & Technology*, 55 (5): 335–344.

Sundell, J. (2004) 'On the History of Indoor Air Quality and Health', *Indoor Air Quality*, 14 (7): 51–58.

Süskind, P. (1987) *Perfume: The Story of a Murderer*, London: Penguin.

Synnott, A. (1991) 'A Sociology of Smell', *Canadian Review of Sociology & Anthropology*, 28 (4): 437–459.

Tafalla, M. (2011) 'Smell, Anosmia, and the Aesthetic Appreciation of Nature', paper presentation at the *Sensory Worlds Conference* at the University of Edinburgh (7–9 December).

Tahbaz, M. (2010) 'Toward a New Chart for Outdoor Thermal Analysis', in *Adapting to Change: New Thinking on Comfort*. Cumberland Lodge, Windsor, UK.

Taiwo, O. (2009) *Carbon Dioxide Emission Management in Nigerian Mega Cities: The Case of Lagos*, Lagos Metropolitan Area Transport Authority (LAMATA), available at: www.unep.org/urban_environment/PDFs/BAQ09_olukayode.pdf (accessed 5 August 2012).

Taylor, N. (2003) 'The Aesthetic Experience of Traffic in the Modern City', *Urban Studies* 40 (8): 1609–1625.

The History Channel (2012) 'Stink: Modern Marvels', US, available at: http://www.youtube.com/watch?v=mQgWc25NGB4&feature=youtu.be (accessed 2 August 2012).

The Washington Times (2008) 'World Class Hype', Washington, US, available at: http://www.washtimes.com/news/2008/mar/17/world-class-hype/ (accessed 17 March 2008).

Thwaites, K. and Simkins, I.M. (2007) *Experiential Landscape: An Approach to People, Space and Place*, London: Taylor & Francis.

Thwaites, K. and Simkins, I.M. (2010) 'Experiential Landscape: Exploring the spatial Dimensions of Human Emotional Fulfillment in Outdoor Open Space', in M.K. Tolba, Abdel-Hadi, A. and Soliman, S.G. (eds), *Environment, Health, and Sustainable Development*, Cambridge, MA: Hogrefe & Huber.

Thibaud, J.P. (2002) *Regards en Action: Ethnométhodologie de l'Espace Public*, Editions A la Croisée, Grenoble.

Thibaud, J.P. (2003) 'La Parole du Public en Marche', in G. Moser and K. Weiss (eds), *Espaces de Vie: Aspects de la Relation Homme-Environnement*, Paris: Armand Colin: 213–234.

Tiesdell, S. and Slater, A. (2004) 'Managing the Evening/Night Time Economy', *Urban Design Quarterly*, 91: 23–26.

Tinsley, J. and Jacobs, M. (2006) *Deprivation and Ethnicity in England: A Regional Perspective*, UK: ONS.

Tippett, J., Handley, J.F. and Ravetz, J. (2007) 'Meeting the Challenges of Sustainable Development – A Conceptual Appraisal of a New Methodology for Participatory Ecological Planning', *Progress in Planning*, 67 (1): 1–98.

Trivedi, B.P. (2002) 'U.S. Military Is Seeking Ultimate Stink Bomb', *National Geographic Today* (7 January).

Truax, B. (1984) *Acoustic Communication*, Norwood, NJ: Ablex Publishing Corporation.

Tseliou, A., Tsiros, I.X., Lykoudis. S. and Nikolopoulou, M. (2010) 'An Evaluation of Three Biometeorological Indices for Human Thermal Comfort in Urban Outdoor Areas under Real Climatic Conditions', *Building and Environment*, 45: 1346–1352.

Tuan, Y.F. (1975) 'Place: An Experiential Perspective', *Geographical Review* 65 (2): 151–165.

Tuan, Y.F (1977) *Space and Place: The Perspective of Experience*, Minneapolis: University of Minnesota Press.

Tuan, Y.F. (1993) *Passing Strange and Wonderful*. Connecticut: Island Press.

Twilley, N. (2010) *How to: Make your own Scratch-and-Sniff Map*, available at: http://urbanheritages.wordpress.com/tag/smellscapes/ (accessed 12 May 2013).

Ulrich, R.S. (1983) 'Aesthetic and Affective Response to Natural Environment', in I. Altman and J.F. Wohlwill (eds), *Human Behavior and Environment: Advances in Theory and Research*, New York: Plenum.

Ulrich, R.S. (1984) 'View Through Window May Influence Recovery from Surgery', *Science* 224: 420–421.

Ulrich, R.S., Simons, R.F., Losito, B.D., Fiorito, E., Miles, M.A. and Zelson, M. (1991) 'Stress Recovery During Exposure to Natural and Urban Environments', *Journal of Environmental Psychology*, 11 (3): 201–230.

United Nations (2008) 'City Dwellers set to Surpass Rural Inhabitants in 2008', *DESA News* 12 (2).

United States Environmental Protection Agency (2004) *Pollution Prevention Practices for Nail Salons – A Guide to Protect the Health of Nail Salon Workers and their Working Environment*, available at: http://www.salonstore.co.uk/PDF/EPA-USA-NailBook.pdf (accessed 12 October 2010).

UNFCCC (2008) 'Kyoto protocol reference manual on accounting of emissions and assigned amount', in *United Nations Framework Convention on Climate Change (UNFCC)* (ed.). Bonn, Germany.

Urban Planet (2007) *New Aroma To Replace Stale Smoke In Clubs*, available at: http://www.urbanplanet.co.uk/showArticle.aspx?loadid=00310 (accessed 13 January 2013).

Urban Task Force (1999) *Towards an Urban Renaissance: Final Report of the Urban Task Force*, London: Spon.

Urry, J. (1990) *The Tourist Gaze: Leisure and Travel in Contemporary Societies*, London: Sage.

Urry, J. (1999) 'Sensing the City', in S.S. Fainstein and D.R. Judd (eds), *The Tourist City*, London: Yale University Press.

Urry, J. (2003) 'City Life and the Senses', in S. Watson and G. Bridge (eds), *A Companion to the City*, Oxford: Blackwell.

Vennemann, M.M., Hummel, T. and Berger, K. (2008) 'The Association between Smoking and Smell and Taste Impairment in the General Population', *Journal of Neurology* 255 (8): 1121–1126.

Vroon, P. (1997) *Smell the Secret Seducer*, New York: Farrar, Strauss and Giroux.

Walsh, D. (2002) 'Blitz on Smoking – Council to Crackdown on Burning of Unauthorised Fuels', Doncaster: *The Star*.

Wargocki, P., Wyon, D.P., Baik, Y.K., Clausen, G. and Fanger, P.O. (1999) 'Perceived Air Quality, Sick Building Syndrome (SBS) Symptoms and Productivity in an Office with Two Different Pollution Loads', *Indoor Air* 9 (3): 165–179.

Weber, C. (2011) 'Augmented Nose Sniffs out Illegal Stenches', *New Scientist*, 2799, available at: http://www.newscientist.com/article/mg20927995.300-augmented-nose-sniffs-out-illegal-stenches.html (17 February).

Weinstein, N.D. (1978) 'Individual Differences in Reactions to Noise: A Longitudinal Study in a College Dormitory', *Journal of Applied Psychology*, 63: 458–466.

Winneke, G., Neuf, M. and Steinheider, B. (1996) 'Separating the Impact of Exposure and Personality in Annoyance Response to Environmental Stressors, Particularly Odors', *Environment International*, 22 (1): 73–81.

Winter, R. (1976) *The Smell Book*, Philadelphia, PA: JB Lippincott.

World Health Organisation (2008) *Air Quality and Health Factsheet No. 31*, available at: http://www.who.int/mediacentre/factsheets/fs313/en/print.html (accessed 16 January 2013).

World Health Organisation (2011) Urban Outdoor Pollution Database, available to download at: http://www.who.int/gho/phe/outdoor_air_pollution/oap_city_2003_2010.xls

Wrzesniewski, A., McCauley, C. and Rowzin, P. (1999) 'Odor and Affect: Liking for Places, Things and People', *Chemical Senses*, 24: 713–721.

Wysocki, C. (2005) *Gender and Sexual Orientation Influence Preference for Human Body Odors*, Philadelphia, PA: Monell Chemical Senses Center.

Wysocki, C.J. and Pelchat, M.L. (1993) 'The Effects of Aging on the Human Sense of Smell and its Relationship to Food Choice', *Critical Reviews in Food Science and Nutrition*, 33(1): 63–82.

Yang, G and Hobson, J. (2000) 'Odour Nuisance – Advantages and Disadvantages of a Quantitative Approach', *Water Science and Technology*, 41 (6): 97–106.

Zardini, M. (ed.) (2005) *Sense of the City – An Alternative Approach to Urbanism*, Montreal: Lars Muller Publishers.

Index

abatement measures 18
abattoirs 91
acoustics 223–4
activity density 186, 188, 191
Adams, M. 42, 69
adaptation 25, 43, 199, 206, 216, 225
additional sensory stimuli 75–6
advertising 160, 165, 204
aerosols 67
Afghan cuisine 94
Africa 59
African people 195
age 10, 27–8, 33, 39, 47, 51, 214
agriculture 78
air 170–3; definition 170
air conditioning 22, 37, 104–6, 148, 158
air fresheners 158, 162, 216
air movement 186–8, 191, 205, 208, 217
air pollutants, definition 60
air pollution 76–8, 83, 154, 202; design tools 175–6; pedestrianisation 78–81; urban design 81–3
air quality 4, 6, 11–14, 16–17; changing expectations 67–8; placemaking 199; pollution 59–84; values 208
Air Quality Management Areas (AQMA) 61–2, 69, 225
Alais, D. 75
allergies 22, 158–9, 167, 180, 202, 204
Alzheimer's disease 28

Amsterdam 55
anaerobic digestion plants 64, 66
annoyance threshold, definition 14
anosmia 9, 29, 47, 88, 225
antagonists 143
anthropologists 60
anti-social behaviour 114, 122, 129, 139
anticipation effect 216
architects 4, 9, 22, 36, 45; air quality 70; design tools 183, 192–3; food odours 110; odour control 164; placemaking 203; policy-making 113; smellwalks 47
aristocracy 12
Aristotle 16
aromatherapy 175
Ascherson, A. 222
Asia 14
Asian people 95, 101
Askins, K. 42
asthma 59, 73, 75, 158
Atkinson, R. 165
atmosphere 170
attention restoration 174
Australia 14, 66
Austria 5, 22
authenticity 197–201, 220
avoidance behaviour 74–5, 158
Axel, R. 24

babies 33
Balez, S. 22, 41, 216
Barbara, A. 11, 21, 36–7, 115, 197, 199

Barcelona 9, 110, 117, 182
base notes 171, 199
BBC 17, 59
Beauchamp, G.K. 25
behavioural change 38, 40, 74–5, 119, 121, 158, 168, 201–2
Beijing 13
being away 174
Belgium 42
belief systems 76
Bell, D. 122, 201
Bentley, I. 186
Berrigan, C. 44–5
Best Street/Outdoor Market Award 86
Bickerstaff, K. 60, 81, 224
binge drinking 114
biodiversity 78
bioeffluents 16
Birmingham 164
Black Minority Ethnicity (BME) 95, 198, 225
blandscapes 204
blindness 29, 42
blog-sites 48, 212
Boddingtons 66
body odour 116, 139, 153–4
body size 28
Bokowa, A. 14
bonfires 76
Bonnes, M. 70, 81
Boring, E.G. 24
Boston 42
Bouchard, N. 45
bourgeoisie 115
breweries 65–6, 81, 145, 164, 171
briefing 215–16
Britain in Bloom 178
Brody, S.D. 81
Brown, L. 223
Brown, P. 224
Buck, L. 24

building control officers 102
built environment professionals 6, 47–8, 51, 53, 84; air quality 70; definition 4, 225; design tools 169–70, 185–6, 192–3; placemaking 212, 214–16; policy-making 117, 124; role 111, 164, 168, 222, 224; values 203, 205, 208
Burger King 108
burger vans 109, 198
Burr, D. 75
burst effect 217
bus stops 71, 79, 159–60, 165, 191, 204, 209, 218, 221–2

café culture 113, 117–18, 130, 132, 134, 138–9, 184
Cain, W.S. 27, 153
Cairo 2
Calcutta (Kolkata) 59–60, 82
Cameroon 16
Canada 4, 14, 20, 39, 45; air quality 71; design tools 190; food odours 101, 106; odour control 166; placemaking 219; smellwalks 53
Canadian Centre for Architecture 20
canals 182, 209
Cantonese cuisine 98
car parks 128–9, 154, 179, 222
Caribbean cuisine 94
Carlsberg 65
Carmona, M. 19
cartographers 54–5
case studies 47–54, 113, 130–8, 153, 157
CCTV 132, 181, 185
changing expectations 93
chemical senses 10, 113, 225
Chemical Sensitivity Scale 40
Chester 79

chewing gum 134, 151
Chicago 12
China 4, 13–14, 17, 101
Chinese Arts Centre 98
Chinese cuisine 94, 98–9, 101, 104
Chinese people 98–100
Chinese Women's Centre 98
Chiquetto, S. 79
city managers 4, 12, 45, 47, 70, 185, 191–2, 224
class 10–12, 59, 214
Classen, C. 5, 9, 11, 143
Clean Air Act 63
cleansing, definition 143
Clerkenwell, London *see* London
climate change 13, 224
clone-towns 110
coal 11, 47, 62, 81
Cochran, L.S. 29
Cockayne, E. 5, 11
coffee 117–18, 124, 135, 162, 164, 200
cognition 32, 36, 38
Cohen, S. 38
Colletti, J. 181
Columbia University 30
commercial odours 154–5, 160–3, 180, 203, 221
compatibility 174
concentration levels 24–5
Condie, J. 224
confidentiality 49
Conflux 44
Control of Substances Hazardous to Health (COSHH) 67
convenience food 106–9
coping strategies 39–40, 174
countryside *see* rural areas
crescendo effect 217
CRESSON Laboratory 43
crowd dispersal 33
crowd-sourcing 54

Cullen, G. 21
culture 33–4, 36, 38, 56, 82; design tools 175, 180, 186; food odours 93–101, 110; odour control 143, 146; placemaking 198, 218; policy-making 115–16, 122, 125, 139; role 84

Dalton, P. 33
Dann, G. 16, 37, 200–1
Davis, F. 31
Day, R. 74, 81
decipols, definition 16
decomposition 34
decrescendo effect 217
Degen, M. 20, 110–11
demography 48, 95, 97, 101
Denmark 16
density levels 169, 186–8, 191
Denver 36
deodorisation 143, 149–53, 166, 193, 197, 218–19, 223
DePalma, A. 30
Department for the Environment, Food and Rural Affairs (DEFRA) 51, 225
departure effect 217
design briefs 215–16
design tools 169–94, 210–20
Desor, J.A. 25
Detroit 101
developed countries 15
developing countries 13, 82
Devlieger, P.J. 42
Diaconu, M. 5, 22, 41
Dickens, C. 92
diffusion effect 217
Diller, E. 110
Dimoudi, A. 176
Disability Discrimination Act 127
diseases 11–13, 28, 73–4
dispersion modelling 18

documentation 212
dog faeces 197
Doncaster 44, 47–54, 56, 60–70, 72;
    air quality 74, 78–9, 82; Copley
    Road 94–8, 100–2, 110–11, 146,
    166, 192–3, 198; design tools 171,
    175–6, 178–80, 184, 190; food
    odours 88–9, 91–3, 105, 107–9;
    odour control 148, 153, 155–7,
    163; placemaking 200–1, 213;
    policy-making 113–14, 116–18,
    120, 123, 125–30, 138; Priory
    Walk/Silver Street 130–9, 145,
    151–2, 165, 176, 184, 186–7
Doncaster Council 128
Doncaster Market 86–7, 111, 128,
    149, 152, 172, 184, 188
Doncaster Metropolitan Borough
    Council (DMBC) 225
Doty, R.L. 25
Douglas, M. 60
Dove, R. 31
drainage 151, 190–1, 193
Drexler, M. 153
drive-through restaurants 106–7
Drobnick, J. 10, 20
dry ice machines 138

earth-banks 187–8
East Germany 222
Eastern Europeans 95
economics 82, 86, 93, 97, 101, 109,
    111, 165, 185
Edinburgh 55, 61, 171
Egypt 2
Ellena, H. 113
Elliot, R. 180
email 33
emotional attachment 155, 177,
    201–2
engagement 212–15
Engen, T. 25, 31–2, 34, 37, 199

Engineering and Physical Sciences
    Research Council (EPSRC) 44,
    225
engineers 4, 47–8, 70
England 5–6, 30, 39, 44–5, 47–54;
    air quality 61, 65, 69; design tools
    170, 176, 182, 193; food odours
    86, 101, 108; odour control 154;
    placemaking 197, 199; policy-
    making 113–15, 117–19, 121,
    125, 138–9; scenting 222; values
    202, 204, 208
English Heritage 19
Enlightenment 10, 12
Enquiry by Design 214
Entente Florale 178
entrance effect 216–17
environmental health officers 17,
    47–8, 66, 72–3, 76, 102–4
Environmental Protection Agency
    (EPA) 67
environmental psychologists 174
environmental scientists 77
epidemics 11
episodic odours 5, 171, 212
epistemology 10
ethanol 67, 70
ethics 40, 49, 162–3, 204
ethnicity 10, 47–8, 51, 66, 94–7,
    100, 165, 214
ethnoscapes 100
Europe 11–12, 14, 16, 30, 33; design
    tools 178; food odours 98, 102;
    odour control 146; policy-making
    113, 117, 119, 138, 140;
    smellwalks 43, 45, 53
European Union (EU) 13
evaluation 219–20
Evans, G. 93
Evans, G.W. 38
evening economy 6, 47, 107–8, 113,
    117; design tools 188; odour

control 148, 152–3; policy-making 129–32, 135, 139; role 223
exhaust fumes 74, 106
extent 174
extraction systems 102, 105, 116, 143, 162, 165
eye irritation 59

Facebook 48
Fanger, P.O. 16–17
Farmer, G. 204
fascination 174, 178
fast food restaurants 20, 85, 106–9, 111, 135, 137, 146, 221
femininity 10
Festival of Jasmine 195
Fifteenth Ward Smelling Committee 45
filming permission 49
fines 126, 151
fish and chip shops 109, 172
fish markets 87–93, 111
Fitzgerald-Bone, P. 38, 202
Fleming, R.L. 20
Fletcher, C. 38–9, 167
flooding effect 217
floral competitions 178
floral scent trails 78
Florence 206
focus groups 48
food odours 28, 34, 47, 102, 110–11; commercial scenting 161–3; design tools 175, 188; placemaking 198, 218; policy-making 114–15, 118, 138; sources 84–112; urban control 155
fossil fuels 68
fountains 195, 197, 206, 209, 219, 222
Fox, K. 16
fragrance companies 38
France 2, 22, 43, 55, 195, 205, 216

Frankfurt Airport 146
French cuisine 94
Freud, S. 10, 166
Furniss, J. 2
future developments 209–12, 215, 217–20, 224

Gary 36
gated communities 110, 165
gender 27, 33, 44, 47, 51, 214
geographers 4, 143
Germany 28, 33, 146
geysers 205
Gibson, J.J. 213
Glasgow 55, 108, 170–1
Global Catwalk 20
globalisation 20–1, 83
Government Office for London 19
graffiti 195
graphic designers 55
Grasse 195, 197, 210, 219
grease emissions 104, 107, 146, 221
Great North Road 61
Greek cuisine 101
greenery 83
greenspace *see* planting; vegetation
Grenoble 22, 205
Grenoble Graduate School of Architecture 43
Grésillon, L. 5
Grimwood, C.J. 51
Guangzhou 17
Guy, S. 204

habituation 25, 29, 43, 88, 166; placemaking 199, 206, 216; role 222, 225
hair/nail salons 66–8, 81, 146
Hall, E.T. 11
Hamel, R. 183
haptics 29, 170, 225
hard branding 93

heart conditions 73
heart notes 171
Hegel, G.W.F. 10
Heili, V. 202
Hellström, B. 206
Helsinki 146
Herbert, S. 165
Herz, R. 33
Hirsch, A.R. 31, 38
historians 5
Hobson, J. 18
holding breath 74, 105
Horlicks 66
horror films 199–200
hot dog vendors 109, 198
hot springs 205
Houses of Parliament 11
Hudson, R. 77
Hull 66
humidity 54, 110
hygiene 12, 14, 92, 165, 219

Iceland 30
iconic effect 217
ideology 56
idling engines 70–1, 82, 209
imagineering 212
immigration 95–7, 100, 195
implementation 216–19
impregnation effect 217
India 4, 13–14, 59, 119, 145
Indian cuisine 94, 96, 101, 104
industrial revolution 13
industrialisation 11
inhalers 75
international district 85
international food 93–101
involuntary odours 5, 171–2
Iran 14
Ireland 119
ISO International Standard 7730
    204

Italian cuisine 94, 101
Italy 206

Jacobs, J. 21
Jacobsen, J.K.S. 16, 37, 200–1
Japan 15, 33, 38, 54–5, 119, 146, 209
Japanese cuisine 104
judgements of place 78–81

Kaplan, R. 174
Kaplan, S. 174
Karmanov, D. 183
kebab shops 108–9
Keep Britain Tidy 125–6
Keller, A. 28
KFC 106, 108, 154
King, P. 31, 36
Kinney, P. 30
Knasko, S.C. 38
Knopper, M. 36
Kouros 157

labelling 143, 201
Labour 113
Lagos 4, 13, 59–60, 82
Laing, D.G. 72
Lambert, P. 20
landfill sites 18, 149
Landry, C. 21, 77, 223
Larssona, M. 27
leadership 164, 195, 203, 205, 208, 210, 222
Leeds 65
Lefebvre, H. 20, 164
legislation 6, 12–15, 19, 51, 60; air quality 63, 81, 83; food odours 105, 111; odour control 145–6, 154; policy-making 115, 118–21, 123, 125–6, 130; role 168; values 208–9
lesser senses 10
Leuven 42

Li, W. 29
Licensing Act 114
Lidén, E. 18
Light, A. 204
limbic system 16, 24
Lisbon 42
listening states 43
litter 107, 113, 125–7, 149, 151, 178, 223
Liverpool 30
London 2, 11, 13, 19, 44; air quality 61, 63, 65, 68–75; case studies 47, 49, 56, 171, 175, 181, 183, 221; design tools 173, 190; food odours 87, 91, 93, 101; odour control 166; placemaking 201; values 204
Low, K.E.Y. 5, 41, 100
Lucas, R. 22, 213
Luminar Leisure 116
lung disease 59, 73
Lush 154, 157–8, 161
Lykoudis, S. 148, 224
Lynch, K. 21, 192

McBean, M. 44–5
Macdonald, L. 108
McDonalds 106, 108, 154
McFrederick, Q.S. 78
Macintyre, S. 108
Mackett, R. 79
McLean, K. 54–5, 170
Malnar, J.M. 21, 171–2, 212
Malone, G. 181
Manchester 44, 47, 49, 54, 56; air quality 65–6, 68–71, 74–5; Chinatown 98–100, 102, 146, 166, 172, 192; design tools 171, 175, 181; food odours 87, 110; policy-making 118
Manchester Council 128
Manchester University 159
mapping studies 54–6, 170

marketing 4, 157, 161–2, 202–3
markets 85–93, 109, 128, 131, 149; design tools 172, 179, 184, 188; odour control 152, 156, 160, 163; placemaking 200–1, 221
masculinity 10
masking effects 77–8, 116, 118, 125, 152–4; design tools 193; odour control 160, 167; placemaking 197, 218; role 223; values 208–9
Massey, D. 160, 165, 197–8, 200–1
materials 186, 189–91, 218
Mean, M. 110
meat markets 90–3
meat rendering plants 63–4, 67, 82
media 116
medication 75
Mediterranean areas 148
megacities 4, 14, 59, 82
Mehrabian, A. 38
memory 27, 31–2, 36, 40, 45; design tools 177; food odours 85–7, 90; placemaking 199–200, 215; policy-making 138–9; role 222; values 202
menstrual cycle 27
meteorology 210
Mexico 13, 77
Mexico City 13, 77
microclimates 148, 186–8, 191
middle notes 171–2
Milan 206
Minton, A. 110, 118, 165–6
mobile interviews 51
modernism 10, 12, 81, 111, 167
Molton Hops 66
Monell Chemical Senses Centre 33
monitoring 70, 219–20
Montreal 71, 190
mood 38, 183
Moore, E.O. 174
Moss, M. 38

Mountain View 106–7
mucus 170
Muiswinkel, W.J. 67
multiculturalism 95–7, 216
multinationals 154, 163
Mumbai 4, 13

nail bars 66–8, 81, 146
Nasal Ranger 18
National Association of British
    Market Authorities 86
National Geographic Smell Survey
    29
nationality 33
natural environment characteristics
    15
natural materials 189
NCP 129
neo-liberalism 167
Nepalese cuisine 94
Netherlands 14, 55, 67
neutralising effect 217
New Economics Foundation 20
New York 12, 21, 30, 44, 48; air
    quality 59, 82; design tools 190;
    food odours 101; policy-making
    119; smellwalks 55
New Zealand 14, 205
Newport 55
Nigeria 4, 13, 59, 145
nightclubs 116, 159
Nike 154
Nikolopoulou, M. 29, 65, 148, 176,
    224
nioi-bu 54–5
nitrogen 170, 176
Nobel Prize 24
noble senses 10
non-food odours 154–6
non-natural restorative odours 183–4
Nordin, S. 18, 38, 40
nose training 29

nostalgia 31, 90
nuisance 14, 39, 67–8, 81, 102–3,
    146, 202
Nutall Mintoes 64

ocular-centricity 10–11, 21, 82, 175
odorants, definition 60, 76
odour pollution, definition 14
odours 15–18, 22, 27, 37–40, 43;
    classification 15–18, 53;
    concentration 26, 38–9, 69, 170,
    186, 193, 208; control 143–68,
    188, 197; definition 60, 76;
    detection 26–7, 29, 31, 37, 40, 48,
    53–4, 56; dilution 18, 173, 186,
    193, 217; extraction 102–6;
    identification 18, 26–7, 29, 31, 50;
    measurement 15–18; objectives
    215–16; perception 111, 161–3;
    placemaking 195–220; receptors
    24–5, 170, 209, 222, 225; values
    106–9, 201–5
Office for National Statistics (ONS)
    95, 225
olfactometry 18
olfactory system 24–31, 77, 170–1,
    225
olfs, definition 16
Oliver, L. 38
Olympic Games 13–14
One Hundred Sites of Good
    Fragrance 15, 209
othering 100
Oxford University 2
oxygen 170, 176

Pakistan 14
Pallasmaa, J. 11, 21
panic attacks 32
Paris 1–2, 5, 11, 55, 114, 143
Parkinson's disease 28
participant recruitment 48

particulate matter (PM) 13, 61, 177, 225
patio heaters 123
Payne, S.R. 175, 193
pedestrianisation 62, 69, 78–81, 83, 130–2, 134, 145, 153, 208
Penwarden, A.D. 29, 186
perfume industry 155–60, 171–2, 195, 197, 221
perfumers 25, 37, 55, 171, 195
Perliss, A. 11, 21, 36–7, 115, 197, 199
Perth 66
Piaget, J. 171
Pizza Hut 108
place perception 36–7, 93, 96–7, 101, 108
placemaking 6, 20, 141, 194–220
planners 4, 47–8, 70, 83, 102, 107, 183, 203
planning permission 64, 108
Planning for Real 214
planting 83, 126–7, 131–2, 134, 140; design tools 171, 175–82, 185, 188; odour control 148; placemaking 208–9
pluralism 204
police 59, 61
policy-making 13–15, 19, 81, 83, 110–40, 145, 164, 183, 222–3
politics 56, 59, 70, 95, 101, 114, 126, 208
pollinators 78
pollution 4, 6, 11–14, 16–17, 20; air quality 59–84; avoidance behaviour 74–5; design tools 177, 182, 188; odour control 149, 151, 154, 156, 158, 165, 167; perspectives 34, 36; policy-making 119, 137, 139; scenting 221; smellwalks 45, 47; values 208–9
pop-up urinals 129, 222

Porteous, J.D. 5, 60, 99
Portugal 42
Positive Soundscapes Project 46
post-traumatic stress disorder 32
Postrel, V. 201, 204, 219
Pottier, J. 85
pragmatism, definition 204
pregnancy 28
Primary Care Trusts 73
prisons 66, 174
private sector/sphere 10, 134
privatisation 110, 118, 165
property values 12
Proust, M. 31
psychologists 37
public art 189
Public Health Act 127
public sector/sphere 127, 134, 139
public toilets 127–30, 138, 152, 166, 172, 184, 197, 223
public transport 69–71, 206
pubs 114–16, 118–23, 125, 129–31, 135; design tool 184; odour control 146, 154, 162; policy-making 138–9
Pugh, T.A.M. 176, 208

qualities of odour 27

race 99–101
racism 10
Radford, C. 180
Rasmussen, S.E. 21
ratchet effect 219
ratings 51–3
reactionary approach 197
recording equipment 48–9
recycling 149
Reinarz, J. 5, 10–11
Relph, E. 20, 198, 200–1
reproductive disorders 67
respiratory illnesses 74, 167, 214, 219

restorative environments 169–94
restorative odours 173–85
Reynolds, R. 82, 178
road works 190
Rodaway, P. 5, 10, 20, 32, 143–4
Rome 206
Romice, O. 22
Rotorua 205
Rotterdam School of Management 157
route-planning 49–50
rural areas 10, 37, 75, 78, 82
Russell, J.A. 38

Sacks, O. 42
San Francisco 159, 165, 204
sanctioned areas 145
Scent Marketing Institute 221
scenting 47, 153–67, 193, 195, 197, 203, 218, 221, 223
Schafer, R.M. 4, 42–3, 45, 99
schizophrenia 28
Schleidt, M. 32–3
Scholder-Ellen, P. 38, 202
Scotland 30, 55, 108, 116, 119, 170–1, 180
Second World War 64
Sennett, R. 4, 11, 114, 166
sensation 32
sensescapes 214
sensewalks 42–6, 49
sensitivity 225
sensory deprivation 9
sensory manipulation 158–9, 161–3, 167–8, 197, 201, 203
Sensory Notation Tool 213
sensory studies 5
separation 144–50, 153, 193, 197, 218, 223
sewage 11, 18, 63, 149
sewerage systems 12, 191
sexual attraction 158, 203

Shanghai 4
Shaw, S. 99
Sheffield 44, 47, 49, 56, 65–6; air quality 68–71, 74, 82; design tools 171, 175, 181–2, 190; food odours 87
Sheffield United 65
Shoenfeld, Y. 28
sick-building syndrome 39
Simkins, I.M. 215
Simon Fraser University 42
Singapore 5, 101, 148
site assessment 212–15
sky scenting 163–7
smell perception 24, 32–5, 225
The Smelling Committee 45
smellmarks 99, 105, 156, 158, 191–2, 200, 217, 225
smellscapes 1–6, 15–18, 24–6, 37–40; air quality 59–84; classification 15–18; definition 5, 225; design tools 169–94; food sources 85–112; historical perspective 9–12; legislation 13–15; mapping 54–5; measurement 15–18; memory 31–2; perception 32–7; performance 26–31; placemaking 195–220; policy-making 113–40; pollution 59–84; representing 42–56; strategic context 205–10; twenty-four hour cities 118–19; urban design 19–22, 81–3, 169–94, 210–20
smellwalks 5–6, 22, 27, 41–56, 71; design tools 175, 178, 181, 183–4, 186, 189–90; food odours 108, 110; odour control 144, 161–4; placemaking 214–16; policy-making 114, 118, 120, 128, 130, 132
Smithfield meat market 91–3
smog 13, 59, 173

smoke 76, 78, 190
smokers/smoking 26, 28, 47, 51, 113;
    odour control 145–6, 151, 154,
    168; placemaking 214; policy-
    making 115–16, 118–27, 130,
    134–5, 138–40; values 202, 223
sniff tests 17–18
social construction 159
social media/networking 33, 48, 212
Sony 154
soundmarks 99
soundscapes 18, 43, 72, 175, 193,
    206, 218, 223
soundwalks 45
South 59
Southworth, M. 42
stakeholders 70, 94, 199, 201, 203,
    210–15, 218, 220, 224
Stallen, P. 65
Starr, C. 65
static effect 217
Stein, M. 33
Steinheider, B. 38
stereotypes 10, 148, 175, 178, 221
Stewart, H. 176
Stockholm 145, 206
strategic context 205–10
street cleansing 12, 126, 138, 197
street furniture 189
street urination 127–30, 136, 140,
    149, 188
street vendors 109, 111, 165, 218
streetscapes 189
stress 4, 81, 174, 183
Strous, R.D. 28
Studio X 48, 55
sub-Saharan Africa 59
subconscious *see* unconscious
surveillance 132
Süskind, P. 195, 203
sustainability 44, 168–70, 211, 218
Sweden 27, 145, 206

sweet factories 64–5, 67–8, 78, 81
synaesthetic associations 170
synergy 212
synthesis, definition 143
synthetic odours 155–63

Tacoma 36
Tafalla, M. 9
Tahbaz, M. 29
Takasago 38
tap-rooms 115
Tastduftwien 22
taxi ranks 209
Taylor, N. 68
Technical University of Denamrk 16
Tetley's 65–6
Thai cuisine 98, 104
Thailand 32
Thames, River 11
theme parks 199–200
Thibaud, J.P. 43
Thorpe Park 199–200
Thwaites, K. 215
Tianjin 101
Tims, T. 110
Tippett, J. 211, 214
toilet provision 127–30, 138, 152,
    166, 172, 184, 197, 223
Tokyo 15, 119, 146
tools for design 169–94
top notes 171–2
topography 54, 83, 186, 190–1
topology 71
Toronto 55, 101, 106–7
tourism 20, 37, 42, 93, 100, 113, 195,
    197, 200–1
trade-offs 68–76, 82, 175
traffic emissions 13–14, 59, 61–2,
    68–76, 79–80
traffic lights 209
transition effect 217
trees 176–82, 185, 188, 195, 208

trigeminal nerve 9, 24–6, 60, 72, 202; definition 226; stimulation 26, 38, 66, 72, 88
Truax, B. 43
Tuan, Y.F. 36, 200–1
twenty-four-hour cities 6, 113–19, 125–30, 138–40, 148, 224
Twilley, N. 55
Twitter 48

UCLA 16
Ulrich, R.S. 174
unconscious 25, 82, 113, 199, 201, 203
United Kingdom (UK) 9–10, 12, 14, 20, 44–5; air quality 59, 62, 67–8, 71, 79; design tools 178; food odours 86, 94, 104–6, 110; odour control 145, 148, 157, 159, 163; policy-making 113, 117–20, 127, 140; scenting 221; smellwalks 51, 53
United Nations (UN) 4
United States (US) 10, 42, 45, 53, 55; air quality 66–7; food odours 101, 106, 110; odour control 145, 159, 166; perspectives 14, 18, 33, 36, 40; placemaking 219; policy-making 119, 121; scenting 221
University College London 44
University of Columbia 48, 55
University of Montreal 45
University of Philadelphia 29
University of Salford 44, 46
urban design 19–23, 47, 54, 81–3, 124; new approaches 192–3; placemaking 195–220; policy-making 139; process 210–20; strategic context 205–10; tools 169–94; values 201–5
Urban Design Compendium 117, 163–4

urban designers 4, 45, 47, 70, 83, 164, 203
urban studies 4, 20
Urban Task Force 113
Urry, J. 37

values 201–5
Vancouver 4, 43
vandalism 185, 218
vegetation 15, 170, 175–8, 181–2, 195, 218, 221
vehicle design 13, 61
Venice 206
ventilation 22, 67, 85, 91, 102–7; odour control 145–6, 148, 155, 161, 167; placemaking 200–1; policy-making 114–15, 138
video recordings 49
Vienna 5, 22
Vietnamese cuisine 94
visual impairment 29, 42
Vivacity2020 Project 44–5, 47
Vodvarka, F. 21, 171–2, 212
Vogt, H. 221
volatile organic compounds (VOC) 13, 76–7, 176, 226
vomit 127–30, 136, 138–40, 149, 151–2, 165, 188, 223

wake effect 217
Walker, G. 60, 81, 224
Ward's Brewery 65–6
warzones 54
waste 34, 97, 102, 107, 125–30; design tools 175, 178; odour control 149–53; placemaking 197; policy-making 140; scenting 221
water vapour 170
water/waterways 182–3, 192, 206, 209
West 9, 12, 54, 66–7, 76, 81–3, 113, 154

JD Wetherspoon 117
Wicklen, G. van 181
wind, definition 173
wind flow 29, 31, 54, 63–5, 140,
    170–3, 186, 208
windows 74
Wise, A.F.E. 29, 186
World Health Organisation 13–14,
    202

World Soundscapes Project 4, 42, 45
Wu, E. 55

Yang, G. 18
York 61

Zabaleen 2
Zardini, M. 9, 20–1
zoning 12, 165, 188, 208